# HISPANIC REALITIES

## IMPACTING AMERICA

*Implications for Evangelism & Missions*

**Daniel R. Sánchez, Ph.D.**

*Preface by* **Jesse Miranda, Ph. D.**

*Cover Design by* **Daniel E. Sánchez,**
**daniel@moonlight-studios.com**

Church Starting Network
www/churchstarting.net
2006

HISPANIC REALITIES IMPACTING AMERICA:
*Implications for Evangelism & Missions*

For more information on materials from Church Starting Network refer to the Church Starting Network website:
www.churchstarting.net

FIN 26 07 06

---

Library of Congress Cataloging-in Publication Data

Sánchez, Daniel R. 1936

HISPANIC REALITIES IMPACTING AMERICA: *Implications for Evangelism & Missions/ Daniel R. Sanchez, with contributing authors Jesse Miranda, Bobby Sena, and Diana Barrera*

ISBN 0-9772433-1-1

# Dedication

We want to dedicate this book to all of the Hispanic Americans who have gone before us and who held tenaciously to a vision of a brighter and more promising future. This includes the religious workers, the educators, the medical professionals as well as the clerks, the farmers, the farm laborers, and the day laborers who worked hard to blaze new trails and to establish inspiring role models. Today we stand on their shoulders as we move to new horizons and respond to new opportunities. We will never forget the sacrifice and the noble spirit of our beloved *abuelitos* (grandparents) and *padres* (parents) who did so much with so little and never gave up. We also want to honor the Anglo pioneers in Hispanic ministry who caught the vision and committed their lives to the glorious task of leading Hispanics to a personal experience of salvation in Jesus Christ. The lives of millions of born-again Hispanics stand today as living epistles of their love and dedication (2 Cor 3:2-3).

# Acknowledgements

This book draws solid information from several studies and surveys conducted by such prestigious organizations as the Brookings Institution, the Hispanic Center of the Pew Charitable Trust, the Harvard University Kennedy School of Government, the Urban Institute, the USC Annenburg School of Communication, the U.S. Department Bureau of the Census, and carefully selected books and articles which are referenced in the endnotes of each section to enable the readers to secure additional information from these sources. The observations, conclusions and applications made in this book reflect the insights and experience of the authors and of numerous religious workers that were interviewed. This information is shared with the hope that those who seek to impact Hispanic Americans with the Gospel of Jesus Christ will take a fresh look at the astounding Hispanic population growth and seek God's guidance in developing innovative and bold strategies to respond to this challenge.

## The Authors

Dr. Daniel R. Sánchez has served as Professor of Missions and Director of the Scarborough Institute of Church Planting and Growth of Southwestern Baptist Theological Seminary for the past twenty-one years. His previous experience includes starting two Hispanic churches in Texas, serving as a missionary in the Republics of Guatemala and Panama, serving as an Associate Director in the Missions Division of the Baptist Home Mission Board, serving as Director of Missions for the Baptist Convention of New York and lecturing and preaching in more than fifty countries. Among the books he has authored are: *Starting Reproducing Congregations: A Guidebook for Contextual New Church Development, Sharing The Good News With Our Roman Catholic Friends,* The *Gospel in the Rosary, Church Planting Movements in North America, Cómo Sembrar Iglesias en el Siglo XXI,* and *Cómo Testificar A Sus Amigos Católicos.* All of these are available through www.churchstarting.net.

Dr. Jesse Miranda is the director of Center for Urban Studies and Hispanic Leadership at Vanguard University in Costa Mesa California. Prior to serving in this strategic position, Dr. Miranda has served as a pastor, as the Director of the Latin American Bible Institute, and as the Superintendent of the Southern Pacific Latin American District Council of the Assemblies of God Church. He is currently serving as the Executive Presbyter of Hispanic Districts for the Assemblies of God. In addition to being founder and president of AMEN, an interdenominational fellowship of Hispanic pastors Dr. Miranda  has served in commissions established by presidents of the United States.

Dr. Bobby Sena serves as North American Mission Board Church Planting Group Field Partner for Western United States and Puerto Rico and as the Leader of the Hispanic Service Team. Prior to serving in this capacity, he served as a pastor of several churches, a church planting strategist, and an Evangelism Consultant for the North American Mission Board. Bobby's passion is seeking, enlisting, training, and deploying the next generation of church planting leaders in the Southern Baptist Convention.

# The Authors

Diana Barrera is the Executive Director of COMHINA which stands for Cooperación Misionera de Hispanos de Norte América (Missionary Cooperation of North American Hispanics). Under her able leadership this missionary organization has focused on awakening the hearts of thousands of Hispanics who have been interceding, giving, going, and sending missionaries to unreached people groups throughout the world.

# CONTENTS

# PREFACE

Dr. Jesse Miranda

The book of Acts is a picture of the Early Church as a revolutionary learning organism and growing organization. Luke also records several of the challenges that threatened its corporate survival. It is the story of a body of believers managing the cultural differences of Jews and Gentiles on its way to becoming the global community that God meant it to be. A key reminder was that the Church's mission was not the Church but the world.

In the 1970s and 80s the Church in North America began to engage the so-called globalization. During those decades, major demographic changes began to take place. People from nations around the world began to move into the neighborhood. As ethnic populations, Hispanic Americans in particular, began to increase in towns and cities across the country, the need for changes in ministry design, procedures, and goals increased.

Many congregations and ministries found it easier to relocate than reinvent themselves to the context, leaving church buildings as empty monuments of a past era. Fortunately, some congregations accepted the challenge and made changes. They have remained to face the ethnic diversity challenge and "stay the course." These congregations continue to provide a faithful witness in the midst of chaotic changes but are in constant need of reinforcement, some to the extent of re-visioning.

This book was written to re-enforce the courageous efforts of the leaders of these congregations. It was written for all ministries, church based or para-church, that are called to witness in old and new Hispanic settlements. It was written for church-planting missionaries who envision a plenteous harvest and are willing to build places to store this harvest.

*The thesis of this book is that biblical and cultural competencies are essential to gather a plenteous harvest.* These competencies interrelate to build God's Kingdom. The stark realities you'll read in this book underscore the importance of effective inter-cultural and/or cross-cultural relations and strategies for ministry in fulfilling the Great Commission among the growing Hispanic community in North America.

In the backdrop of these chapters is the fact that church organizations are having to struggle to understand their identity and purpose regarding ethnic ministry. Questions abound. How do we maintain historical identities and mission while seeking to embrace increasing diversity for our very survival? How do we address the new challenges by the growing Hispanic population in society? There is concern about having unity in the midst of this diversity? I believe that unity develops where there is biblical and cultural competency.

Bob Sena's chapter entitled "Diversity among Hispanics," helps us to understand the factors that contribute to assimilation, the various levels of assimilation among Hispanics, and the implications of assimilation for Hispanic families as well as Hispanic churches. He makes it clear that there is significant diversity among the various segments of the Hispanic population. Sena affirms that this diversity must be addressed.

But first there must be a decision if ethnic diversity in the church body is a matter of political correctness or a mandate of the Great Commission. We must decide if it is a problem to be fixed or a key to the success of our ministry. Is addressing this ethnic diversity a potential organizational "problem" to be avoided or a potential ministry advantage? Is this effort to address diversity a fad or a public relations emergency to be handled, or is it a resource for the Church to grow?

Managing ethnic diversity is the most significant factor affecting the evangelical church today. It is essential for the success of ministry in the Hispanic context. This book is presented with leaders in mind. It seeks to aid leaders who are already successful but want to fine tune their vision and skills. It provides for leaders who desire sharpness in their ministry among Hispanics. It speaks to leaders who realize they have been operating with a dated mindset of the world and the people around them. It seeks to aid leaders who wish to hone-in on the nature of ministry and the ministerial process in a Hispanic context. The book relates to leaders who understand that practices developed in one culture may not easily transfer to another.

To these ends Dr. Daniel Sanchez writes several chapters which contain eye-opening realities of the Hispanic community. He underscores the noticeable changes in the Hispanic population and the implications of these changes resulting in church planting in traditional Hispanic enclaves such as the Southwest, Chicago, and New York. He recounts the novel, yet welcome surprise, that Spanish-speaking congregations are sprouting in places such as North Carolina, Arkansas, and Iowa.

Sanchez' chapters will overwhelm you with a virtual reality or with a forceful revisit of the purpose and identity of your ministry. Who are we as a church or ministry? What are we here for? What ought to be our relationship to this growing and increasingly diverse population? What contribution might we make to meet this new challenge? Are you aware of the budding movement taking place in many metro centers across the country - a new urbanism with a twist? These urban places, known as the "Latino new urbanism" or "Hurban areas" (for Hispanic urban), exist in cities where Hispanics are fast becoming the majority capitalizing on Latino cultural preferences for compact neighborhoods, large public plazas, and a sense of community. "Latinos are comfortable living near stores and businesses and riding buses and trains" says Katherine Perez, director of the Transportation and Land Use Collaborative of Southern California.[1]

In my chapter entitled "The Samaritan Analogy," I intend to help you understand Latino attitudes and engagements (or lack thereof) in public and religious life by highlighting, what I term, "the Samaritan complex"—an identity resulting from a contextual history and ensuing psychological identity. As is true of all people groups, the historical memory and collective social experience of Hispanics underpin their activities and explain much of behavior. More specifically, a legacy of conquests and a following social stigma has contributed to the perception many Hispanics have of themselves as being a devalued minority group. As a group, Hispanics remain for the most part an undigested minority in the life of this country. As individuals, many Hispanics have acculturated and still others have been assimilated into U.S. life. These facts all points to the reality that the Hispanic Community is anything but homogeneous.

The fundamental human needs have been shaped by this unique historical, social, and psychological background and have contributed in making Hispanics the ethnic group most responsive to the Gospel. A similar example is found in the story of the Samaritan people, a people also living in the margins. The Samaritans were social and religious outcasts of their time. Today, their stories are symbols of the transformational power of the Gospel. Because of the transformational nature of the Gospel, we should describe anew the social world we inhabit with the help of the biblical story.

In Sanchez' chapter entitled "The Hellenistic Analogy," he posits a biblical paradigm for those Hispanics who have experienced a significant degree of assimilation into the North American society while at the same time retaining much of the language and the culture of their parents. Those who are bi-lingual and bi-cultural will find in this chapter positive affirmation of their identity and a sense of purpose in being *"gente puente"* (bridge people). Like the Apostle Paul, they have the privilege and the opportunity of communicating the gospel of salvation in a wide variety of cultural settings. Instead of being a liability, their bi-culturalism and bi-lingualism becomes a marvelous asset in the furtherance of the Kingdom of God across cultural barriers in this country and throughout the world.

So it is that in these essays we describe our social world in a fresh new way (a re-vision) and we relate it to the biblical story. The most critical and difficult issues facing the church, as a global organization, are internal, that is, a re-vision that results in the reconfiguration and redeployment of its spiritual and human resources. Re-vision does not hinge solely on accelerating one's own ethnic learning curves and broadening one's own information pool. Re-visioning is also not the re-engineering of organizational processes or a continual re-equipping of people.

A re-vision of Hispanics results from a biblical competency that harnesses a shared framework of beliefs, values, and ministry goals and a cultural competency that allows initiatives, methods, and strategies to translate into practice essential to the creation and maintenance of any group. It is moving beyond a mere conscious-raising process; beyond just coping with cultural differences. It is embracing the wellspring of diversity and competently converting ethnic diversity into a positive force enhancing communication and community. More importantly, this goes beyond the worldly tactics of "blame and shame" in which someone is the victim and another, the perpetrator. Rather, it is the Gospel tapping into each ethnic spiritual bank and cultural capital to build God's Kingdom with the help of the biblical story and with the help of the Holy Spirit.

---

Endnotes
[1] Katherine Perez, "New Urbanism Embraces Latinos," USA TODAY, 2/15/2005.

# INTRODUCTION

The explosive growth and rapid expansion of the Hispanic population is transforming the social, economic, and religious panorama of America. Hispanic Americans are now the largest minority group in America[2] and are projected to comprise one fourth of the American population by the year 2050.[3] According to a the latest Census Bureau report, "the U.S. Hispanic population passed the 45 million mark and accounted for half of the growth of the US population since 2000, indicating that the nation's largest minority group is increasing its presence even faster than in the previous decade."[4]

Through a combination of high birth rates and continuous immigration, Hispanic Americans are experiencing a higher annual growth rate than the Baby Boom generation of the 40's and 50's which was approximately 2 percent annually. "The Hispanic growth rate for the past 12 months was 3.6 percent compared with the overall population growth of 1 percent.[5] Referring to the rapid expansion of the Hispanic population throughout the country, Harry Pacon, president of the Tomas Rivera Policy Institute states,

> It's going to have profound effects on America. They are no longer regionally centered in places like California and New York. There are more Hispanics in Cook County, Chicago, than in Arizona or Colorado, or New Mexico... The major significance is that it's a national presence."[6]

The astounding growth and rapid expansion of the Hispanic population across America is impacting not only the large cities with long-standing Hispanic concentrations such as Chicago, Houston, Los Angeles, Miami, and New York but such unlikely places as Raleigh, Atlanta, Orlando, Las Vegas, Nashville, Portland, and Washington, D.C. to name but a few. In addition to the urban areas, many of the suburban and rural areas of America are experiencing sudden and substantial growth. This explosive growth has motivated such highly reputable organizations as the Brookings Institution, the Hispanic Center of the Pew Charitable Trust,[7] the Harvard University Kennedy School of Government, the Urban Institute, the USC Annenburg School of Communication, and the U.S. Department Bureau of the Census to conduct extensive surveys and studies on the Hispanic population in America. From these and other studies as well as personal observation I have gleaned ten "Hispanic Realities" that are transforming the social, economic, political, and religious life of America today.[8]

*This book analyzes these realities and explores their implications for leading Hispanics to a personal experience of salvation in Jesus Christ, establishing biblically sound, culturally relevant, reproducing congregations among them, enabling these congregations to experience healthy growth and meaningful ministry in their communities, and encouraging them to participate in the implementation of the Great Commission by sending Hispanic missionaries to highly strategic parts of the world.*

"The face of America is changing and it's changing rapidly," says Gary Cowger, president of General Motors North America. "You ignore diversity at your own risk..."[9]

# INTRODUCTION

Let us keep this in mind as we analyze the ten most significant Hispanic Realities in America today, acquaint ourselves with the Hispanic culture, and design biblically sound and culturally contextualized strategies to lead the largest number of Hispanics to a personal faith in Jesus Christ.

Endnotes

[2] Dallas Morning News, "Report: Hispanic Population Surging," June, 9, 2005, 13A.

[3] Pew Hispanic Center/Kaiser Family Foundation, 2002 National Survey of Latinos, December 2002, 53.

[4] D'vera Cohn, "Hispanic population keeps gaining numbers," Star Telegram, June 9, 2005, 5A.

[5] D'vera Cohn, "Hispanic population keeps gaining numbers," Star Telegram, June 9, 2005, 5A.

[6] Harry Pacon, cited in D'vera Cohn, "Hispanic population keeps gaining numbers," Ft. Worth Star Telegram, June 9, 2005, 5A.

[7] "Latino Growth in Metropolitan America," The Brookings Institution Center on Urban & Metropolitan Policy and the Pew Hispanic Center.

[8] The terms "Hispanic" and "Latino" are used interchangeably in this book. While some prefer one term over the other, both terms are used extensively and convey the encompassing of all national origin groups among Hispanics. Pew Hispanic Center/Kaiser Family Foundation, 2002 National Survey of Latinos, December 2002, 6.

[9] Gary Cowger, Diversity Inc., May 2005, 20.

# PART ONE
# HISPANIC REALITIES

# CHAPTER 1

# REALITY # 1

The growth of the Hispanic American population has exceeded even the boldest projections of demographic experts.

*Between 1950 and 2008,*
*The Hispanic Population*
*Grew By 41.5 Million*
**From 4.6 Million to 45.5 Million.**[10]

This growth equals to the entire population of Canada and is greater than the total population of a large number of countries throughout the world.

This makes Hispanics the largest minority group in America today.[11]

Two main factors have contributed to this unprecedented growth—the unprecedented birth rate among Hispanics and the unrelenting immigration of Hispanics.

**1. The Hispanic birth rate continues to contribute to unprecedented population growth.**

In 1995, one in every six births in America was Hispanic. Demographers project that by the year 2050, one in every three births will be Hispanic. The high Hispanic birth rate is resulting in numerical growth that exceeds any of the other sociocultural groups in America today.

**Table 1**
**Hispanic Birthrate**

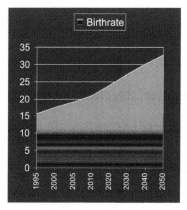

Table 1 reveals that, in the year 1995, slightly over 15 percent of the births in American were Hispanic. By the year 2050, the projections are that 33 percent (or one third) of the births in America will be Hispanic. Another startling fact has to do with the Hispanic population increase due to births in comparison to the increase related to immigration.

*"Births have overtaken immigration this decade as the largest source of Hispanic growth."[12]*

2.  **The second factor that is contributing to explosive growth among Hispanics is immigration.**

Currently four of every ten immigrants into America each year are Hispanic. The projection indicates that if this trend continues, in ten years half of all immigrants to North America will be Hispanic.[13]

## Table 2
## Hispanic Immigration Rate

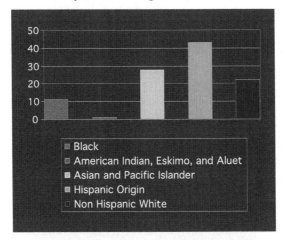

- **4 of every 10 immigrants each year are Hispanic**

- **In 10 years half of all immigrants will be Hispanic**

Table 2 shows the immigration rate of Hispanics in comparison to other cultural groups. In the year 2000 the Black immigration rate was 10 percent, the American Indian, Eskimo, and Aluet was less than 1 percent, the Asian and Pacific Islander was 28 percent, the Non-Hispanic White was 21 percent, and the Hispanic immigration rate was *42 percent.*

What makes Hispanic population growth different from that of previous immigrant groups is that *Hispanics have experienced both biological growth and immigration growth simultaneously.* Most immigrant groups (e.g., Irish, German) have come in one or two major waves which have slowed to a trickle. Hispanic Americans have, however, enter the United States through some major immigration waves and also by a rather constant on-going immigration. This continuing immigration, combined with high birth rates, has contributed to unprecedented and continuous growth. As will be seen later in this document, the steady flow of immigrants from Latin America has continued to reinforce the Hispanic culture as well as the use of the Spanish language in this country.

> *The Census Bureau projects that*
> *102.6 million Hispanics*
> *will live in the United States in 2050.*

The Hispanic population, according to projected net gain estimates, will increase by 67 million in the period between 2000 and 2050. The projected Hispanic population of 102.6 million by the year 2050 is almost triple the Hispanic population of 35.3 million in 2000.[14]

> *Hispanics have not only experienced*
> *an astounding growth rate in the*
> *past 30 years, but are projected*
> *to nearly triple their population*
> *within the next 45 years.*

By then Hispanics will comprise nearly one fourth of the population of the United States. In June of 2005 the Census Bureau reported that one in every seven people in the United States is Hispanic.[15]

In other words, Evangelical Christians face not simply an imperative of catching up with the explosive Hispanic population growth, but also an imperative of developing strategies that will help make significant gains in leading Hispanics to a personal faith in Christ in the next four and a half decades.

**Table 3**
**Hispanic Population Projections (1990 – 2050)**

| Year | Population Estimate/Projection | Percent of Total Population |
|------|------|------|
| 1990 | 22.4 Million | 9.0% |
| 1995 | 27.1 | 10.3 |
| 2000 | 25.3 | 12.5 |
| 2003 | 39.9 | 13.7 |
| 2010 | 47.7 | 15.5 |
| 2020 | 59.8 | 17.8 |
| 2030 | 73.1 | 20.1 |
| 2040 | 87.6 | 22.3 |
| 2050 | 102.6 | 24.4 |

Table 3, shows the estimated Hispanic population and the percentage of the total population that will be Hispanic by the year 2050. The truth of the matter is that these population projections have been increased in the last few years indicating that the Hispanic population is growing faster than Demographic experts had projected.

*By the year 2050 Hispanics are projected to comprise nearly one fourth of the population of America.*

Sound evidence indicates that this trend is well underway. ***Between 2000 and 2004 Hispanics grew from 35.6 million to 41.3 million***[16]

*Table 4.*

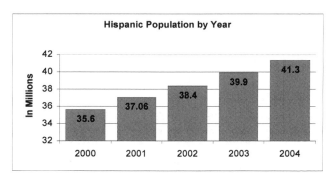

### *Hispanic Population by Year*

Table 4 shows the steady increase in the Hispanic population from the year 2000 to the year 2004. The total number of Hispanics in the United States obviously is increasing steadily and notably from 35.6 million to 41.3 million in just five years. The growth rate of the Hispanic population is certainly one of the Hispanic Realities of the present period.

This same growth rate is clearly seen in table 5.

### Table 5.
### *From July 1, 2003 to July 1, 2004 the*

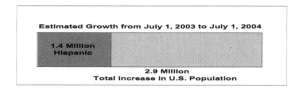

*Hispanic Population grew by 1.4 million[17]*
*"The nation's largest minority group accounted for nearly half (1.4) of the overall population growth of 2.9 million between July 2003 and July 2004, according to a Census Bureau Report released today"[18]*

In a Washington Post article entitled "Hispanic population keeps gaining numbers," D'Vera Cohn stated:

> Last July Hispanics numbered 41.3 million out of a national population of 293.7 million. They have the fastest growth rate among the nation's major racial and ethnic groups. In the 1990s they accounted for 40 percent of the country's population increase, from 2000 to 2004, that figure grew to 49 percent. According to a Census Bureau report to be released today, Hispanics have accounted for about half of the growth in the U.S. population since 2000, indicating that the nation's largest minority group is increasing its presence even faster than in the previous decade.[19]

While there are those who have predicted a significant decrease in the Hispanic population rate, the facts show that the opposite is true. The Hispanic growth rate has increased faster than was expected.

*People seeking to reach the population of this country for Christ will be very wise to develop contextualized strategies and allocate personnel and resources to reach the rapidly growing Hispanic population in America today.*

Endnotes

[10] Pew Hispanic Center, Roberto Suro and Jeffery S. Passel, *The Rise of the Second Generation*, October, 2003, 3. (), 3.

[11] U.S. Census Bureau cited in "Report, Hispanic Population Surging," Dallas Morning News, June 9, 2005, 13A.

[12] D'Vera Cohn, "Hispanic population keeps gaining numbers," Washington Post, cited in Fort Worth Star Telegram, Thursday, June 9, 2005, 5A.

[13] Source: Current Population Survey, March 2000, PGP-5

[14] Source: Current Population Survey, March 2002, PGP-5

[15] U.S. Census Bureau cited in "Report, Hispanic Population Surging," Dallas Morning News, June 9, 2005, 13A.

[16] "Report, Hispanic Population Surging," Dallas Morning News, June 9, 2005, 13A.

[17] Associated Press, "Census: Hispanic population reaches record level." Fort Worth Star Telegram, Thursday, June, 9, 2005, A1.

[18] Ibid

[19] D'Vera Cohn, "Hispanic population keeps gaining numbers," Washington Post, cited in Fort Worth Star Telegram, Thursday, June 9, 2005, 5A.

# CHAPTER 2

# REALITY # 2

*Hispanics have spread throughout the country*
*faster than any previous immigrants group.*

Several facts emerge as we look at the rapid expansion of the Hispanic population. Hispanics have grown in every type of metropolitan area: Established Hispanic Metros; New Hispanic Destinations; Fast Growing Hispanic Hubs, and Small Hispanic Places. [20]

## Table 6
## Types of Metropolitan Areas

| Types of Urban Descriptions | Descriptions of Areas | Locations of Areas |
|---|---|---|
| Established Hispanic Metros (16) | Large Base/ Slow Growth | New York, Los Angeles, Miami, Chicago, etc. |
| New Hispanic Destinations (51) | Small Base/Fast Growth | Atlanta, Birmingham, Charlotte, Ft. Lauderdale, Greenville, etc |
| Fast Growing Hispanic Hubs (11) | Large Base/Fast Growth | Austin, Bakersfield, Dallas, Houston, Phoenix, Riverside, San Diego, etc. |
| Small Hispanic Places (22) | Small Base/Slow Growth | Akron, Buffalo, Detroit, Newark, Philadelphia, etc. |

Table 7 shows the percent of the Hispanic population and the percent of growth in the past two decades as well as the areas in which this growth has occurred. [21/22]

### Table 7
### Hispanic Urban Growth

| Area Type | % of Hispanic Population | % Growth 1980-2000 |
|---|---|---|
| Established Hispanic Metros | 52% | 97% |
| New Hispanic Destinations | 19% | 303% |
| Fast Growing Hispanic Hubs | 25% | 235% |
| Small Hispanic Places | 04% | 81% |

**Average Urban Growth (all areas) 145%.**

Table 7 also shows the percent of the Hispanic population that is concentrated in each type of urban community and the rate of growth of the Hispanic population between the year 1980 and the year 2000. In the Established Hispanic Metros, Hispanics grew by 97% between the years 1980 and 2000. Particular urban areas within these Established Hispanic Metros showed remarkable growth. For example: Albuquerque 55%; Chicago 143%; Denver 142%; El Paso 98%; Fresno 143%; Jersey City 67%; Los Angeles 105%; McAllen 118%; Miami 123%; New York 60%; Oakland

138%; San Antonio 67%; San Francisco 75%; San Jose by 78%; Tucson 122%; and Ventura 122%.

These Established Hispanic Metros grew to a total of 14,119,006 or 43% of the Hispanic population in the year 2000.[23]

In eighteen New Hispanic Destinations, Hispanics grew by 505% between the years 1980 and 2000. Particular urban areas in these regions showed remarkable growth in Hispanic populations.  For example, Raleigh experienced the greatest rate of growth with 1180% during these two decades. It was followed by: Atlanta 995%; Greensboro 962%; Charlotte 932%; Orlando 859%; Las Vegas 753%; Nashville 630%; Fort Lauderdale 578%; Sarasota 538%; Portland 437%; Greensville 397%; West Palm Beach 397%; Washington D.C. 346%; Indianapolis 331%; Fort Worth 338%; Providence 325%; and Tulsa 303%.

The 505% increase in Hispanic populations in these 18 New Hispanic Destinations during these two decades brought their Hispanic total to 2,750,664 by the year 2000.[24] While these were the New Hispanic Destinations with over 300% growth, there were actually 33 other areas that fit under this category all of which experienced more than 100% growth. These include Albany, NY, which grew by 185%; Allentown, PA, by 261%; Baltimore by 148%; Bergin Passaic by 162%; Birmingham by 183%; Boston by 181%; Columbus, GA, by 220%; Grand Rapids by 283%; Harrisburg, PA by 226%; Hartford CT by 148%; Jacksonville by 198%; Knoxville by 157%; Little Rock by 200%; Louisville by 193%; Memphis by 214%; Hunterdon by 233%; Milwaukee by 170%; Minneapolis St. Paul by 331%; Monmouth-Ocean NJ by 200%; Nassau-Suffolk by 175%; New Haven by 190%; Norfolk-Virginia Beach-Newport

News by 163%; Oklahoma City by 281%; Omaha by 213%; Providence by 437%; Richmond by 235%; Salt Lake City by 233%; Scranton by 189%; Seattle by 274%; Springfield MO by 203%; Tacoma by 192%; Tampa by 209%; WV PSMA by 346%; Wichita, KA by 280%.

The combined percentage growth of all of the 51 New Hispanic Destinations is 303%. What is astounding is that even in some of the most unlikely metro areas in terms of previous Hispanic presence, they have grown at very rapid rates in the last two decades.[25]

While many people are accustomed to the large concentrations of Hispanics in the Established Hispanic areas, New Hubs are growing so rapidly that their impact needs to be taken into account by mission strategists wishing to reach Hispanics for Christ. In alphabetical order, these Fast-Growing Hispanic Hubs are: Austin which grew by 211% between the years 1980 and 2000; Bakersfield by 192%; Dallas by 358%; Houston by 211%; Orange County by 206%; Phoenix by 261%; Riverside-San Bernardino by 324%; Sacramento by 172%; San Diego by 174%; Stockton by 158%; and Vallejo by 197%. These Fast-Growing Hispanic Hubs grew by a combined rate of 235% and a total of 6,818,961 Hispanics by the year 2000.[26]

A fourth category of Hispanic Metropolitan growth is the "Small Hispanic Places." These are cities where there was a small number of Hispanics in 1980, yet they have experienced significant growth between that year and the year 2000. In alphabetical order they are Akron which grew by 44%; Ann Arbor by 54%; Baton Rouge by 74%; Buffalo by 44%; Charleston by 75%; Cincinnati by 154%;

Cleveland by 47%; Columbus by 152%; Dayton by 61%; Detroit by 58%; Gary by 50%; Honolulu by 8%; Mobile by 106%; New Orleans by 19%; Newark by 65%; Philadelphia by 59%; Pittsburg by 50%; Rochester by 81%; St Louis by 59%; Syracuse by 56%; Toledo by 49%; and Youngstown by 77%. The combined rate of growth for the Small Hispanic Places was 54%.

## Conclusions that arise from this information are:

1. **The Hispanic population grew in all metropolitan areas by a combined rate of 145% between the years 1980 and 2000.** In the Established Hispanic Metros they grew by 97%; in the New Hispanic Destinations by 303%; in the Fast-Growing Hispanic Hubs by 235%; and in the Small Hispanic Places by 81%. Every metropolitan area of America today is faced with the challenge of leading more Hispanics than ever to a personal faith in Christ and enabling them to start churches that minister to their communities.

2. **New patterns of growth have developed.** Hispanics are not only growing in the Established Areas (e.g., Los Angeles, New York City, Chicago, Miami), but are going to "New Destinations," areas where they had not concentrated in large numbers in the past. Cities such as Atlanta, Georgia; Charlotte, North Carolina; Las Vegas, Nevada; Nashville, Tennessee; Raleigh-Durham, North Carolina; and Washington D.C. are experiencing sudden and explosive growth. This increase in population is posing significant challenges for the native residents who have not had significant previous contacts with Hispanics but do have a commitment to

lead Hispanics to a personal faith in Christ and to start churches among them.

3. **Many Hispanics are bypassing the "Gateway Cities" (e.g., Los Angeles, New York, Chicago and Miami) and are going straight to "New Destination" areas. Washington DC and Atlanta among others are emerging immigration gateways for Hispanics.**[27] **One of the implications of this is that many Hispanics are not just new arrivals to these areas but to this country itself. This has significant implications in terms of the adaptation of Hispanics to the predominant culture of the United States and to an area of the country that has not had previous experience of relating to Hispanics.**

4. **Hispanics are not just experiencing significant growth but are undergoing new types of growth.** The perception that most Hispanics lived in rural areas was dispelled at least three decades ago when they started to concentrate in the urban areas of America. Today we discover that there has been yet another shift. Hispanics are now spreading to the suburbs. Approximately 54% of all Hispanics live in the suburbs.[28] It is also interesting to note that Hispanic men outnumber Hispanic women by 17% in the new Hispanic Destination Metro Areas.[29] Male immigrants arrive first and families follow. This fact has implications for church ministries that need to relate to the men first and then to their families when they arrive.

5. **Long-term residents in the "New Destination Areas" face the dual task of adjusting to the significant influx of a cultural group with whom they were not previously acquainted and of seeking to relate to a**

family structure that is somewhat atypical. Organizations, whether social or religious, that are able to relate to the new arrivals will find that this will enable them to serve and minister to entire families in the future. It has been proven that people who are in a state of flux are often more open to new ideas and relationships.

*The rapid and widespread growth of the Hispanic population coupled with the emerging new forms of growth and new areas of settlement present an unprecedented challenge for those who wish to lead Hispanics to a personal faith in Christ, enable them to establish churches, and encourage them to impact their communities with vibrant, compassionate ministries.*

Of the growing Hispanic populations, Harry Pacon declares: "The major significance is that it's a national presence."[30]

---

Endnotes

[20] "Latino Growth in Metropolitan America," The Brookings Institution Center on Urban & Metropolitan Policy and the Pew Hispanic Center, 3.

[21] Ibid., 4

[22] Ibid.

[23] Ibid., 12.

[24] Ibid., 5.

[25] Ibid., 12,13.

[26] Ibid., 16.

[27] Ibid., 5.

[28] "Latino Growth in Metropolitan America," The Brookings Institution Center on Urban & Metropolitan Policy and the Pew Hispanic Center. 1.

[29] "Latino Growth in Metropolitan America," The Brookings Institution Center on Urban & Metropolitan Policy and the Pew Hispanic Center. 1.

[30] Harry Pacon, cited in D'vera Cohn, "Hispanic population keeps gaining numbers," Star Telegram, June 9, 2005, 5A

# CHAPTER 3

# REALITY #3

**The First Generation (the immigrants) has become the largest segment of the Hispanic population in America today.**[31]

Although the ancestors of some Hispanics were permanent residents of what is now the southwestern United States when this territory was annexed, many Hispanics are descendents of those who have immigrated since the early 1900s.

In the middle portion of the 20th century, the third generation (grandchildren of the immigrants) constituted the largest segment of the Hispanic population and had the deepest roots in U.S. culture. This is the generation that is more assimilated into the predominant society, is bilingual, or prefers to speak English.

*By 1990, however, those who are first generation immigrants became the largest segment of Hispanic population.*[32] This is the generation that is the least assimilated and is basically Spanish speaking.

Table 8 shows the current Hispanic population by generations and percentage of the Hispanic population for each generation.

### Table 8
### Current Hispanic Population by Generations

| Generation | Percent of Hispanic Population | Total |
|:---:|:---:|:---:|
| First | 14.2 million | 40% |
| Second | 9.9 | 28% |
| Third | 11.3 | 32% |

Demographers predict that until 2020 the first generation will continue to be the largest segment of the Hispanic population. From 2020 on, the second generation will be the largest. From 2010 on, the third generation will constitute about one third of the Hispanic population as seen in Table 9

### Table 9
### Projected Hispanic Population by Generations

| Generation | 2000 | 2010 | 2020 |
|:---:|:---:|:---:|:---:|
| First | 40% | 38% | 34% |
| Second | 28% | 32% | 36% |
| Third | 32% | 30% | 30% |

In Table 9 we see the projected percentage of the population for the three generations of Hispanics.

*This generational shift among Hispanics strongly challenges the assumption that all Hispanics are becoming assimilated and that social services and ministry in Spanish and specialized strategies to relate to them are no longer needed.*

Following the assimilation patterns of previous groups, many people concluded that within two generations, the majority of the Hispanic population would become a part of the predominant society and Spanish ministries as well as Spanish-speaking churches would no longer be needed. What they did not take into account is that Hispanic immigration patterns have been different from those of other groups coming to America. Their geographical proximity to their mother countries, unlike the Germans, Italians, and Irish to name but a few, has contributed to on-going immigration which has continually reinforced the culture and the language of the Hispanics that were already in America.

The large number of immigrants in just three decades has resulted in the immigrant generation outnumbering the two previous generations. This, in a very real sense results in a repetition of the immigration process over and over again as Hispanics continue to arrive in America. *The need for Spanish-speaking ministries and Spanish-speaking churches is even greater today than it was three decades ago!*

At the same time, however, the growth of the second generation and the consistent percentage of the third generation underscore the fact that the use of the English language will continue to be indispensable in relating to them. "Regardless of nativity or country of origin, Hispanics who reside in the United States are engaging the English language and American ways to varying degrees."[33]

> *While, on the one hand, there is a desperate need for Spanish-speaking churches, there is also a desperate need for bi-lingual and English-language/Spanish-culture congregations as well as for English-language/Predominant-culture churches to reach the more assimilated Hispanics in America today.*

Reality # 4 sheds additional light on this striking need among Hispanic workers.

---

Endnotes

[31] Source: Pew Hispanic Center, Roberto Suro and Jeffery S. Passel, *The Rise of the Second Generation*, October, 2003, 4.

[32] Source: Pew Hispanic Center, Roberto Suro and Jeffery S. Passel, *The Rise of the Second Generation*, October, 2003, 4

[33] Pew Hispanic Center/Kaiser Family Foundation, 2002 National Survey of Latinos, December 2002, 6.

# CHAPTER 4

# REALITY #4

## The use of the Spanish language in America has increased in the past two decades.[34]

Contrary to the perception of many, the use of the Spanish language is not declining but in fact is increasing due to the influence of the first generation. The statistics on Table 10 clearly point this out.

### Table 10
### Spanish Language by Generations[35]

| Generation | Percent of Population | Spanish | Bilingual | English |
|:---:|:---:|:---:|:---:|:---:|
| First | 72% | 24% | 04% | 40% |
| Second | 07% | 47% | 46% | 28% |
| Third | 0% | 22% | 78% | 32% |

**These facts relating to the use of Spanish language by generations confront us with a dual challenge:**

1. Communicating with the immigrant generation requires primarily utilizing the Spanish language.

Major corporations in America have realized the importance of using Spanish in communicating with the immigrant generation. Those corporations that have neglected the use of the Spanish language have been ineffective in relating to the Hispanic American community. One example of the former is K-Mart:

> Kmart Corp, which is reconstructing from bankruptcy protection, said Wednesday that it will publish its weekly circular in Spanish for the first time, in a bid to reach out to the growing Hispanic market. The discount retailer said the advertising circular will be translated into Spanish. The circular will be available in 160 stores located in large Hispanic populations and appear in 10 Spanish-language newspapers throughout the U.S., K-Mart is expanding its effort to reach this influential group. *More than 55 percent of all Hispanics living in the United States are within 15 minutes of one of its stores (italics mine). As the $500 billion Hispanic market continues to grow in the U.S., Kmart is expanding its efforts to reach this influential consumer group.*[36]

2. Communicating with the second and third generation requires the use of bi-lingual and English-dominant strategies.

In an article entitled "Spanish Spoken Here," a spokes person for General Motors outlines their strategy to communicate bilingually:

> General Motors (GM) hopes to entice more Spanish-speaking employees and, as a result, customers, to its

Chicago-area dealerships through a new jobs program. Through the Bilingual Employment Sales Training (BEST) program, GM will work with its dealers in attracting, recruiting, and training 200 bilingual sales personnel. Latinos comprise 16 percent of Chicago's population, 1.8 million people, according to GM.GM will appeal to job candidates through television, radio, and print advertising and direct marketing efforts. Successful candidates will receive career training and counseling as sales associates. "The Hispanic market is expected to continue growing in the coming years. GM has a great opportunity to grow with it, but we also have a responsibility to provide job opportunities so that the Hispanic community can prosper with us," said Dora Ann Sanchez-Mead, GM training manager.[37]

Geoffrey Jones stresses the fact that the use of Spanish is increasing in North America:

> Last season, Spanish-language network Univision captured more teens nationwide than MTV, more men than ESPN, and three times as many new viewers as CNN... Spanish-language radio also is booming; it's among the top stations in Los Angeles, New York, and Miami. Univision has about 90% of the Spanish-language viewing audience.[38]

It is important to be aware of the fact that Hispanics (as well as other cultural groups) make a distinction between the trade language (that of the predominant society) and their heart language (their mother tongue).

A study by Daniel Lund of MUND Americas and Sammy Papert of Belden Associates found that

Hispanics prefer Spanish when they are seeking a service, such as an Internet provider of a travel agency. But when buying a product, like a car or a cell phone, they prefer English, a language they associate with rational decisions. To put it another way, Latinos use Spanish for the emotional transactions, while English is the tongue of calculation and dispassionate choice.[39]

These facts about the use of Spanish language among Hispanics have significant implications for those who are seeking to sell products to Hispanics versus those who are trying to provide counseling or to minister to them spiritually. The fact that many Hispanics have learned to function in English on the job does not mean that they do not use their heart language in their primary relationships and in their religious practices. *It is an established missiological fact that people respond more rapidly and completely to the Gospel message when it is presented to them in their mother tongue.*[40]

Many corporations are learning that it takes more than translating materials into Spanish. An understanding of the culture is indispensable:

"In culture" means speaking to Hispanics in their native language or the language they respond to most when making decisions. In culture means being sensitive to ethnic or nationality sensitivities and not making cultural gaffes. In culture means reaching out to social organizations or civic leaders to make sure your marketing campaign or editorial slant won't trigger a boycott by disgruntled community activities.[41]

Churches seeking to minister to Hispanics face the dual challenge of communicating with those who are predominantly Spanish speakers and with those who are more proficient in English than in Spanish. The Pew Foundation Survey states:

> Spanish remains the predominant language in the adult Hispanic population. English, however, clearly gains ground even within immigrant households. The second generation – the U.S. – born children of immigrants – predominantly speak English or are bilingual. Indeed, Hispanic parents, even those who are immigrants, report that English is the language their children generally use when speaking to their friends.[42]

In light of the fact that Hispanics are experiencing immigration and assimilation simultaneously, ministries among Hispanics need to provide for people at all the stages of this continuum.

---

Endnotes

[34] Source: Pew Hispanic Center, Roberto Suro and Jeffery S. Passel, *The Rise of the Second Generation*, October, 2003, 7.

[35] Source: Pew Hispanic Center, Roberto Suro and Jeffery S. Passel, *The Rise of the Second Generation*, October, 2003, 8.

[36] Fox News, "Kmart Reaches Out to Hispanic Customers, August 28, 2002.

[37] DiversityInc, May 2005, p.20.

[38] Goeffrey Jones, "DL's Jones On Boom In Spanish-Language Broadcasting," Invester's Business Daily, October 18, 1999.

[39] Guy Garcia, *The New Mainstream*, rayo, an Imprint of Harper Collins Publishers, 2004, 44.

[40] Donald McGavran, *Understanding Church Growth*, Grand Rapids: William Eerdmans, 1970, 198.

[41] Guy Garcia, *The New Mainstream*, rayo, An Imprint of Harper Collins Publishers, 2004, 9,10

[42] Pew Hispanic Center/Kaiser Family Foundation, 2002 National Survey of Latinos, December 2002, 8.

# CHAPTER 5

# REALITY #5

**Second and third generation Hispanics have made significant strides in educational attainment, yet the first generation lags behind.**[43]

While it is true that second and third generation Hispanics have made significant strides in improving their educational status, the same is not true for first generation Hispanics. Table 11 shows that 54 percent of the immigrant generation has less than a high school education, 24 percent are High School graduates, 13 percent have received some college training, and 9 percent are college graduates. The percentages change dramatically for second and third generation Hispanics with many more graduating from High School and getting some college training or graduating from college.

**Table 11**
**Education among Hispanics (Ages 24-65)**[44]

| Generation | Less Than High School | High School | Some College | College Graduation |
|:---:|:---:|:---:|:---:|:---:|
| First | 54% | 24% | 13% | 09% |
| Second | 23% | 33% | 29% | 15% |
| Third | 25% | 35% | 27% | 13% |

As we look at educational attainment, we face a dual challenge in training Hispanics for Christian ministry:

1. We need to encourage second and third generation Hispanics to avail themselves of existing educational programs in universities and seminaries. As can be seen in Table 11, the percentage of second and third generation Hispanics who have completed their High School education is appreciably higher than that of first generation Hispanic. These second and third generation Hispanics, therefore are better prospects for existing training programs in colleges and seminaries in America today.

2. We need to make provision for entry-level training for First generation Hispanics who are called to ministry. This is the group that is most responsive to the gospel message. Consequently, more churches are being started among them, yet most denominations do not have strategies to start training persons at the entry level and provide a way (a ramp) for them to continue their studies at the college and seminary level.

Corporations are recognizing the need for contextualized training for Hispanics. For example, food and facilities management provider Sodexho is rolling out "Sed de Saber" (Thirst for Knowledge), an English-as-a-second-language program for its Spanish-speaking frontline employees. More than 100 employees in California, Arizona, Texas, Massachusetts and Washington, D.C., will participate in the initial stage of the program, which will eventually be available to all Spanish-speaking employees. Those who complete the 6-month program receive a certificate and a cash award. "We have a vested interest in the success of our employees," says Richard Macedonia, Sodexho USA's CEO. "As the demographics of our work force continue to change, we are concentrating on developing our employees ... not just for better jobs, but for careers."[45]

3. While the focus of this book is leading Hispanics to a personal faith in Christ and enabling their congregations to minister to their communities more effectively, one fact that cannot be ignored is, *the High School dropout rate for Hispanic youth is twice as high as the dropout rate of comparable non-Hispanic whites.*[46]

In his study entitled "Hispanic Youth Dropping out Of U.S. Schools: Measuring the Challenge," Richard Fry states:

> Latino youth in the U.S. is [sic] more likely to have dropped out of school than other youth. In 2000, 21 percent of Hispanic 16- to 19- year olds were drop outs, in comparison to 8 percent of white youth, and 12 percent of African American youth.

Fray shares three items of information that are very useful in understanding the current status of Hispanic youth education:

1. Focusing on data for Hispanics who have dropped out of U.S. schools before completing high school reveals a problem that is quite grave and has serious long-term implications for the education system, Latino communities, and the nation as a whole. However, these numbers show that the problem is not as disturbing as commonly thought. Simply put, dropout rates of 30 percent or more are frequently cited for Hispanics overall. These figures,

however, include many immigrants who never began studies in a U.S. school. Counting only Latinos who dropped out of school after engaging in the American educational system, one finds a drop-out rate of only about 15 percent among 16- to 19-year olds.[47]

2. Among the native-born Hispanic 18- to 19- year olds, those who completed high school rose from 54.7 percent to 60.0 percent from 1990 to 2000. Among foreign-born Hispanic 18- to 19-year olds, the high school completion rate rose from 32.0 to 38.1 percent over the decade.[48]

3. *The lack of English-language ability is a prime characteristic of Latino dropouts.* Almost 40 percent do not speak English well. The 14 percent of Hispanic youth 16- to 19-year olds who have poor English language skills have a dropout rate of 59 percent.[49]

Fry's study provides bad news as well as good news. The bad news is that a disproportionately high percentage of Hispanic young are dropping out of school. The good news is that there is a trend toward improvement. From the stand-point of those seeking to minister spiritually to the Hispanic community, there are two areas of serious concern.

First, if the youth who never attend school upon arriving in this country are factored in, there are at least 30 percent in any given area who have not finished high school. This points to the need to have GED type programs in our churches as well as providing ramps in the ministry training programs in such a way as to make up for educational deficiencies and enable Hispanics with a calling to ministry to start at a basic level and then plug into existing educational programs at the baccalaureate, masters, and doctoral programs.

Second, since proficiency in the English language is one of the crucial factors in obtaining a high school education for our Hispanic youth, we must ask the question, what are the churches doing to address this need?

**The educational needs of Hispanic youth provide a challenge as well as  an opportunity for those ministering in Hispanic contexts. Ministries that teach English as a second language, that encourage students to stay in high school, that tutor those who have special needs, or that provide a ramp for those who need to start their training at entry levels will not only help the Hispanic community socially and economically but will establish bridges that will facilitate the communication of the gospel message.**

Endnotes
[43] Pew Hispanic Center, Roberto Suro and Jeffery S. Passel, *The Rise of the Second Generation*, October, 2003, 8.
[44] Pew Hispanic Center, Roberto Suro and Jeffery S. Passel, *The Rise of the Second Generation*, October, 2003, 8.
[45] DiversityInc, May 2005, 20.
[46] Richard Fry, "Hispanic Youth Dropping Out Of U.S. Schools: Measuring The Challenge," Pew Hispanic Center, 2003, iii.
[47] Ibid., iii.
[48] Ibid., iii.
[49] Ibid., iv.

# CHAPTER 6

# REALITY # 6

*Hispanics are showing more receptivity
to the Evangelical message than ever
before in the history of this country*

## Evidences of Receptivity

Never in the history of this nation have Hispanics been more receptive to the evangelical message than they are now. A study done by Priest/Sociologist Andrew Greeley indicates that 23 percent of the Hispanic population now identifies with non-Catholic denominations, mainly Evangelicals.[50] This fact has been confirmed by more recent studies such as the Pew Hispanic Center's National Survey of Latinos. The results of this study are demonstrated in table 12.

### Table 12
### Religious Preference of Hispanics by Origin[51]

| Religion | Total | Foreign Born | Native Born |
|----------|-------|--------------|-------------|
| Catholic | 70% | 76% | 59% |
| Evangelical | 14% | 11% | 20% |
| Other Christian Religions | 06% | 05% | 09% |
| Non-Christian | 02% | 01% | 03% |
| Jewish | 0% | 0 | 01% |
| No Religion | 08% | 07% | 08% |

Table 12 shows that among Hispanics 70 percent identify themselves as "Catholics;" 20 percent as "Evangelical or Born Again;" 9 percent as "Other Christian;" 2 percent as "Some other non-Christian religion;" and 8 percent as having "No Religion."[52]

### Table 13
### Hispanic Religious Preference by Countries/Regions[53]

|  | Catholic | Evangelical | *Protestant Not Evangelical | Total Evangelical Protestant |
|---|---|---|---|---|
| Mexico | 76% | 11% | 05% | 16% |
| Puerto Rico | 55% | 21% | 08% | 29% |
| Central America | 51% | 25% | 04% | 29% |
| South America | 70% | 13% | 05% | 18% |
| Cuba | 64% | 15% | 05% | 20% |
| Dominican Republic | 74% | 12% | 03% | 15% |
| All Other | 46% | 25% | 13% | 38% |

\* "Protestant" includes "Other Christian Religion/Protestant (Not Evangelical)."

As we look at the religious preference of Hispanics we can rejoice over several facts:

• Hispanics are responding to the Evangelical message more than ever.

• Many who come from Latin America are already Evangelical Christians. For example, almost one third of the immigrants from Central America are already Evangelical Christians. Many of these either join existing churches or start new churches upon their arrival.

- Hispanics have the potential of positively influencing the American society.

The perception of many is that "immigration is transforming American religion." In his article "A New Spirituality: Hispanic Americans are influencing religious trends," Phillip Jenkins points out that the media have been trumpeting the country's new religious diversity. This does not sound too startling in light of this country's hospitality to Muslims, Buddhists, Sikhs, and adherents of other faiths. Jenkins, however, makes this insightful statement:

> While mass immigration is indeed having an enormous religious impact, the main beneficiary of the process is unquestionably Christianity. Far more than most observers yet appreciate, the vast majority of the new immigrants are Christian or have become so after their arrival on these shores – and it's a Christianity with a powerfully traditional bent... The vast majority of Latin Americans come from Christian cultures, either Catholic or Protestant. And although not every one is equally pious – or even notionally a believer – they have all been formed in a cultural matrix that is clearly Christian. [54]

In light of the statistics cited in Table 12, we know that approximately 20 percent of Hispanics can be counted as born again Christians.[55] It is also encouraging to know that the vast majority of Hispanic Americans have a religious background that favorably predisposes them to the Evangelical message if it is presented adequately. Therefore, instead of being pessimistic about the religious diversity of our nation, we need to acknowledge the fact that immigration from Latin America is increasing the possibility of vast numbers of persons being reached with the Gospel and transforming America in a positive way.

## Challenges to Evangelical Christians

In light of this receptivity, Evangelicals should accept two intense challenges. The challenges involve:

- Equipping Hispanic Evangelicals to share their faith in a more positive and effectively way with those people with a Roman Catholic background who have not had a personal experience of salvation in Jesus Christ.

- Developing contextualized evangelistic, church planting, and church growth strategies that will accelerate outreach to all of the Hispanics and enable them to establish churches with effective and compassionate ministries in their communities.

## Conclusion

Increased responsiveness demands increased evangelization. Donald A. McGavran insisted that good missionary practice involved winning the winnable now. McGavran felt that response rather than need should determine the utilization of missionary resources.[56] Following this missionary principle of action, Evangelicals today should move to seize the opportunity presented by the current Hispanic response to the Gospel.

---

Endnotes
[50] Andrew Greeley, "Defection Among Hispanics," *America* (July 30, 1988).61.

[51] Pew Hispanic Center/Kaiser Family Foundation, 2002 National Survey of Latinos, December 2002, 53.

[52] Pew Hispanic Center/Kaiser Family Foundation, 2002 National Survey of Latinos, December 2002, 53.

[53] Pew Hispanic Center/Kaiser Family Foundation, 2002 National Survey of Latinos, December 2002, 53.

[54] Philip Jenkins, "A New Spirituality: Hispanic Americans are influencing religious trends in the United States," *Hispanic Trends*, Hispanic Publishing Group/Hispanic Online.com.

[55] George Barna, "The Faith of Hispanics is Shifting," ., 2/26/2003

[56] Donald A. McGavran, *Understanding Church Growth (Grand Rapids: Eerdmans, 1970).*

# CHAPTER 7

# REALITY # 7

## Hispanics are typically very conservative regarding social values[5]

A 2003 survey of U.S. Latinos by the Pew Hispanic Center of the Kaiser Family Foundation found that immigrants from Latin America were "overwhelmingly committed to strong family ties, religious beliefs, education, and hard work and were actually worried that the coming to the United States would have a negative impact on the moral values of their children."[58]

### Table 14
### Importance of Religion to Hispanic/Anglos[59]

|  | Hispanics | Anglos |
|---|---|---|
| Most Important | 21% | 20% |
| Very Important | 47% | 41% |
| Somewhat | 25% | 28% |
| Not At All | 06% | 11% |

The survey cited above also demonstrated the importance Hispanics assign to religion in their lives. As Table 14 indicates 21 percent of Hispanics consider religion "most important," in comparison to 20 percent for their Anglo counterparts. This table also indicates that 47 percent of Hispanics consider religion "very important," in comparison to 41 percent for their Anglo counterparts. It is also important to note that of Hispanics only 6 percent considered religion "not at all important," compared to 11 percent of their counterparts. As one adds the first two categories, one finds that for 68 percents of Hispanics religion is either "most important" or "very important" compared to 61 percent for their Anglo counterparts. It can be safely stated that Hispanics are strong when it comes to the conservation of religion as an important social value.

For Hispanics, family unity and loyalty are important values. A strong attachment to family is evident among Hispanics who predominantly speak English and are generations removed from the immigrant experience.[60] This is an example of the selective assimilation in which many Hispanics participate. While they desire to incorporate many of the values of the predominant society, they also choose to retain some values, among which is the importance of family. A majority of Hispanics maintain that children growing up in the US will stay close to their families[61]

Recent studies by the PEW Foundation's Hispanic Center reveal that Hispanics in general have more conservative social values than Anglos in general. As seen in table 15, Hispanics regard as unacceptable divorce, homosexuality between adults, and abortion.[62]

### Table 15
### Attitudes Regarding Social Practices
### Percent who found these practices unacceptable:

|  | Hispanics | Anglos |
|---|---|---|
| Divorce | 35% | 24% |
| Homosexuality | 66% | 58% |
| Abortion | 69% | 52% |

With regard to social issues that Hispanics considered important in the last presidential election, 58 percent stated that education was vital as compared to 40 percent for Anglos; 39 percent said that the economy was vital as compared to 38 percent for Anglos; 23 percent said that Health Care and Medicare were important as compared to 22 percent for Anglos, and 20 percent said that Social Security was vital as compared to 19 percent for Anglos.[63] As one can see from this survey, "on some social issues Hispanics express a conservatism that sets them apart from their Anglo counterparts."[64]

A 2003 survey of U.S. Latinos by the Pew Hispanic Center of the Kaiser Family Foundation found that immigrants from Latin America were overwhelmingly committed to strong family ties, religious beliefs, education, and hard work and were actually worried that coming to the United States would have a negative impact on the moral values of their children.[65]

A similar study conducted by Drs. Gaston Espinoza, Virgilio Elizonda, and Jesse Miranda confirmed the findings of other studies that concluded that Hispanic Americans strongly support conservative values. They state:

> Although Latinos tend to vote politically progressively, they clearly support traditionally and conservative pro-family, moral, and social issues such as school prayer, school vouchers, and the charitable choice initiative. Despite the unique character of the Latino community, it shares many of the same goals, aspirations, and social political views as a cross-section of American society.[66]

As Evangelicals lead Hispanics to a personal experience of salvation in Jesus Christ, they will find committed allies in retaining many of the conservative social values in America.

---

Endnotes

[57] Pew Hispanic Center/Kaiser Family Foundation, 2002 National Survey of Latinos, 47.

[58] Guy Garcia, *The New Mainstream*, rayo, An Imprint of Harper Collins Publishers, 2004, 130. Simon Romero and Janet Elder, "Hispanics in the U.S. Report Optimism," The New York Times, August 6, 3003.

[59] Pew Hispanic Center/Kaiser Family Foundation, 2002 National Survey of Latinos, December 2002, 53.

[60] Pew Hispanic Center/Kaiser Family Foundation, 2002 National Survey of Latinos, 13.

[61] Pew Hispanic Center/Kaiser Family Foundation, 2002 National Survey of Latinos, 13.

[62] Pew Hispanic Center/Kaiser Family Foundation, 2002 National Survey of Latinos: The Latino Electorate, October 2002, Chart 14.

[63] Pew Hispanic Center/Kaiser Family Foundation, 2002 National Survey of Latinos: The Latino Electorate, October 2002, Chart 17.

[64] Ibid., 1.

[65] Guy Garcia, *The New Mainstream*, rayo, An Imprint of Harper Collins Publishers, 2004, 130. Simon Romero and Janet Elder, "Hispanics in the U.S. Report Optimism," The New York Times, August 6, 3003.

[66] Gastón Espinoza, Virgilio Elizondo, Jesse Miranda, Hispanic Churches in American Public Life: Summary Findings, Interim Reports, Vol. 2003.2, 2nd Edition, March 2003, 11-24.

# CHAPTER 8

# REALITY # 8

**Second and third generation Hispanics have made significant strides financially yet newly arrived Hispanics have typically the most difficult time financially[67]**

1. First Generation Hispanics who do not speak English are more likely to have lower incomes, to rent living quarters, to have financial difficulties, and to avoid using bank accounts.

2. Second Generation Hispanics and those who speak English (or are bilingual) are more likely to have higher incomes.

3. This has significant implications for evangelism and church planting strategies as well as for stewardship development.

4. Ministries such as Teaching English-as-a-Second-Language can have the effect of leading people to Christ as well as helping them to improve their economic status.

### Table 16
### Hispanic Household Income[68]

|  | Native Born | Foreign-Born |
|---|---|---|
| Less than 30,000 | 57% | 37% |
| 30,000 - 49,000 | 20% | 28% |
| 50,000+ | 11% | 27% |
| Don't Know | 12% | 09% |

### Table 17
### Hispanics by Occupation[69]

|  | Foreign Born | Native Born |
|---|---|---|
| White-Collar | 31% | 69% |
| Blue-Collar | 65% | 28% |
| Other | 03% | 03% |

*While it is important to find ways to
minister to Hispanics who are
at the bottom of the Socioeconomic scale,
it is also imperative to develop a strong
sense of stewardship among the
Hispanics whose earning power
is increasing rapidly.*

Many of the nation's leading corporations have begun to recognize the increasing economic potential of Hispanic Americans and are developing specialized strategies to tap into the Hispanic market. Quotes such as the following are now appearing in the nation's most influential periodicals:

*"According to the U.S. Bureau of Economic Analysis,
Latino buying power, or total income after taxes,
will rise from $700 billion to $1 trillion by 2010."[70]*

*"US Hispanic population and purchasing power
are both rising faster than that of the general
population. And because US Hispanics are
younger as a group than the rest of America,
the prime wage-earning years are
still ahead of them."*[71]

The strategies that are being developed by some of these
corporations are based on solid research of current Hispanic
American cultural characteristics. For instance, in her article
entitled "Banks make push for Latino Customers," Ilene
Alshire states the following:

> Banks across North Texas are trying to tap into a
> market that is largely unfamiliar to them... So
> they're adding Spanish-speaking employees and
> offering products to better serve Hispanics and to
> make people more comfortable about saving and
> borrowing money from banks.[72]

In a subsequent article entitled "Thinking Biculturally Is the
Key to Serve," Ilene Alshire quotes a study by Mintel, a
market-research firm which found that:

> Only half of U.S. Hispanics are bank customers,
> compared to 80 percent of the population as a
> whole. Only 27 percent of Hispanics have a
> mortgage, and fewer than 50 percent have some
> type of a loan.[73]

Alshire adds:

> Bankers and researchers cite several reasons for
> the high percentage of Hispanics without bank

connections: language barriers, wrong marketing tools and programs, immigration from countries where checking accounts were reserved for the well to do or where financial institutions were mistrusted, and a lack of awareness of what banks have to offer. Several banks are working hard to address these needs. Chase, for example, has its Bankmobile, a converted recreational vehicle that is staffed with bilingual employees and has the tools to take customers through, for example, the mortgage process... Chase puts a heavy emphasis on financial education, creating an awareness of banking products... "And we are doing it in Spanish, so they don't feel embarrassed about not being able to speak English well." The bank has also tried direct mail and advertising with a Spanish-language radio station, and grassroots efforts to increase its share of the Hispanic market. Bank of America has a Spanish-language Web site designed with some features specifically for customers who are either unfamiliar with or mistrustful of banks.[74]

Bank of America is taking extraordinary measures to relate to Hispanics. Recognizing the need to strengthen credit history within the Latino community, Bank of America announced the launch of its Electiva Visa Platinum, a full-service rewards credit card designed for Latinos. The card offers bilingual services, including welcome kits, a reward-redemption site, program materials, communications, check offers, and monthly statements.

"Establishing and managing credit is essential to living a successful life in this country, and this credit card can help Hispanics enjoy the perks of cash while strengthening their credit," says Jose Ruiz, senior vice president, Bank of America.[75]

Two crucial lessons can be learned from the manner in which these institutions are approaching Hispanics:

*First, financial institutions are making serious efforts to understand the cultural needs of the Hispanic population.*

*Second, these institutions are willing to employ the staff and to design the strategies that will facilitate communication and enhance trust between the institutions and the Hispanic population.*

*The actions of these financial institutions have significant implications for missionary agencies in terms of evangelism, discipleship, church planting, and stewardship development. Will Evangelicals learn from these corporations or will they continue to use traditional approaches even if they are no longer effective?*

---

Endnotes

[67] Pew Hispanic Center/Kaiser Family Foundation, 2002 National Survey of Latinos, 13.
[68] Pew Hispanic Center/Kaiser Family Foundation, 2002 National Survey of Latinos, 12.
[69] Pew Hispanic Center/Kaiser Family Foundation, 2002 National Survey of Latinos, 17.
[70] Ambar Hernández, HISPANIC, May, 2005, 38.
[71] Guy Garcia, The New Mainstream, rayo, An Imprint of Harper Collins Publishers, 2004,5
[72] Ilene Alshire, "Banks make push for Latino customers, Fort Worth Star Telegram, January 10, 2005, 1
[73] Ilene Alshire, "Banks make push for Latino customers, Fort Worth Star Telegram, January 10, 2005, 1
[74] Ilene Alshire, "Thinking Biculturally Is The Key To Service", Fort Worth Star Telegram, January 10, 2005, 1-C

[75] DiversityInc., volume 4 number 4, May 2005, 10

[75] Pew Hispanic Center/Kaiser Family Foundation, 2002 National Survey of Latinos, 13.

[75] Pew Hispanic Center/Kaiser Family Foundation, 2002 National Survey of Latinos, 12.

[75] Pew Hispanic Center/Kaiser Family Foundation, 2002 National Survey of Latinos, 17.

[75] Ambar Hernández, *HISPANIC*, May, 2005, 38.

[75] Guy Garcia, *The New Mainstream*, rayo, An Imprint of Harper Collins Publishers, 2004,5

[75] Ilene Alshire, "Banks make push for Latino customers, Fort Worth Star Telegram, January 10, 2005, 1

[75] Ilene Alshire, "Banks make push for Latino customers, Fort Worth Star Telegram, January 10, 2005, 1

[75] Ilene Alshire, "Thinking Biculturally Is The Key To Service", Fort Worth Star Telegram, January 10, 2005, 1-C

[75] DiversityInc., volume 4 number 4, May 2005, 10.

# CHAPTER 9

# REALITY # 9

## Hispanic Americans are the group with the largest percentage of children and young people.[76]

### *The median age for Hispanics is 26.7 years*

As seen in Table 18, the median age for Hispanics is lower than that of the other major cultural groups in America today. For non-Hispanic Whites the median age is 39.6 years; for African Americans it is 30.5 years; and for Asians it is 32 years. Of Hispanics, 10.4% are under age 5, compared to non-Hispanic Whites, 5.7%.

### Table 18
### Hispanic Median Age

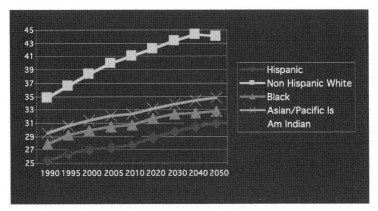

Of Hispanics, 5.2% are 65 years and over, compared to non-Hispanic Whites, 15.0%. Percentage wise, therefore, Hispanics have many more children and significantly fewer seniors than the non-Hispanic White population.

"The new census figures show a Hispanic population dominated by the young: Half are under age 27. By comparison, half of Anglos are over 40. That reflects a demographic divide that could have broad implications, experts say. And the speedy growth of the Hispanic population beyond the enclaves of the past could put their concerns into a more national spotlight."[77]

These statistics produce several observations:

First, the fact that half of the Hispanic population is under 26.7 years of age has very significant implications for the staffs and programs that churches have to minister to them. Churches that have children's ministers and ministers of youth are in a much better position to meet the needs of Hispanic children and youth. The implication of this is that such churches have programs that are specifically focused at ministering to Hispanic children and youth.

Second, Hispanic children and youth are typically more receptive to the Evangelical Message than other age groups including their parents. The willingness as well as the availability of time of the children and youth to become involved in activities that have a spiritual content is a factor in their responding more enthusiastically to the Evangelical message.

Third, Hispanic young people who fall between the cracks of their parent's culture and that of the predominant society are more prone to be involved in gangs which are an attempt to form a third culture. Coupled with the disproportionate dropout rate of Hispanic youth, the desire to belong makes many of them susceptible to the recruiting efforts of the gangs in their neighborhoods. Conversely, Hispanic youth who are meaningfully involved in religious and social activities in churches will have a sense of belonging and will not feel the need to join gangs in their communities.

Fourth, contextualized strategies for reaching Hispanic children and youth are desperately needed. Implications of the need for contextualized strategies are:

- One of the factors that need to be contextualized is the use of the language that is employed. "In 2000, 86 percent of Hispanic 16- to 19-year-olds spoke English at least well. The other 14 percent have poor language skills in English." [78]

- Second, churches that want to minister to Hispanic youth will need to be able to reach both ends of the spectrum. First generation Hispanic churches will need to use English in ministering to many of their young people.

- Conversely, second and third generation churches will need to use Spanish to reach that segment of the Hispanic youth that are basically Spanish speakers.

Fifth, more churches than ever before need to join forces with the schools in their communities to encourage Hispanic young people to finish their high school education and go beyond if possible. 14 percent of Hispanic 16- to

19-year-olds have poor language skills and also have a very high dropout rate. About 60 percent of these youth are high school dropouts.[79] Among Latino youth fluent in English skills, about 15 percent are high school dropouts. For the latter group, teaching English as a second language would address some to the vital needs among immigrant Hispanic youth.

Sixth, there is a dire need to minister to Hispanic children. Government statistics show that "twenty-seven percent of Hispanic children reside in poverty."[80] Churches that minister to the physical and emotional needs of children will find that it will be quite natural to minister to their spiritual needs as well. Their receptivity is seen in their readiness to participate in such activities as Vacation Bible School, Backyard Bible Clubs, and church-related recreational activities.

Seventh, the presence of such large numbers of Hispanic youth has significant implications for the workforce of America in the future. Lewis Goodman, an American University expert on U.S.-Latin American relations states:

> If we didn't have those elements, we would be moving into a situation like Japan and Europe... where the populations are graying in a way that is very alarming and endangering their productivity and endangering even their social security systems.[81]

*Almost all the growth in the number of U.S. youth within the next 20 years will be Hispanic.[82]*

# CHAPTER 9
*Reality #9*

The Census Bureau projects that the school age population will increase by 5.6 million children out to 2025. Of that increase, Latino children will increase by 5.2 million. [83]

What are Evangelicals doing to meet the challenge now and within the next two decades?  What changes in ministries are needed to take advantage of these realities in the Hispanic population?  Children and youth should become a priority for Evangelicals as they minister among Hispanics in this day.

---

Endnotes

[76] Current Population Survey, March 2002, PGP-5

[77] D'Vera Cohn, "Hispanic population keeps gaining numbers," The Washington Post, cited in Fort Worth Star Telegram, June, 9, 2005, A5.

[78] Richard Fry, "Hispanic Youth Dropping Out Of U.S. Schools: Measuring The Challenge," Pew Hispanic Center, 2003, 8.

[79] Ibid

[80] Ibid., 12.

[81] Lewis W. Goodman, cited in "Report: Hispanic population surging," Dallas Morning News, June 9, 2005, 13A.

[82] Ibid., 12.

[83] Ibid., 12

# CHAPTER 10

# REALITY # 10

**Hispanics have much in common with one another yet there is significant diversity among them.**[84]

*Hispanic Americans face the dual challenge of immigration and assimilation simultaneously.*

On the one hand, new immigrants function almost exclusively within their native culture and language while on the other hand their children immediately upon arrival embark on a rapid assimilation process promoted by public education, the media, and peer group pressure. This presents an awesome challenge for Hispanic churches.

Table 19 shows the degree of assimilation experienced by each generation. First generation Hispanics typically have very few social contacts outside their own group and the majority of them are Spanish speakers. Second generation Hispanics have some social contacts outside their own group and are bilingual with perhaps more mastery of the Spanish than the English language. Third generation Hispanics have many social contacts outside their own group and may be bilingual with more fluency in English or even be predominately English speakers. Fourth generation Hispanics have most of their contacts outside their group and are generally English speakers.

## Table 19
## Hispanic Assimilation by Generations

| Generation | Outside Social Contacts | Language |
|---|---|---|
| First | Few | Spanish |
| Second | Some | Bilingual Spanish Dominant |
| Third | Many | Bilingual English Dominant |
| Fourth | Most | English Only |

**These data give rise to important observations:**

1.  Hispanics are neither monolithic nor a hodgepodge of distinct national origin groups.

2.  Their common culture shares a diversity of views that is most evident in the contrasts between immigrant and native born.

3.  They share a range of attitudes and experiences that set them apart from the non-Hispanic population.

4.  Different types of churches are needed for Hispanics in the various assimilation stages. This will be discussed more fully in chapter 12.

While the information on Table 19 can be helpful in analyzing the various segments of the Hispanic population, Christian workers should remember that there are numerous exceptions due to the variants in the Hispanic community. Typically the rate of assimilation is affected by factors such as:

- Patterns of residence (do they live in isolated communities?)
- Length of residence (how long have they been in the U.S.?)
- Attitudes of the predominant society (are they receptive to the immigrant group?)
- Attitudes of the immigrant group (to what extent do they want to assimilate?)
- Socioeconomic levels (how similar are they to the predominant society?)
- Values (how similar are their values to those of the predominant society?)

## General Suggestions

The following suggestions were made by researchers related to the Brookings Institution's Center on Urban and Metropolitan Policy, the Pew Hispanic Center, and Kaiser Family Foundation in the research projects entitled "The Rise of the Second Generation," and "Latino Growth in Metropolitan Areas." While originally addressed to government and education policy makers, these suggestions have significant application for mission strategists seeking to respond to the challenge presented by the astounding growth, dispersion, and diversification of the Hispanic population in this country.

- *Overall findings suggest the need for new ways of thinking about the Hispanic population in this country.*[85]

- *Newly arrived immigrants are bringing new energy to the Spanish language and to attitudes shaped in Latin America.*[86]

- *Two processes – assimilation and immigration – are taking place side-by-side in the Hispanic communities, often within a single family.[87]*

- *The vast and widespread growth of America's Hispanic population also signals new forms of growth and new areas of settlement across the nation's metropolitan landscape.[88]*

- *These Hispanic population trends seem to follow discernable pathways likely to carry into the future. [89]*

- *The need for policy makers to adapt quickly to vast change presents special challenges in metro areas that started with miniscule Hispanic populations and that experienced sudden, substantial growth.[90] This applies to mission strategists as well.*

- *Public officials responsible for planning the allocation of services and resources need to tailor their decision-making to the particular growth variation in their service area.[91] This has special application to mission strategists.*

- *Due to the explosive growth of the Hispanic population, unprecedented cooperative efforts are going to be needed between international mission agencies, national mission agencies, state missions organizations, local mission groups and existing Hispanic churches.[92]*

## Conclusion

The cultural, socio-economic, and generational diversity among Hispanic Americans requires that a variety of strategies and congregational models be employed to lead the largest number possible to a personal experience of salvation in Jesus Christ.

---

Endnotes

[84] Pew Hispanic Center/Kaiser Family Foundation, 2002 National Survey of Latinos, 6.

[85] Pew Hispanic Center/Kaiser Family Foundation, 2002 National Survey of Latinos, 6.

[86] Pew Hispanic Center/Kaiser Family Foundation, 2002 National Survey of Latinos, 6.

[87] Pew Hispanic Center/Kaiser Family Foundation, 2002 National Survey of Latinos, 7.

[88] *"Latino Growth in Metropolitan America," The Brookings Institution Center on Urban & Metropolitan Policy and the Pew Hispanic Center, 10.*

[89] *"Latino Growth in Metropolitan America," The Brookings Institution Center on Urban & Metropolitan Policy and the Pew Hispanic Center, 11.*

[90] *"Latino Growth in Metropolitan America," The Brookings Institution Center on Urban & Metropolitan Policy and the Pew Hispanic Center, 10.*

[91] *"Latino Growth in Metropolitan America," The Brookings Institution Center on Urban & Metropolitan Policy and the Pew Hispanic Center, 11.*

[92] This observation is made by the members of the Hispanic Task Force

# PART TWO
# UNDERSTANDING
# HISPANICS

# CHAPTER 11

# HISTORY OF HISPANIC AMERICANS

In order to understand Hispanics it is essential to be acquainted with their history. Knowing how the Hispanic groups have become a part of the American scene is indispensable for an understanding of their pilgrimage and for the development of contextualized strategies to lead them to a personal faith in Christ resulting in the establishment of culturally relevant churches among them. This chapter provides a brief historical sketch of Spanish Americans, Hispanic Americans, Puerto Ricans, Cubans, Central Americans, and South Americans.

As we provide this information, perhaps a caveat is needed. While the historical facts that will be discussed have been documented, the description of the various cultural groups under the rubric of "Hispanic Americans," needs to have room for interpretation. There is no absolute consensus among Hispanics regarding the terms that are used to describe each group. Some might even have differences of opinion regarding the question of historical relevance. Since this is a very brief overview, a number of historical facts have not been included. If this promotes dialogue, one of the goals for writing this book has been achieved. With this in mind, let us review the history of Hispanic Americans.

## Spanish Americans

Hispanics have been in the Southwest since the early 1600's. In 1528 explorations of what is now the Southwestern United States (New Mexico, Texas, and California) began.[93] In 1598 Juan de Oñate (who married Hernán Cortéz' niece) established the first colony in what is now New Mexico.[94]

Subsequently *villas* (provincial towns) were established in Santa Fe, Santa Cruz (Española valley), and San Felipe de Neri, which is now Albuquerque. In California the famous Franciscan missionary Fray Junípero Serra founded 21 missions along the California coast (the mission of San Diego was founded in 1769 and Monterrey in 1770). By 1821, four principal areas of settlement had developed. The first and most heavily populated was New Mexico consisting of towns, ranches, and farms. Next in size was California, consisting of missions, military fortress communities, towns, and ranches. Third was the northeastern settlement of Texas with its center in San Antonio. The smallest was the Arizona colony which was established in Tucson.

Descendants of the colonial Spanish Americans still live in California, Colorado, Arizona, New Mexico, and Texas. Many of these are now found in urban centers such as Los Angeles, San Diego, Salt Lake City, Denver, and San Antonio. The Spanish Americans who live in the smaller towns (former land grant villages) "are generally more conservative, of their traditional values of the extended family, the Catholic faith, the Spanish language, and home and community, than the other Spanish-speaking groups."[95]

Educational achievement among Spanish Americans has risen substantially since the early 20th century. This period has also seen the movement of Spanish Americans from rural (farm) oriented employment to skilled and professional types of employment. It appears as though Spanish Americans will retain their distinctiveness within the Hispanic population in the U. S. while continuing to join other Hispanic groups in their quest for an improved quality of life and the recognition of their shared values.[96]

## Hispanic Americans

Speaking chronologically, the first group one needs to focus on in terms of its residence in this country is the Spanish American group. The second group, which at times is difficult to isolate totally from the first, is the Hispanic American group. This is due to several factors. First, a variety of backgrounds were represented in the early colonies. These included the *peninsular* (a person born in Spain); the *criollo* (a person born in the New Spain of pure Spanish ancestry; and the *mestizo* (a person of Spanish and Indian ancestry).[97] These three backgrounds therefore were represented in the colonies. The second reason why it was difficult to differentiate between Spanish and Hispanic Americans is that the territories of the Southwest belonged to Spain until 1821 when Mexico gained its independence from Spain at which time the inhabitants of this area officially became citizens of Mexico.

After Mexico won its independence from Spain, it invited Anglo Americans to settle in its northern provinces (now the Southwest).[98] The large influx of settlers and their subsequent disagreement with the restrictions set by Mexico led to the Texas Revolution which resulted in the formation of the Republic of Texas in 1845.[99] Fighting between the two nations continued until 1848 when the Guadalupe-Hidalgo treaty was signed and the Southwest was annexed to the U. S. It was at this time that the Hispanic inhabitants of this territory technically became "Mexican-Americans." Currently this group comprises 66.9 percent of the Hispanic population in America.

## Puerto Ricans

The third group, in terms of its length of affiliation with the U.S., is the Puerto Rican community. Puerto Rico was discovered and claimed for Spain by Columbus in 1493. It remained a Spanish colony and was used primarily as an outpost until 1889.

Puerto Ricans have held legal status as immigrants to the continental United States since 1889 when Puerto Rico became a U.S. possession. They have been U.S. citizens since 1917 and are able to travel freely between the island and the mainland. While there had been some political exiles who had sought refuge in New York,[100] the first large wave of migration took place in the 1920s and 30s. Those who came were motivated by the high rates of unemployment in the island caused in part by two hurricanes in 1928 and 1932 which devastated the coffee plantations that had been the main source of income.

Following World War II, large numbers of Puerto Ricans came to the mainland as contract farm workers. Some of them stayed and became permanent residents in the cities that were closest to them. With the advent of cheaper air fares, the number of those traveling to and from the island increased dramatically. "The movement can best be understood in terms of a continuous internal migration within the United States."[101]

The largest Puerto Rican community is found in New York City, which continues to be the most important settlement for Puerto Ricans in the mainland. Other concentrations of Puerto Ricans are found in New Jersey, Connecticut, Massachusetts, Florida, Ohio, and California. Socioeconomic variations exist within (e.g., Harlem) and between (e.g., New York vs. California) the Puerto Rican communities in terms of educational attainment and socioeconomic levels. While Puerto Ricans are not considered "immigrants," when they come to the mainland their cultural characteristics and language often contribute toward making their experience similar to that of other Hispanic immigrants. As Fredrickson and Knobel explain:

> Puerto Rican identity in the United States is a compound of class, cultural, and racial distinctiveness. To some extent the ethnic group displays the characteristics of the inner-city poor generally. But their Hispanic culture makes them stand out from the other working-class elements. Residential concentration and the continued accretion of new comers from Puerto Rico reinforce cultural uniqueness in the urban environment.[102]

In addition to linguistic and cultural factors, the adjustment of Puerto Ricans to life in the mainland is compounded by differences in climate, social organization, educational attainment, and socioeconomic status. Migration from a tropical island to the cold states of the Northeast by itself requires a significant amount of adjustment. This migration is often from a rural (often agricultural) setting to industrial urban centers. Except for a select few, many who come from Puerto Rico do not have the educational attainments which are needed to secure the professional and high-skill jobs which are available in the industrial, eastern cities of the mainland where job opportunities for unskilled labor are rapidly declining.

Unless the younger generation attains a higher level of education, the poverty cycle continues to affect their lives. While the number of second generation Puerto Rican high school and college graduates is steadily growing, there is a need for continued emphasis of educational attainment.

Despite the fact that Puerto Ricans have had a legal status in the United States since 1898, many of them continue to struggle like other immigrant groups to improve their quality of life. Their positive disposition toward evangelical Christianity makes their communities fertile grounds for evangelism and church planting. One of our greatest needs is to train Puerto Rican pastors and church leaders to reach their communities for Christ. Puerto Ricans constitute 8.6 percent of the Hispanic American population.

## Cuban Americans

The second place Christopher Columbus visited during his first voyage was the island of Cuba, which he claimed for Spain. Thinking that they were in China his men explored Holguín in search for the city of Peking. Instead, they found natives smoking cigars. This was the first time that Europeans had seen tobacco. Spaniards began to settle the island in 1511. For the nearly 400 years Spain ruled Cuba. In 1898 Cuba obtained its independence from Spain with the help of the United States.

As early as 1830 there were Cubans living in Key West, Florida. Later in the waning years of Spanish colonial rule, other Cuban political refugees settled in the Tampa area. Still Other Cubans came during the 1930s when Cuba came under control of dictator, Flugencio Batista. In 1959, Fidel Castro and a band of rebels overthrew Batista.

When it became evident that Castro intended to establish a communist government, large numbers of people sought asylum in the United States. Between 1959 and 1962 more than 155,000 Cubans immigrated to the U.S. As a result of the missile crisis direct flights between Cuba and the U. S. were suspended. In 1965, following the signing of a "memorandum of understanding," the air-lift was resumed bringing more than 257,000 Cubans to our shores. In 1980 an additional 200,000 Cubans arrived in the U. S. as a result of the Mariel boat-lift.

The arrival of the Cubans differed in several significant ways from that of other Hispanic groups. Due to the antipathy of Americans to Communism and the fact that diplomatic relations between the two countries were severed, Cubans were accorded the status of refugees and were received with open arms. Several evangelical denominations participated actively in sponsorship programs which led to the conversion of many Cubans and the establishment a numerous churches along the east coast.

A second factor which distinguished Cubans from other Hispanic immigrants is that disproportionately large numbers of people from the middle and upper socioeconomic classes were among the first wave of refugees. These were the ones who felt the greatest aversion to Castro's political views and had the means to leave their native land. The fact that many of these were skilled (professional, managerial, entrepreneurial, commercial) workers contributed to facilitating their adjustment and employment in this country.

A third factor which distinguishes Cuban Americans from other Hispanics is that among them there is a disproportionately large number of elderly persons. This situation resulted from the selective emigration practiced by Cuban officials which made it easier for the elderly to leave the island.

A fourth factor is that there are more Cuban females of marriageable age (20-29) than there are males (76 males to every 100 females).[103] This condition springs from the fact to a large extent males of military-service age were not allowed to leave the island.

While there are some characteristics which distinguish Cuban Americans from other Hispanic groups, they have a number of things in common. First, many of them were political and economic refugees. Second, though there are slight linguistic differences, Cubans were immediately able to communicate with other Spanish-speaking groups. Third, many of the customs and traditions were similar to those of other Hispanic groups. Fourth, along with other Hispanics, Cubans faced the challenge of adjusting to linguistic, social, political, and economic patterns of the predominant society.

Today, 3.6 percent of the Hispanic American population is made up of Cuban Americans.[104] While the greatest concentration of Cuban Americans is found in Miami, there are significant clusters of them in such states as New York, New Jersey, and California.

## Central and South Americans

It was not until his third and fourth journeys that Columbus reached the lands in which Central and South Americans live. The colonies which were established and the countries which developed subsequently differed greatly in terms of geography, size, history, language, and sociopolitical factors. Central and South Americans, therefore, represent differing social strata, regional attachments, and ethnocultural backgrounds.[105] Despite this diversity, these Central and South American groups have been deeply affected by the Spanish and Portuguese traditions, which transcend national boundaries and ethnic origins.

Today Central and South Americans constitute 14.3 percent of the Hispanic population in the U.S. They constitute a variety of national and ethnic groups representing 18 different countries. Immigration from Central America began in the 1830s and continued at a slow rate. Following World War II the number of immigrants from Central America increased rapidly.

In the 1980s this number increased at an even faster rate due to the political turmoil in such countries as Nicaragua, El Salvador, Honduras, and Guatemala. At present, there are concentrations of Central Americans in New York City, Los Angeles, San Francisco, Miami, and Chicago. It is of interest to note that groups from certain countries tend to concentrate in certain U. S. cities. Guatemalans, for instance, favor Los Angeles, Hondurans are concentrated in the Gulf Coast, and Panamanians tend to congregate in New York City. It is also important to know that the number of females coming from Central America outnumbered that of males significantly. Of the occupations of Central Americans in this country 30-40% are professional and white-collar workers and 15-28% are domestic servants.[106]

In the early 1900s the number of South Americans in this country far outstripped that of Central Americans. This demographic fact means that many of the South Americans who are here are third and fourth generation Americans. South Americans have tended to concentrate in such cities as New York, Chicago, San Francisco, and Los Angeles. In comparison to the Central Americans, more South Americans are found in the professional ranks (38%) and fewer in the domestic service rank (4-5%).[107] The largest numbers of South Americans in this country are from Colombia, Ecuador, and Argentina.

While there are numerous differences between Central and South Americans, they share some common patterns of migration, settlement, and social characteristics. A significant number of South Americans exhibit, to a large extent, middle-class characteristics. This is due, in part, to the fact that significant numbers of those who have come are in the highly trained and skilled job category. Many of these work long hours as family units (husband and wife), living in a frugal manner in order to make it possible for their relatives to join them from abroad and to achieve a greater social mobility than their parents were able to achieve.[108]

## Other Hispanics

The category entitled "other Hispanics" is used by the Census Bureau to include Hispanics of other national and regional origins who are not represented in such large numbers that they require a separate designation. This category includes Hispanic people who trace their origin to one of the following countries: Spain, Germany, Portugal, Jamaica, Trinidad/Caribbean Islands, Italy, or "other countries."[109]

These people, therefore, may come from a wide variety of places where the Spanish language and culture are predominant. This fact, however, does not mean that they are not significant for together they constitute 6.5 percent of the Hispanic population in this country. As is true of the other groups discussed above, effective ministry among these groups requires an understanding of their history, culture, and religious orientation. The fact that they come from a Spanish-speaking area means that they have some things in common with other Hispanic Americans. Their differences, however, need to be studied and taken into account in doing ministry among them.

# Conclusion

The term Hispanic American encompasses all of the groups mentioned above. These became a part of the American scene at different times in history and under different circumstances. As will be pointed out in the next chapter, there is some diversity among these groups in terms of country of origin, customs, and length of residence in the United States. A cultural basin (from Spain) and a common language (Spanish) provide a common ground for the group known today as "Hispanic Americans." Despite the commonalities, it is helpful to know the historical pilgrimage of each of these groups and to take this into account while seeking to minister in Hispanic communities.

Endnotes

[93] See *World Book Encyclopedia* s.v. "Christopher Columbus" by Samuel Eliot Morison.

[94] See *The World Book Encyclopedia*, s.v. "Juan de Oñate" by Richard A. Bartlett.

[95] Harvard Encyclopedia, s.v. "Spanish," p. 953.

[96] Ibid., p. 953.

[97] See Virgilio Elizondo, *Galilean Journey: The Hispanic American Promise* (Maryknoll, NY: Orbis, 1983), pp. 9-18.

[98] David Nevin, *The Texans*, Chicago: Time-Life Books, 1975, 51-75.

[99] Don C. Locke, Increasing Multicultural Understanding, Newbury Park: SAGE Publications,1992, 128,29.

[100] See *Harvard Encyclopedia*, s.v. "Puerto Ricans," pp. 859-60.

[101] Ibid.

[102] *Harvard Encyclopedia*, s.v. "Prejudice and Discrimination History of," by George M. Fredrickson and Dale T. Knobel, p. 839.

[103] *Harvard* op. cit., p. 259.

[104] 1990 U. S. Census, Bureau of the Census, Washington D. C., "Commerce News," March 11, 1991, Table 2.

[105] *Harvard Encyclopedia of American Ethnic Groups*, s.v. "Central and South Americans," by Ann Orlov and Reed Ueda, pp. 210-217.

[106] *Harvard*, op. cit., p. 312.

[107] Ibid.

[108] Ibid, p. 217.

[109] Pew Hispanic Center/Kaiser Family Foundation, 2002 National Survey of Latinos, December 2002, 19.

# CHAPTER 12

# DIVERSITY AMONG HISPANICS

Bobby Sena

The descriptions of the various groups in the previous chapters indicate that Hispanic groups have many things in common. These groups, however, also have many things in which they are different. These commonalities and differences have significant implications for those who seek to minister among Hispanic Americans.

## Factors That Contribute to Diversity

Significant factors contribute toward diversification among Hispanic Americans.

First, each Hispanic group has a unique history related to its residency in the United States. Hispanics have come to America from a wide variety of countries during different periods in the history of this nation and have, therefore, experienced different pilgrimages. As presented in chapter 11, some became citizens as a result of the annexation of the Southwestern territory, others came as political refugees, others may be put in the category of economic refugees, and still others have been born in this country. These factors have contributed to certain personality traits which distinguish each group.

Some groups, for example, are generally very extroverted while others are more reserved. Some groups typically use more formal terms for greeting people while others are more informal in their approach. Some groups are more open to assimilation into the predominant society of this country than others. It cannot be assumed, therefore, that all Hispanic groups are alike. The various groups follow different patterns related to the establishment of relationships, the manner in which decisions are made, the way in which they organize themselves, the way in which they worship, and the manner in which they exercise leadership. The differences between these groups, therefore, have significant implications for evangelism, church planting, church growth, and missionary efforts.

Second, Hispanics are not a biologically homogeneous group. There is a great deal of variety among Hispanics in general and among the sub-cultural groups. For example, among Puerto Ricans, Cubans, and some Central Americans there are those who have phenotypical characteristics of their Spanish ancestry, others of their African ancestry, others of their Indian ancestry, and others of a combination of these. Among Mexican Americans and some Central and South Americans one finds phenotypical characteristics of the Spaniards, the Indians, and a blend of the two. Technically, therefore, there is no such thing as the "Hispanic Race." While some use the term "*la raza*" for the purpose of self-identity, biologically Hispanics do not constitute a specific race.[110] Another way of saying this is that Hispanics are a group with common cultural and linguistic characteristics (a culture and a language that originated in Spain) rather than a specific racial group as such.

A third factor which has contributed to the sociocultural variety among Hispanics is the fact that each group has had a unique pilgrimage toward establishing residency in the United States. Sociologist R. A. Schermerhorn points out that modes of entry and goal orientations have a bearing on the manner in which minority groups relate to the predominant society.[111] The mode of entry refers to the status which was assigned to the minority group when it became a part of the life of this country. Did this group become a part of the United States as a result of *annexation, forced political migration, forced economic migration, voluntary immigration, birth* or some other reason? What is their current status: citizens, permanent residents, refugees, or undocumented residents? What was their socio-economic level at the point of entry into this country? Were they in the higher, middle or lower socio-economic level? Each of these factors signals a specific pilgrimage for each of these Hispanic sub-groups. It is not difficult to see that agricultural workers at the lowest rung of the socio-economic scale face the greatest challenges as they seek to live and work in the context of a middle to upper middle class dominant society. It may take a generation or two before agricultural workers become middle class. Conversely middle class (and in some cases professionals) immigrants generally adapt quicker to life in this country and experience economic progress more rapidly. The mode of entrance into this country has a bearing on the manner in which these groups adjust to the social, cultural, political, economic and religious setting in America. This needs to be taken into account in seeking to understand the pilgrimage of each of these groups.

Goal orientation is also a factor which affects the lives of Hispanic Americans. What are the goals of the predominant society with regard to the Hispanic groups? Are they forced assimilation, voluntary assimilation, forced segregation, or cultural pluralism?[112] During different periods of its history America has had different attitudes toward the immigration of the various groups. In times of economic prosperity or times of war when laborers have been needed, America has had a more receptive mood than in times of economic down turns. A concomitant question is "what are the goals of the Hispanic groups *vis-à-vis* the predominant society?" The various sub-groups have had a variety of goals ranging from total separation to total assimilation. In most instances, however, with the passing of time, most Hispanics have practiced a form of selective assimilation which has allowed them to incorporate many of the values of the predominant society while retaining those values from their culture that they consider essential. If the goal orientations of the predominant society and those of the Hispanic groups coincide, then there is harmony. If they differ, then there is conflict. This has social as well as religious implications.

A fourth factor which has contributed to cultural variety among Hispanics is assimilation. When Hispanics become permanent residents in this country, they and their children immediately embark in the process of adaptation to their new socio-cultural environment. Sociologists such as Andrew Greeley and R. A. Schermerhorn have developed categories for the different stages of assimilation within a cultural group.[113] These can be useful in an analysis of the various segments of the Hispanic American community. For the purpose of this discussion, I have modified the nomenclature of these categories.[114] Utilizing the insights of these sociologists, Hispanic Americans can be classified under the following categories:

**1. "Traditional."** (First Generation Immigrants)
When they arrive in this country they speak only Spanish and their social contacts (close friends) are confined primarily to their own cultural group.

**2. "Bi-Cultural ."** (Second Generation - U.S. Born, or came as children[115]). They are bilingual (perhaps a bit more fluent in Spanish than in English) and have social contacts in both their cultural group and the predominant society.

**3. "Marginal ."** (Third Generation - U.S. Born). They are more proficient in English than in Spanish and have more social contacts in the predominant (Anglo) society than in the Hispanic American community.

**4. "Acculturated."** (Fourth Generation - U.S. Born). They basically speak only English and have the majority of their social contacts outside of the Hispanic American community.

These stages of assimilation can be helpful in determining what language to use and what methods to employ in leading Hispanics to a personal faith in Jesus Christ. It needs to be pointed out, however, that some Hispanic sub-groups will progress more rapidly along the assimilation ladder than others. Educational, economic, and even residential patterns will either accelerate or delay the assimilation process.

## The Impact of Assimilation

Assimilation can be described as the process by which an immigrant group adopts some of the cultural characteristics of the host group. This involves seeking to learn the language as well as the customs of the predominant society.

## *Assimilation of Adults*

Unless the immigrant group lives and works in total isolation from the host group, a certain degree of assimilation is needed. Immigrant persons often find it necessary to learn the language of the host group (English) in order to find employment and function adequately in the new environment. Language learning may relate primarily to that which is needed to carry out the requirements of a job and to function in the basic activities of life related to travel (getting a driver's license) to financial dealings (purchasing goods) and availing themselves of needed services (medical, legal). For adult immigrants, a basic understanding of the language and customs of the host society, therefore, is essential for life in the new cultural setting.

## *Assimilation of Children*

For the children of immigrant parents, the process of assimilation has even stronger and more extensive implications than for adults. There are at least three factors that contribute to assimilation among the children of immigrants: 1) Schooling; 2) Media; and 3) Peer Group. Let's study these for a moment.

### 1. Schooling

As soon as the immigrants arrive, the law requires them to enroll their children in school. Immediately after enrollment the children are faced with the task of learning English. Even schools that have bilingual programs require students to learn English as soon as it is possible. That along with the fact that children have a great capacity to learn languages contributes to the fact that within a short period of time they can become proficient in their new language.

## 2. Media

An additional factor that contributes to the rapid assimilation of the children of immigrants is the media. This means that children began to watch English television programs and movies, to listen to music and programs in English speaking radio stations, and to read English language books and magazines. This, in addition to the reading assignments that children do in school contributes toward a preference for English in the things that they hear and read.

## 3. Peers

The children of immigrant families, like all other children, are greatly influenced by their peers (friends, classmates, and those of their own age in society in general). This peer-group influence relates to they way they dress, comb their hair, interact with others, and talk. Because the children of immigrant parents are surrounded by other children who speak English and have some of the characteristics of the predominant society, they soon become very much like them. So what happens?

# Implications of Assimilation

The assimilation process has implications for the families, the churches, and the denominational life of Hispanics.

## Implications for the Families

The assimilation process has implications for Hispanic families. It impacts both children and parents.

### Impact on Children

The children of immigrant parents are directly impacted by the assimilation process in several ways. First, these children face the challenge of living in two cultures. In school they function in the English language and relate to teachers American, who in addition to teaching the subject matter of their courses, also communicate the history and cultural values of the predominant (American) society. The positive value of this emphasis is the preparation of the children to function and to be successful in their jobs and in society in the future. At home, however, children often find themselves needing to communicate in Spanish and to relate to Hispanic cultural values and customs. Typically children spend more time functioning in the English language and relating to Anglo cultural values than they do to those in the Hispanic environment in their homes.

### Impact on Parents

Not only children, but also parents are affected by the assimilation process. This manifests itself in several ways. First, parents feel at time frustrated because their children are learning English quicker than they are. Second, parents often face the challenge of helping their children do their homework and other school tasks without the benefit of having the proficiency in English that is required. This often leads to communication problems not with the parents but with the grandparents who feel that they cannot communicate with their grandchildren.

## *Implications for the Church*

If the assimilation process poses challenges for Hispanic families it poses challenges for Hispanic churches also. It must be kept in mind that there have been Hispanic churches in the U.S. for many generations. For example, the First Hispanic Baptist Church of San Antonio, Texas was established in 1861.[116] Other Hispanic churches, however, were established last week. To be effective, Hispanic churches must take into account the implications of the assimilation process.

One of the most important challenges that the Hispanic church faces relates to the language that will be utilized in its teaching ministry and worship services. Often the Hispanic church is pressured by immigrant parents to "preserve the Hispanic language and culture." At this point several very important questions need to be addressed.

### Linguistic Implications

**First, what is the primary mission of the church, to preserve the culture or to communicate the Gospel?**

From a biblical perspective, the answer should be to communicate the Gospel. Jesus did not send out his disciples to preserve their culture but to communicate the Gospel (Matthew 28; Mark 16). The Apostle Paul understood this principle when he stated that he was willing to adapt himself to the people who needed to hear the Gospel so that they would be saved (1 Cor. 9:20).

**Second, whose task is it to preserve the culture?**

There is absolutely no question that it is a tremendous blessing for the children of immigrant parents to become proficient in both languages and to function in both cultures. The Apostle Paul was bilingual and bicultural. That is one of the reasons why the Lord was able to use him in such a marvelous way. Children who are bilingual and bicultural have a tremendous advantage in terms of their employment and ministry.

*The responsibility for accomplishing this bilingual and bicultural status rests on the shoulders of the parents and not the church.* It is absolutely not realistic to believe that in one or two hours a week the church can match the influence that the school, the media, and peer groups have on the children the rest of the week. Parents who are diligent in teaching their children Spanish in the home can accomplish this. Those who are not, cannot expect the church to accomplish this in the few hours it has every week.

**Third, what happens when churches are not willing to be flexible in order to reach and teach children and young people in the language that they best understand?**

History has demonstrated over and over again with many immigrant groups that churches that are inflexible with regard to the language that they use in their worship and discipleship programs *lose their children and young people.* Some young people will go to Anglo churches, but regrettably most will become totally unchurched.

So what options do Hispanic churches have with regard to the language(s) that they should use?

## Table 21
## Hispanic Assimilation and Church Planting

| Generation | Outside Social Contacts | Language | Church |
|---|---|---|---|
| First Traditional | Few | Spanish | Hispanic Culture |
| Second Bi-cultural | Some | Bilingual SPANISH Dominant | Bicultural HISPANIC Dominant |
| Third Marginal | Many | Bilingual ENGLISH Dominant | Bicultural ANGLO Dominant |
| Fourth Acculturated | Most | English | Anglo |

In Table 21 we can see the various options open to reaching the Hispanics in their various states of assimilation:

**First, Hispanic churches that are totally made up of immigrant families obviously need to utilize the Spanish language in their worship services and discipleship activities (such as Sunday School ).** This type of church, however, needs to be aware that it does not take long for the children of immigrant parents to communicate better in the English language than in Spanish. Is this church willing to teach Spanish classes on Saturdays like some of the Greek and Hebrew congregations do? If not, it should begin to make plans to utilize English in its activities with children and young people.

**Second, Hispanic churches that are made up of members who are in the "Bi-cultural" assimilation**

**category need to become bilingual.** These churches may lean more heavily toward the use of Spanish, but they will need to use some English in their worship services and have Sunday School classes in English for the children and young people who are more proficient in that language.

**Third, Hispanic churches that are made up of members who are in the "Marginal" assimilation category need to use more English than Spanish to reach and keep this group.** These churches will recognize the needs of all groups within their fellowship and seek to maintain Christian connections between the groups.

**Fourth, Hispanic people who are in the "Acculturated Category" could be better prospects for the Anglo churches.** This is due to the fact that this type of Hispanic has more in common with Anglo culture than with the Hispanic culture.

Are Hispanic churches willing to say like the Apostle Paul, "I have become all things to all people, to the Jew I have become like a Jew, to the Gentile, like a Gentile in order to reach as many as I can with the Gospel?" (1 Cor. 9:20). If so Hispanic churches would say: "To the traditional ethnic, I have become like a traditional ethnic, to the median ethnic like a median ethnic, and to the marginal ethnic, like a marginal ethnic in order that I might win the largest number possible to Christ."

## Leadership Implications

The assimilation process also has very significant implications for the leadership of the church. What happens when the pastor and the congregation are at different stages of assimilation? For example, what happens when a pastor who is a member of the immigrant generation (traditional ethnic) is called to pastor a median or marginal generation congregation? The answer to this is that this can result in a great deal of conflict.

# Reasons for Conflict

**First, the linguistic capabilities of the pastor and the congregation may be different.** This, obviously, can lead to lack of communication and conflict. The best solution is for the pastor to learn English as quickly as possible in order to address this challenge.

**Second, the cultural values of the pastor may be different.** This is not to say that the cultural values of the pastor were not valid in his country of origin. The truth of the matter is that there are some cultural differences if the congregation is median or marginal ethnic and the pastor is traditional ethnic. In other words, the fact that the members of the congregation have been in this country for several generations means that they have assimilated not only in terms of language, but in terms of cultural values and practices. As a missionary who goes to another country, the pastor in this case needs to learn the language and culture of the group he is going to minister to if he is going to be successful in his ministry.

**Third, the preference of leadership style may be different.** The immigrant pastor may be accustomed to the more autocratic leadership style of the country from which he came. The congregation, on the other hand, may have a stronger preference for a more democratic (participatory) leadership style. This preference may be due to the fact that the congregation is more accustomed to American cultural values that emphasize democratic leadership patterns. It may also be due to the fact that many Hispanic congregations were started by Anglo churches and have adopted the form of government and leadership style that is found in many Anglo churches. In other words, many Hispanic churches have also experienced a degree of assimilation into the predominant society.

**Fourth, the preferences regarding the organizational life of the church may be different.** Due to the fact that many Hispanic churches in the U.S. have existed for many years (some over 100 years) they have incorporated into their organizational life many of the programs that have been very effective in Anglo churches. This includes Sunday School, Church Training, Missionary, Youth, and Ministry organizations and programs. The way these are structured and operated reflects to a large extent what these Hispanic churches have learned in training sessions as well as in observing the example of Anglo churches. This does not mean that changes cannot or ought not be made. It does mean that rapid and abrupt changes without taking into account historical patterns can be disrupted and lead to conflict.

# Implications for Churches

An ideal situation is when the pastor and the congregation are at the same level of assimilation and have similar understandings with regard to culture, leadership styles, and organizational patterns. If this is not the case, the immigrant pastor needs to become aware of these differences and make the necessary adjustments if conflict is to be avoided. Orientation sessions similar to the ones missionaries go through could be very helpful for immigrant pastors.

## Conclusion

As we can see, then, there is a great deal of variety between the Hispanic groups (and even among them). This stems, not only because their countries of origin are different, but also because they have encountered different sets of circumstances when they became a part of the life of this country. It is important, therefore, that we study these factors in order to understand these groups better and to design more effective strategies for evangelism, discipleship, church starting and church growth.

---

Endnotes

[110] Pew Hispanic Center/Kaiser Family Foundation, 2002 National Survey of Latinos, December 2002, 8

[111] R. A. Schermerhorn, *Comparative Ethnic Relations: A Framework for Theory and Research* (New York, NY: Random House, 1970).

[112] Ibid., p. 83.

[113] Andrew Greeley, "Is Ethnicity Un-American?" New Catholic World 219, no. 1311 (May/June 1976), 106-112, utilized the terms "total ethnic," "fellow traveler," "marginal ethnic," and "assimilated ethnic," to chart movement into the dominant culture; R. A. Schermerhorn, *Comparative Ethnic Relations: A Framework for Theory and Research* (New York, NY: Random House, 1970) utilizes similar categories to chart movement away from the group's cultural heritage.

[114] I am essentially using the categories posited by John C. Locke in *Increasing Multicultural Understanding,* Newbury Park: SAGE Publications, 1992, 6. The only category that I modified was that of "Marginal" since he uses it to refer to marginalization to both cultures while I use it as it relates only to the culture of origin,

[115] Some call this the 1.5 generation because they arrived as children, yet were not born in the host country.

[116] Josué Grijalva, *Ethnic Baptist History*, Atlanta: Home Mission Board, 1985.

# Chapter 13
# Needs in the Hispanic Community

Those who serve in Hispanic communities encounter a wide variety of needs. Some of these needs are physical, others are psycho-social, others are spiritual, and many a combination of the three. One of the best ways to reach people in any community is:

- to discover their felt needs,
- to minister to them by addressing these needs,
- to build bridges of friendship and understanding,
- to share the good news of salvation with an attitude of compassion and concern.

By utilizing a holistic approach in ministry, Christians and churches can meet the needs of many Hispanics and aid them in experiencing life transformation as they become open to a personal relationship with Jesus Christ.

## Physical Needs

A survey of Hispanic pastors conducted by the Research Department of the North American Mission Board, revealed the following needs in the order of priority that the pastors established.[117] The percentages indicate the number of pastors who agreed that a certain need should be placed at a particular slot in the order of priorities.

1. Helping persons to get jobs or better jobs - 68%
2. Helping new immigrants establish themselves 60.8%
3. Helping persons to have better access to basic social services (health care, Social Security, Medicare) 60.8%
4. Counseling programs. 60.8%
5. Ministry-based evangelism (e.g., Block Parties) 59.2%
6. English or citizenship classes 58.3% 6.
7. Evangelistic services 56.7%
8. Helping students to stay in school 53.3%
9. Church/community sports programs 51.7%
10. Job training 50.0%
11. After-school programs for teenagers 49.2%
12. Drug/ alcoholic rehabilitation programs 45.0%
13. Day-cares or child care programs 45.0%
14. Reduce violence among the families.40.85
15. Food distribution 37.5%
16. Programs for the elderly 32.2%
17. Providing shelter for the homeless. 30.8%
18. Reduce violence in the community (e.g., gangs) 29.2%
19. Adequate housing 25.5%
20. Voter registration 20.8%
21. Other community needs 15.8%

This list reveals the existence of a variety of physical, psychological, and spiritual needs in America's Hispanic communities. Categorizing these needs is helpful. This effort to categorize or view the needs in isolation, however, is often difficult for they overlap to a large extent. With this caveat in mind, it is interesting to note that many of the needs listed above relate to the adaptation of new Hispanic immigrants to life in this country.

This relationship is evident in that the top six needs listed in the survey relate to adaptation to life in the new culture.

These needs include helping persons to get jobs or better jobs; helping new immigrants to establish themselves; helping persons to have better access to basic social services (health care, Social Security, Medicare); counseling programs; ministry-based evangelism (e.g., Block Parties); and English or citizenship classes.

A significant number of ministries have been developed to address these needs in Hispanic communities. The Woman's Missionary Union based in Birmingham, Alabama has developed training materials for those wishing to be involved in such ministries as teaching English as a Second Language and assisting immigrants in their adjustment to life in this country.[118]

The Evangelism Unit of the North American Mission Board based in Alpharetta, Georgia, has developed materials for Special Evangelistic Events including Block Parties (Fiesta Evangelística de la Comunidad), Special Day Celebrations (such as Thanksgiving and Christmas), and Evangelistic Events (such as Street and Open Air Evangelism, Musical Concerts, Evangelistic Meals, Sports Evangelism, Media Evangelism Events, Evangelistic Drama Events, Evangelistic Felt Needs Seminars).[119]

An excellent resource is found in the Biblical Counseling Keys provided by the Hope for the Heart ministry. These keys address such areas of need as Alcoholism, Drug Addiction, Domestic Violence, Conflict Resolution, and many others.[120]

## Psycho-social Needs

In additional to physical needs, there are psycho-social needs that Hispanics face as they seek to adjust to life in America. The multi-faceted transition which Hispanic Americans have experienced in their pilgrimage has impacted their lives in a number of ways. The search for a sense of identity is at the heart of their socio-historical experience.[121] The serious questions this group has had regarding its identity have affected its social, economic, political, and religious life.

Several themes emerge as one studies the psycho-social needs of the Hispanic Americans:[122]

- a search for a sense of identity,
- a search for a sense of dignity,
- a desire to overcome a sense of marginality,
- a desire to attain a spirit of brotherhood (*carnalismo*)[123].

A brief analysis will be made of these needs in order enable the reader to have a better understanding of the Hispanic American community.

## *A search for a Sense of identity*

One of the first challenges Hispanics face when they become permanent residents in the United States is that of developing a clear sense of identity. Typically when immigrants arrive in this country as adults, they identify themselves in terms of their country of origin. Some for instance will say that they are "Peruvians" or "Salvadorians," or whatever their country of origin might be. After they have been here for a while, they began to search for a term that describes them more adequately, for they are not longer just "Peruvians," but Peruvian-Americans. Often as they seek to identify themselves with the broader group of Latin American or Spanish origin they will utilize the term "Latino," or "Hispanic."[124]

Usually the children of the immigrant generation have the greatest struggle in defining their identity. This is due to the fact that they do not have strong ties with the culture (and perhaps the language) of their parents' country of origin. For example, are they Peruvians or Americans or a part of both cultures?

The search for identity has led some to attempt to discover their socio-historical heritage. Reverend Virgilio Elizondo describes this search:

> They began to dig into their past, to penetrate the development and meaning of their historical process. . . . Who are we, they asked themselves. And they began to search for their roots—not in order to go backward, but in order to go forward. Just as the rediscovery of its Greco-Roman origins had brought a new vitality to Europe, so too Hispanic Americans realize that they have to rediscover their origin in order to appreciate and celebrate their historical process and their true existential identity.[125]

Hispanic Americans have more than a mere academic interest in ascertaining their socio-historical heritage. They feel that their existential identity is closely connected with this discovery. The manner in which many Hispanic Americans are affected by an inadequate understanding of their socio-historical heritage is described by Gloria López-McKnight when she states: "So many of us feel cut off from the past, confused with the present, and uneasy about the future."[126]

The search for a socio-historical heritage, however, is complicated by the fact that most Hispanic Americans are the product of several cultural traditions: Spanish, Indian, *mestizo,* and Anglo American.[127] In their search for a socio-historical identity, some have tended to emphasize the Spanish culture.[128]

The ambivalent attitude some Hispanic Americans have had toward the *mestizo* strain has caused them to deny this part of their heritage.[129] Others, however, have sought to repudiate the Spanish part of their heritage. Some, for instance, have attempted to create an ideology which places greater (if not exclusive) emphasis on the Indian heritage. Some have proposed the concept of *la raza* (the people, race, or clan) which stresses a compelling feeling of belonging to a group but may not conceptualize the cultural (or racial) identity of this group adequately.[130]

Confusion exists among some Hispanic Americans as to whether the concept of *la raza* refers to a racial or cultural group or both. It has not been scientifically proven, for instance, that Hispanic Americans are a racial entity.[131] The concept of *la raza*, though still relatively vague, has captured the imagination of some Hispanic Americans who yearn to be a part of a cultural group which they define for themselves and of which they can be proud.[132]

Another dimension of their heritage which some Hispanic Americans apparently do not seem to be cognizant of is that which has been contributed by the predominant society, the Anglo American culture. Even though the schooling and enculturation of many Hispanic Americans has taken place in the United States, some believe they can return to the culture of their ancestors without incorporating vital Anglo American cultural elements.[133]

The task of ascertaining the Hispanic American socio-historical heritage is a complex one.[134] It has not been established that there are sufficient commonalities among the various cultural tributaries to provide *a single, specific socio-historical heritage.* Furthermore, a common heritage with which most Hispanic Americans can identify has not been articulated with sufficient clarity to date.

There is the possibility that stressing one heritage to the exclusion of the others may lead to the development of a false identity.[135] There is a sense in which each segment of the Hispanic American population has a tendency to focus on its own socio-historical heritage. Perhaps the most that can be said is that a definable, Hispanic American socio-historical identity is still in its formative stages.[136]

The desire to discover their socio-historical heritage, however, remains strong among Hispanic Americans. Rodolfo Alvarez expresses this aspiration when he states: "I have a unique psycho-historical experience that I have a right to know about and to cultivate as part of my distinctive cultural heritage."[137] Elizondo believes that efforts toward finding this cultural heritage are currently being made. He states:

However mixed or confused or undefined may be the innermost self-identity of the Hispanic American people, elements of its composition are now coming to light at a more rapid pace than ever before. Poets, artists, and musicians are bringing out, through the language of the arts, many ethnic elements which are still beyond scholarly analysis and synthesis.[138]

## *A sense of marginality*

Another dimension of the Hispanic American search for an identity relates to their efforts to overcome a sense of marginality. From the time of the annexation of the Southwest, Hispanic Americans have had to define their identity in terms of the predominant society. Due to the fact that they were rapidly outnumbered by Anglo American settlers in what is now the Southwestern United States, Hispanic Americans found themselves occupying a minority status socially, economically, and politically.

Two dimensions to the sense of marginality which Hispanic Americans have experienced are with regard:

- to the predominant society in the United States
- to the culture of their country of origin.

Several factors have contributed to the sense of marginality which Hispanic Americans feel with regard to the predominant society in the United States. One of these factors is rejection by some members of the predominant society. In some instances, the predominant society has been more willing to allow *cultural* assimilation than *structural* assimilation (i.e. allowing Hispanics to adopt the language and the customs of the predominant society but resisting their entrance into the social institutions of the predominant society). Having done virtually everything which the predominant society has expected of them (speaking and acting like Anglo Americans) and yet feeling that they are still not fully accepted, some Hispanic Americans have a sense of marginality.

An additional factor which has contributed to the Hispanic American sense of marginality from the predominant society has been an incomplete cultural and structural assimilation into this society. While some Hispanic Americans have assimilated into the predominant society to the extent that they identify with it and participate in its social, economic, and political structures, others have achieved only partial cultural assimilation. Pressured by the structures of the predominant society to assimilate culturally,[139] yet restrained by their inability or unwillingness fully to relinquish their own culture, some Hispanic Americans find themselves in a cultural limbo.[140]

The reluctance or inability of many Hispanic Americans to give up some aspects of their cultural heritage keeps them from participating fully in the predominant society. Still, the fact that they live in the American context forces them to incorporate some of the social, political, and linguistic elements of this predominant society.[141] Hispanic Americans face a dilemma.

In some instances this sense of marginality has led to creative adaptive responses (e.g., Tex-Mex culture).[142] In many cases it has led to disorientation,[143] a sense of rootlessness,[144] and, for some, a pervasive sense of rejection.[145] In the 2002 National Survey of Latinos conducted by the Pew Hispanic Center, 31 percent of Hispanics reported that "they or someone close to them had suffered discrimination in the last five years because of their racial or ethnic background."[146]

An incomplete cultural and structural assimilation into the predominant society, therefore, has caused many Hispanic Americans to experience a sense of marginality. In some instances, two contributing factors to this have been the rejection by some members of the predominant society and the unwillingness on the part of some Hispanic Americans to assimilate. In the case of the former it can be said that some Hispanic Americans feel that they have been marginalized by the predominant society while in the case of the latter, some Hispanic Americans have marginalized themselves.

Still others feel marginalized by the culture of their country of origin. The sense of marginality in the lives of many Hispanic Americans can be described as a "triangular conflict"[147] which includes the American predominant society, the culture of the Hispanic's country of origin, and the Hispanic American culture. In the 2002 National Survey of Latinos, 47 percent of the Hispanics interviewed said that discrimination by Hispanics against other Hispanics was a major problem.[148] "They are most likely to attribute this type of discrimination to disparities in income and education."[149]

Some segments of the Hispanic American group feel alienated from the predominant American society. Other segments feel marginalized from the people and culture of their country of origin. Others feel marginalized by other Hispanic Americans. Still other segments feel this sense of marginality from their own culture as well as the host culture.[150] They have not achieved structural assimilation with the predominant society in the United States, yet are not fully accepted by the people of their country of origin.[151]

Many Hispanic Americans, therefore, are struggling to overcome the various dimensions of the sense of marginality which afflict their lives.[152] While some Hispanic communities (especially those populated by second and third generation Hispanics) have experienced significant assimilation, other communities continually find themselves at the starting point of the assimilation process with the arrival of new immigrants. Some churches, therefore, face the challenge of ministering in communities where the process of immigration and that of assimilation continue to occur simultaneously. Dr. Jesse Miranda deals with this sense of marginalization more extensively in chapter 14.

## *A search for a sense of dignity*

The Hispanic American search for a sense of identity is also a search for dignity and self-worth.[153] The socio-historical experience of some Hispanic Americans has contributed to the development of a sense of unworthiness as a cultural group.[154] This is consistent with the observation of some social scientists that "sociocultural alterations and losses may seriously harm an identity."[155]

Some psychologists have found what appears to be evidence of this in some Hispanic Americans. Augustine Weilbert, for instance, observes that "one of the most common traits discovered in some Hispanic Americans has been a very low self-esteem, and a very modest self-image."[156] R. D"az-Guerrero echoes this when he asserts that self-esteem is one of the greatest needs among Hispanic Americans.[157] The recognition of this need, as Ysidro Mac"as points out, has led many Hispanic Americans to strive to attain a positive self-image and self-respect.[158]

The Hispanic American search for a sense of dignity has several dimensions. One of these is overcoming the effects on the Hispanic American self-image of the negative stereotypes held by some members of the predominant society[159]

In the past, the predominant society's stereotypes of Hispanic Americans perpetuated especially in some educational systems,[160] commercial advertising,[161] and mass media reporting[162] have contributed toward the formation of the negative image which the latter have of themselves. Vigil states that ethnocentric attitudes of teachers and educational curricula which "emphasized the value of the predominant group and denigrated the minority one" have contributed toward the development of negative self-images on the part of many Hispanic American students.[163]

While it is important to avoid the extreme of a "victimological"[164] interpretation of the manner in which this negative self-image has been formed, the influence of some segments of the predominant society has been well documented.[165] This has led some Hispanic Americans to internalize the negative stereotypes which the predominant society has of them.[166] Elizondo explains: "If you hear again and again that you are inferior, good for nothing, incompetent, and lazy, you may eventually begin to believe it yourself."[167] The comments of an eighth grade student in a Southwestern school reflect the internalization of this negative self-image:

> To begin with, I am a Mexican. That sentence has a scent of bitterness as it is written. I feel that if it weren't for my nationality I would accomplish more. My being Mexican has brought about my lack of initiative. No matter what I attempt to do, my dark skin always makes me feel that I will fail.[168]

Many Hispanic Americans have overcome the effects of a negative self-image and have accomplished much personally as well as collectively. Others, at times, have used their cultural background to rationalize their lack of effort and discipline. Manuel A. Machado, for instance, points out that some Hispanic Americans "look for scapegoats to blame for their own failures; thus society and American racism become the simple answers to their simple minds."[169]

For some, having a Hispanic ancestry has become such a strong a symbol of shame and inferiority that it interferes with their ability to achieve even moderate goals.[170] Others, however, have developed an appreciation for their Hispanic heritage and have learned to function effectively in the context of the predominant society. The Hispanic American search for a sense of identity, therefore, involves not merely the discovery of their socio-historical heritage but the shedding of negative stereotypes. López-McKnight expresses this conviction when she states that Hispanic Americans must come to be viewed by the predominant society "as dignified human beings."[171]

The Hispanic American search for a sense of dignity is closely connected with their desire to retain their cultural identity. Hispanic Americans want their culture to be respected by the predominant society. They aspire to be considered first class citizens while retaining their cultural heritage. Different approaches have been utilized by the various generations in their effort to attain a sense of dignity. Some have felt that it was up to the predominant society to grant them a sense of dignity.[172] Others attempted to attain a sense of dignity by incorporating many cultural elements from the predominant society. For others, however, a sense of dignity appears to be heavily dependent upon their ability to discover and retain their cultural heritage. The search for a sense of dignity has been expressed differently in each of the generations discussed above.

## A desire to attain a spirit of unity (carnalismo)

The desire to attain a spirit of unity among Hispanic Americans is another dimension of their search for identity. Feeling a sense of powerlessness[173] and marginality with regard to the predominant society, many Hispanic Americans believe that their identity can be enhanced and their socioeconomic status can be improved if they attain unity as a sociocultural group.[174] López-McKnight explains that unity among the Hispanic American community is a prerequisite in order to be more effective in addressing its bicultural and bilingual social and economic needs.[175] This desire for unity is expressed perhaps most clearly in the concept of *carnalismo*.[176]

The Hispanic American spirit of *carnalismo* has its roots in the Indian concept of *compadrazgo* and the Spanish concept of the extended family. Dating back to the time of the Spanish settlements, the concept of *compadrazgo* (co-parenthood or Godparent age)[177] was developed to establish social ties with non-family members.[178] This had the effect of "knitting the family together normatively and of formalizing informal ties of friendship."[179]

The Spanish concept of the extended family includes more than just blood relatives.[180] In addition to grandparents, aunts, uncles, and cousins, it includes in-laws (father, mother, aunts, uncles, and cousins in law), and *hijos de crianza* (orphans brought up in the family).[181] The extended family is the "main focus of obligation and also a source of emotional and economic support as well as recognition for accomplishment.[182]

The notion of *carnalismo* appears to utilize the concepts of *compadrazgo* and the extended family as it seeks to promote a type of brotherhood within Hispanic American community which is characterized by a deep feeling of allegiance to other *carnales*.[183]

The spirit of *carnalismo*, however, faces serious challenges from within the Hispanic American community. There are divisions between the various segments of the Hispanic American community.[184] Elizondo's description of the spirit of *carnalismo* acknowledges that there is divisiveness among Hispanic Americans: "We recognize one another; there is a bond, a sense of *familia*, which we all experience, but there is also an area of self-identity that we do not agree on."[185]

The areas of disagreement, however, go beyond that of self-identity. There are significant generational, socioeconomic, and nationalistic differences which divide Hispanic Americans.[186] At times the conflicts between Hispanic American groups have been as heated as those occurring in the national arena.[187] Grebler's study of marriage patterns, for instance, indicates that "the social distance between different generations of Hispanic Americans is greater than the social distance between some categories of Hispanic Americans and Anglos."[188]

An additional distance between segments of the Hispanic community relates to their status as native born (English dominant) and foreign born (Spanish dominant) persons. This distance is greater than any distance which might exist because of differences related to the country of origin of the Hispanic Americans.[189]

Another challenge which comes from within is that of *envidia* (envy), an attitude resulting from the belief that there is "limited good." Consequently an individual or family can improve only at the expense of others.[190] This attitude, which affects the poor generally,[191] often results in great rivalries among leaders and groups thus preventing the type of cooperation which could help them overcome oppressive conditions.

The tendency on the part of Hispanic Americans who have achieved middle class status to disassociate themselves from those in the lower socioeconomic levels constitutes yet another internal challenge to the spirit of *carnalismo*. López y Rivas chastises middle class Hispanic Americans for "turning their backs on the poor."[192] Mac"as criticizes the Hispanic American who believes that "just because he makes it, the system is valid for all Chicanos."[193]

The spirit of *carnalismo* faces challenges from outside the Hispanic American community as well. The changes brought about by urban life constitute one of these challenges. Changes which occur in employment patterns, family roles, patterns of residence, and social services have militated against the functions of the extended family. Employment patterns in urban areas unlike those in agricultural communities are generally based on ability rather than status in the family. The shift in family roles is from patriarchal orientation to the norm of equality. Residential patterns have changed from single family housing to multiple family housing. Social services have often assumed some of the functions of the extended family. [194]

Despite the fact that there are many challenges to the spirit of *carnalismo*, its proponents[195] believe that it is essential for the establishment of a common sense of identity and for mutual assistance.[196] This ideal is expressed in the *Plan Espiritual de Aztlán* which reminds Hispanic Americans that brotherhood unites them and that love for their brothers is what motivates them to struggle on their behalf.[197]

## Spiritual Needs

As is true of all people groups, Hispanic Americans have spiritual needs that can only be met through a proper relation with God. In chapter 6 we pointed out that Hispanics are by and large a religious group of people. The recent studies of the Pew Hispanic Center's National Survey of Latinos reveals that among Hispanics 70% identify themselves as "Catholics;" 20% as "Evangelical or Born Again;" 9% as "Other Christian;" 2% as "Some other non-Christian religion;" and 8% as having "No Religion."198198 Pew Hispanic Center/Kaiser Family Foundation, 2002 National Survey of Latinos, December 2002, 53.

Only 8% stated that they had no religion. This fact lends credibility to the statement that more Hispanics claim to be religious than many other cultural groups in America today.

While it is evident that such a large percentage of Hispanics identify themselves with a religious group, the fact remains that a significant percentage of them have not had a personal experience of salvation in Jesus Christ. Many of them are like the Samaritan woman described in John chapter 4. She had a very limited understanding of the truths about God revealed in the Old Testament and a vague hope about the future. Whatever religion she practiced (a mixture of Judaism and paganism) did not seem to influence her lifestyle or satisfy her spiritual yearnings.

The religious experience of other Hispanic perhaps resembles that of Nicodemus. With great devotion they take a legalistic approach to their religious experience but have a void in their lives. They have not responded in repentance and faith to Jesus Christ as their personal Savior and Lord and do not have a lifestyle that demonstrates a sense of freedom from the guilt of sin, relief from the fear of judgment, and joy in their relationship with God.[199] As a result of this, they often feel confused and alienated when they face the trials and tribulations of life and either have a false hope or do not have a sense of assurance when they think about their eternal destiny.

Christians who try to convince Hispanics that their religious tradition is wrong or simply to try to get them to switch from one religion to another usually end up alienating them. As we point out in chapter 17, our emphasis should not be on *religion* but on *relationship*. Leading people to receive Jesus Christ as their personal Savior and Lord is the most effective way to help them to have the spiritual resources they need to face the challenges of life on this earth and have a strong sense of assurance about their eternal destiny.

# Conclusion

Several observations can be made from the analysis of the cluster of themes which relate to the Hispanic American search for identity:

- First, many Hispanic Americans appear to be striving to find an anchor for their sense of identity.
- Second, different segments of Hispanic Americans have attempted to gain a sense of dignity through the employment of different strategies. These strategies include efforts to get the predominant society to change the negative stereotypes it has of Hispanic Americans, efforts to join the predominant society through the process of cultural and structural assimilation, and efforts to revitalize their own culture.
- Third, some Hispanic Americans are experiencing a sense of marginality with regard to the predominant society, to the culture of their country of origin, or to other segments within their own cultural group. Some of the contributing factors to this sense of marginality are the attitudes of the predominant society, the desire of Hispanic Americans to retain their cultural characteristics, and the different rates of assimilation to the predominant society among Hispanic Americans. The sense of marginality, which is pervasive in the lives of many Hispanic Americans, is complex and at times destructive.
- Fourth, some Hispanic Americans believe that their sense of identity and their ability to overcome their sense of marginality are dependent upon their ability to achieve a spirit of unity as a group (*carnalismo*). Efforts to achieve this spirit, however, have been severely hampered by obstacles which come from within the

group. Despite these obstacles many Hispanic Americans continue to strive to attain a spirit of *carnalismo*. The concerns reflected in these themes will be the focus of the study of scripture which is to follow.

The Hispanic American search for a sense of identity is a continuous and complicated one. As Floristan states, "The quest for identity never ends because it consists not only in tracing our roots but also in looking to the future."[200] As they look to the future, many Hispanic Americans are optimistic about their ability to survive as a cultural group by "fashioning syncretic, adaptive strategies"[201] to the many changing conditions.[202]

Hispanics view the variety of cultural perspectives with which they have had to deal as a "core strength"[203] which enables them to confront life and to attain a true spirit of *carnalismo*.[204] This quest can find inspiration and guidance in the concept of the new community of the kingdom which is made possible by the life and ministry of Jesus. This new community is not based on racial or political factors. Instead, it breaks down the walls of partition between the cultural groups and enables them to have a sense of appreciation for their cultural heritage.

This new community is not confined to those who share a particular sociopolitical experience. In it racial and cultural factors are revitalized for the sake of a higher priority.[205] The messianic banquet theme, which was a corrective to the motif of the eschatological pilgrimage of the nations to Zion, places Gentiles on equal footing with Israelites.[206] They are invited to become members of the body of Christ which includes men and women from all peoples of the world in a reconciled and reconciling community.[207]

In their search for identity, therefore, Hispanic Americans can emphasize the reality of a new creation in Christ in whom all are children of the same God and there is neither Jew nor Greek, male nor female. There is the possibility for them to develop a positive sense of identity and dignity knowing that Jesus accepted *mestizos* and identified with them. They are assured that they can become a part of the kingdom and have an equal share in the fundamental dignity of membership in the family of God.[208]

At the same time, their search for identity is challenged by the teachings and actions of Jesus who refused to confine his ministry to one sub-cultural group (e.g., Galileans), and offered compassion and friendship across the existing lines of exclusion. This dignity of membership in the family of God can lead Hispanic Americans toward a positive identity which overcomes excessive preoccupation with self, transcends and celebrates cultural differences, and seeks to become involved in ministry to others.

Understanding socio-historical pilgrimage of Hispanic Americans is the first step toward the communication of the gospel in manner which will be relevant to their lives. Many ministries provided by compassionate congregations can be instrumental in addressing these needs and provide bridges for leading Hispanic to a personal faith in Jesus Christ. As Hispanic Americans anchor their identity in Christ, they will be in a position to affirm the positive elements of their culture, correct or shun the un-biblical elements, and experience the freedom from self-preoccupation that allows them to minister to others with compassion and understanding.

Two biblical analogies provide valuable insights and inspiration for Hispanic Americans who are searching for a positive and empowering sense of identity. In chapter 14, Dr. Jesse Miranda describes the Samaritan analogy. In chapter 15, Dr. Daniel Sanchez posits the Hellenistic analogy.

---

Endnotes

[117] Survey conducted by Richie Stanley and Daniel R. Sanchez, in November of 2004.

[118] The Woman's Missionary Union's e-mail address is: www.wmu.com

[119] For more information contact the North American Mission Board at www.namb.net

[120] For more information contact www.hopefortheheart,org

[121] For a more in-depth treatment of this subject see Daniel R. Sanchez, An Interdisciplinary Approach to Theological Contextualization with special reference to Hispanic Americans, Ph. D. thesis, Oxford Centre for Mission Studies, April 17, 1991.

[122] This is not intended to be an exhaustive list of psycho-social needs, but one which focuses on some of salient needs related the Hispanics' adjustment to life in the midst of the dominant culture in America.

[123] The term "carnalismo" is used especially by Mexican Americans to refer to those who are like biological brothers "hermanos carnales." This means that a strong bond exists between friends and neighbors that is a kin to that which exists between biological brothers.

[124] Pew Hispanic Center/Kaiser Family Foundation, 2002 National Survey of Latinos, December 2002, 2.

[125] See Virgilio Elizondo, Galilean Journey (Maryknoll, NY: Orbis Books, 1983), p. 20.

[126] See Gloria López-McKnight, "Communication: The Key to Social Change," chap in La Causa Chicana, ed. Margaret M. Mangold (New York, NY: Family Service Association of America, 1971), p. 192.

[127] López-McKnight, op. cit., p. 193.

[128] See James D. Vigil, From Indians To Chicanos: A Sociocultural History (London: C. V. Mosby Company, 1980), p. 230.

[129] See Joan W. Moore and Alfred Cuellar, Hispanic Ameri-cans (Englewood Cliffs, NJ: Prentice-Hall Inc., 1970), p. 159.

[130] See Moore and Cuellar, op. cit., pp. 158-59.

[131] See Gilberto López y Rivas, The Chicanos: The Life and Struggle of the Hispanic Minority in the United States (London: Monthly Review Press, 1973), pp. 77, 93; Harvard Encyclopedia of American Ethnic Groups, 1980 ed., s.v. "Hispanics," by Carlos E. Cortés.

[132] Perhaps the imprecision of this concept has con-tributed to its acceptance by large numbers of Hispanic Americans. If it were defined in more precise cultural or racial terms a number of Hispanic Americans would quite likely not identify with this term.

[133] Ironically, as Alvarez points out, the Renaissance Generation, is "even more acculturated than the previous [Assimilation] generation." Rodolfo Alvarez "The Psycho-Historical and Socioeconomic Development of the Chicano Community in the United States." Social Sciences Quarterly 53 (March 1973): pp. 936-37.

[134] See Vigil, op. cit., p. 231.

[135] Those, for instance, who stress the Indian but deny the Spanish side of their heritage do not have a sense of identity which is true to history.

[136] See Elizondo, Galilean Journey, p. 21. The very terms which are employed (Hispanic, Hispanic American, Spanish American, Chicano, and Hispanic) demonstrate not only varieties of backgrounds but also ambivalence regarding the identity of this group. See Moore and Cuellar, op. cit., p. 8.

[137] Rodolfo Alvarez, "The Unique Psycho-Historical Experience of the Hispanic American People," Social Science Quarterly 52 (June 1971): p. 25.

[138] Elizondo, Galilean Journey, pp. 22-23.

[139] Some of the ways in which the dominant society influences the subordinate group toward cultural assimilation are through the news media (radio, television, newspapers, films), and the education-al systems.

[140] Philip D. Ortego, "The Chicano Renaissance," Social Casework 52, no. 5 (May 1971), p. 296.

[141] Ortego, op. cit., 296. While Ortego adequately describes some of the factors which produce this conflict, he fails to acknowledge that there are those in the Hispanic American community who do not have a clear sense of "who they really are." This identity crisis is portrayed vividly in the poem "Joa-quin," in which the author states that he is "lost in world of confusion, struggling to decide between economic progress and cul-tural survival." Rodolfo Gonzáles, I Am Joaquín (Denver, CO: Crusade for Justice, 1967), p. 3.

[142] The syncretistic culture and language represented by Tex-Mex (Texas Hispanic) represents a creative effort to overcome a state of confusion by drawing elements from both cultures and languages. See Vigil, op. cit., p. 165. See also E. Galarza, Barrio Boy (Notre Dame, IN: Univer-sity of Notre Dame Press, 1971), p. 31.

[143] Vigil explains that intoxication, fighting, anomie, drugs, and other forms of cultural disorientation often occur in the lives of individuals who are not securely rooted in either Hispanic or Anglo culture. Vigil, op. cit., p. 163.

[144] See E. Wolf, Sons of the Shaking Earth (Chicago, IL: University of Chicago Press, 1959), p. 237.

[145] See Elizondo, Galilean Journey, pp. 20-23.

[146] Pew Hispanic Center/Kaiser Family Foundation, 2002 National Survey of Latinos, 8.

[147] See George I. Sánchez, Forgotten People: A Study of New Hispanics (Albuquerque, NM: Calvin Horn Publishers, 1967), p. 75.

[148] Pew Hispanic Center/Kaiser Family Foundation, 2002 National Survey of Latinos, 8

[149] Ibid.

[150] The Renaissance Generation may be more prone to experience a sense of marginality from both cultures. On the one hand, the Renaissance Generation states clearly that its culture is neither Hispanic nor Anglo American, while on the other hand, its principal source of identity stems from a sense of continuity with the Aztec-Hispanic culture. See Moore and Cuellar, op. cit., p. 155. Shibutani and Kwan explain that "individuals in this vanguard occupy a marginal status, a position dangling between two social worlds." T. Shibutani and K. M. Kwan, Ethnic Stratifica-tion: A Comparative Approach (New York: Macmillan, Inc., 1965), p. 352.

[151] Vigil explains that some groups such as the vatos locos (crazy dudes) have become marginal to all three cultures. Vigil, op. cit., p. 212, 230.

[152] Vigil, op. cit., p. 162.

[153] See Sandoval, op. cit., p. 11.

[154] See Vigil, op. cit., p. 230.

[155] M. León-Portilla, cited in Vigil, op. cit., p. 230.

[156] Augustine Weilbert cited in Elizondo, Galilean Journey, p. 23.

[157] See R. Díaz-Guerrero, Psychology of the Hispanic Culture and Personality (Austin, TX: University Press, 1975); Joel L. Martinez, Jr., Richard H. Mendoza, eds., Chicano Psychology (London: Academic Press, Inc., 1984).

[158] Ysidro Ramon Macías, "The Chicano Movement," A Docu-mentary History of Hispanic Americans, ed. Wayne Moquin and Charles Van Doren (London: Praeger Publishers, 1971), p. 388.

[159] See Armando Morales, "The Collective Preconscious and Racism," in La Causa Chicana: The Movement of Justice (New York, NY: Family Services Association of America, 1971), pp. 15-29.

[160] See Vigil for a discussion of the contribution of the Anglo American educational system to the formation of negative stereo-types in Hispanic American students. Vigil, op. cit., pp. 173-74.

[161] Margaret Mangold, M, ed, La Causa Chicana: The Movement for Justice, New York, NY: Family Service Association of America, 1971, 25.

[162] For a discussion of the utilization of mass media reporting to foster negative Hispanic American stereotypes see Mirandé, op. cit., pp. 70-90.

[163] Vigil, op. cit., pp. 173-74.

[164] This interpretation would view Hispanic Americans only as victims without any personal responsibility for what happens to them. See R. A. Schermerhorn, Comparative Ethnic Rela-tions (New York, NY: Random House, 1970), pp. 8-9.

[165] This may be the result of discriminatory attitudes which date back to the Spanish settlement period as well as to the denigrating stereo-types which developed during the time of the annexation. See Vigil, op. cit., p. 175; Moore and Cuellar, op. cit., p. 141; Elizondo, Galilean Journey, p. 68; Margaret M. Mangold, ed., La Causa Chicana: The Movement for Justice (New York, NY: Family Service Association of America, 1971), pp. 8-10.

[166] Grebler's study indicates that many Hispanic Americans agree with the stereotype that Anglo Americans have of them. It showed, for instance, that more than 75% of the Hispanic Americans interviewed in Los Angeles and San Antonio felt that Hispanic Americans are more emotional than other Americans and less progressive than Anglos. See Leo Grebler, Joan W. Moore, and Ralph C. Guzman, The Hispanic American People (London: Collier-Macmillan Ltd., 1970), p. 388.

[167] Elizondo, Galilean Journey, p. 23. See also Mirandé, op. cit., p. 89.

[168] Report of the NEA-Tucson on the Teaching of Spanish Speaking, "The Invisible Minority," in Hispanic Americans in the United States: A Reader, ed. John H. Burma (Cambridge, MA: Schenkman Publishing Co., 1970), p. 103.

[169] Manuel A. Machado, Jr., Listen Chicano (Chicago, IL: Nelson Hall, 1978), p. 182.

[170] See J. D. Forbes, Aztecas del Norte: The Chicanos of Aztlán (New York, NY: Fawcett Books, 1973).

[171] López-McKnight, op. cit., p. 209.

[172] They felt that the negative stereotypes which the dominant society had of Hispanic Americans had been internalized by the latter to the extent that for them to make some progress toward attaining a sense of dignity these stereotypes (in the minds of the dominant society) would need to be changed.

[173] See Vigil, op. cit., pp. 330-331, Elizondo, Galilean Journey, p. 25.

[174] See López-McKnight, op. cit., p. 209. Moore and Cuellar explain that appeals for political action, economic progress, and reorientation of cultural identity have been cast in terms of a common history, culture, and ethnic background. Moore and Cuellar, op. cit., p. 153.

[175] López-McKnight, op. cit., p. 208.

[176] While this is a term that is more prevalent among Hispanic Americans, the concept of unity is cherished by most Hispanic Americans.

[177] Moore and Cuellar explain that "as a religious act, it symbolizes formally a promise of the godparents that the child would be brought

117

up as a Christian should anything happen to the child's parents." See Moore and Cuellar, op. cit., pp. 104-5.

[178] See Vigil, op. cit., p. 73.

[179] Moore and Cuellar, op. cit., p. 104.

[180] See Virgilio P. Elizondo, Christianity and Culture (Huntington, IN: Our Sunday Visitor, Inc., 1975), p. 159.

[181] Elizondo, Christianity and Culture, pp. 159-64.

[182] Moore and Cuellar, op. cit., p. 104.

[183] See Aguirre, op. cit., p. 261. The term carnal is often used by Hispanic Americans to mean brother. Carnal is a derivative of the word carne (flesh), hence the idea of a brother in the flesh or blood brother. This term has been expanded to refer to others who belong to La Raza.

[184] See J. Gómez-Quiñones, Hispanic Students por La Raza: the Chicano Student Movement in Southern California, 1967-1977 (Santa Barbara, CA: Editorial La Causa, 1978), p. 43.

[185] Elizondo, Galilean Journey, p. 21.

[186] See Vigil, op. cit., pp. 200-201.

[187] There is a debate, for instance, between structurally assimilated Hispanic Americans and Chicanos who repudiate the option exercised by the former. Some Hispanic American writers (e.g., López y Rivas, The Chicanos, Rodolfo Gonzales, "Chicano Nation-alism: The Key to Unity of La Raza," in Chicano [London: Monthly Review Press, 1973]) feel that the price paid by those who achieved structural assimila-tion into the dominant society was too high (in terms of what they had to "give up" culturally in order to achieve economic success). There does not appear to be sufficient written evidence to indicate that this is in fact the feeling of assimilated Hispanic Americans. See Gómez-Quiñones, op. cit., p. 43.

[188] Grebler, op. cit., p. 409.

[189] Pew Hispanic Center/Kaiser Family Foundation, 2002 National Survey of Latinos, 13.

[190] See Vigil, op. cit., p. 228.

[191] See George Foster, "Peasant Society and the Image of Limited Good," in Peasant Society: A Reader, eds., J. M. Potter, M. N. Díaz, and G. M. Foster (Boston, MA: Little Brown and Company, 1967), p. 305. Foster's observations are consistent with Oscar Lewis's concept of "culture of poverty." See Oscar Lewis, Five Families: Hispanic Case Studies in the Culture of Poverty (New York, NY: Basic Books Inc., Publishers, 1959).

[192] López y Rivas, The Chicano, p. 73.

[193] Macías, "The Chicano Movement," p. 388. While some Hispanic Americans may view their social and economic progress as a fulfillment of the "American dream," others view it as an indication of self-centeredness and greed. Hispanic Americans who are interested primarily in their personal advancement and who have experienced

extensive assimilation (e.g., Assimilated Ethnics) have a tendency to view their experience as a fulfillment of the American dream. Those who have not experienced extensive assimilation (e.g., Total Ethnics) and those who have experienced some assimilation (e.g., Revitalized Ethnics) but remain committed to the advancement of Hispanic Americans as a group have more of a tendency to view individual advancement as an indication of self-centeredness and greed.

[194] See Moore and Cuellar, op. cit,. pp. 116-17. See also Grebler, op. cit., p. 237. Another chal-lenge comes from the model of the dominant society which focuses on the individual and views "carnalismo "as a hindrance to full participation in the Anglo American society." V. M. Briggs, W. Fogel, Jr., and F. H. Schmidt, The Chicano Worker (Austin, TX: University of Texas Press, 1977), p. 23.

[195] Macías, op. cit., p. 338; López y Rivas Chicanos, p. 73; Aguirre, op. cit., pp. 1-5.

[196] Macías links self-awareness and carnalismo as founda-tions for the Chicano ideology. Macías, op. cit., p. 389.

[197] See López y Rivas, op. cit., p. 66. Macias echoes this when he stresses that "the Chicano is a part of a brother-hood that has an obligation to work for the betterment of his people in whatever way he can." Macías, op. cit., p. 388.

[198] Pew Hispanic Center/Kaiser Family Foundation, 2002 National Survey of Latinos, December 2002, 53.

[199] For an excellent book on the assurance of salvation, see Donald S. Whitney, How Can I Be Sure I'm A Christian? (Colorado Springs: NAVPRESS, 1994).

[200] Casiano Floristan cited in Sandoval, op. cit., p. 68.

[201] The negative side of the adaptive strategies, however, is that there is a legacy of inadequate adapta-tions which have plagued the Hispanic American community causing conflict, anguish, and con-fusion. There continues to be a need for theological reflection regarding these and other vital concerns in the Hispanic American community. See Virgilio Elizondo, The Future Is Mestizo (Blooming-t-on, IN: Meyer-Stone Books, 1988), p. 110.

[202] Vigil, op. cit., p. 231.

[203] Vigil, op. cit., p. 231.

[204] Audinet expresses this hope for Hispanic Americans when he states: "Finally your mission is related to our hope for the survival of this planet. More and more power is shifting from East and West to North and South. You are right in the middle of this alignment. By your roots, you are of the South. By your life you are a part of the North. The paradox is this: while you belong to the most powerful empire that has ever existed, and are one of its least powerful elements you have a crucial role. You act not of yourselves alone but for the world." Jaques Audinet cited in Sandoval, op. cit., p. 78.

[205] Donald Senior and Carrol Stuhlmueller, The Biblical Foundation for Mission, Maryknoll, NY: Orbis Book, 1984, 53.

[206] Ibid.

[207] See Minutes and Report of the Meeting of the Assembly of the Commission on World Mission and Evangelism, Bangkok, Thailand, December 31, 1972 and January 9-12, 1973 (Bangkok: n.p., 1973), p. 73.

[208] Elizondo, Galilean Journey, p. 62.

# Chapter 14

# Modern-Day Samaritans

## Dr. Jesse Miranda

## El Camino Real

During the decade of the 80s, when immigration from Latin America was at its zenith, I met a Hispanic woman at a Los Angeles airport. She had come to the United States from Cuba five years earlier. I asked her what she liked about her new country and she readily mentioned many things she enjoyed. Freedom and opportunity were highest on her list.

Then I asked her what she didn't like and she adamantly said, "I don't like being called a Mexican." She felt that being identified with Mexicans devalued her. I surprised her when I informed her that I am of Mexican descent. She then added, "Oh, but I see you are not like the others (of Mexican descent)." What did she see?

This short conversation revealed some truths, realities, and subtleties of the life of Hispanics in the United States. The truth is that all Hispanics are not exactly the same. We identified a Mexican, a Cuban American, and a Mexican American in the course of our short conversation. The reality is that a prevailing collective identity exists in U.S.

121

society that considers all Hispanics as Mexicans. Further, in general the dominant feeling holds the idea is that all immigrants are of lesser value. In a period of five short years, the Hispanic woman had categorized herself and other Hispanics.

This Cuban woman unintentionally viewed Mexicans as being different. This is not surprising since Mexican Americans are the oldest and largest group. Understandably, they cast perceptions, good and bad, and identity markers, accurate or not, for Hispanics in this country. What she and many others fail to understand are the subtleties that are behind a stigma imposed upon Mexican Americans resulting from their historical and social experience in the life of the U.S. Mexican Americans actually are unlike other Hispanics.

As mentioned in previous chapters, Hispanic Americans come from all races and dozens of nationalities. Among Hispanics, Mexican Americans are the most indigenous to the continental U.S. This chapter picks up on this unique story and some of the effects on the Mexican-American community. The risk always exists that in attempting to address the broader issues of diversity, and in this case Hispanic diversity, the perspective of particular groups, Puerto Ricans, Cubans, Salvadorans, Argentines, etc. will become too generalized.

The reality is that important differences exist in the histories, experiences, and consequences of these specific groups. A chapter could be written for each of the 22 Hispanic nationalities. Although this chapter is about Mexican Americans, as Latinos we need to know each other because as Carlos Fuentes, prominent Mexican writer once said, "None of us will ever be able to find the humanity within us unless we are able to find it first in others."[209] We are *familia* and members of the human race.

As I write, immigration is one of the hottest national political issues in the nation and Mexican immigration is the primary target of the policies being discussed. In the 90s, efforts to reduce Mexican influence with the numerous anti-immigrant political propositions only served to spread Latinos beyond the Southwest to new settlements throughout the nation. Since then, the INS has been joined by Homeland Security to keep watch on the borders between Mexico and the United States. Minutemen and vigilantes are stationed along the Southern borders. The governors of Arizona and New Mexico have called these immigration issues states of emergency.

The new immigrant experiences taking place in this country and their increasing numbers have made Hispanics highly visible and the topic of many conversations and debates. For Mexican Americans, history is only repeating itself. As mentioned, they are the oldest and largest among Hispanics in the United States. They originally settled along *El Camino Real* (The King's Highway) where the Spanish built their missions. Later these people became Americans when the Southwest, Arizona, California, New Mexico, and Texas, became part of the U.S. Those of us born since that time became citizens of the U.S. Present birth rates and immigration factors indicate that Mexican Americans will continue to be the majority Hispanic group for many years to come. They will exert vast and increasing influence on how society views Hispanics in general and the contributions Hispanics will make toward the future of this country.

For example, one of the most prosperous counties in the nation, Orange County, California, recently focused on a study and published a book that examines the future: *California 2025*. The OC business journal, which has wide circulation, carried the cover story, "The Key to California's Future: It Depends upon How Far Latinos Take Us."[210]

In the light of increasing and changing demographics the stakes are high for every institution of society. The challenges and consequences of diversity have dramatic implications at all levels of society. Some glorify diversity to be politically correct. Others institutionalize inequality paying little attention to diversity. Still others struggle to understand and involve diverse populations.

This challenge calls for the creation of institutions in which individuals and group differences are respected and allowed to coexist. What are the implications for the Church? It was born to be global in nature and for the creation of the community such as the one envisioned by the Apostle Paul in Ephesians 4. Creating such a community, however, requires decisions and interactions that address fundamental values, preferences, and rights.

The early Church experienced some of this kind of conflict and had to call the Council of Jerusalem (Acts 15) to deal with it. To the Church diversity can become either a problem to be solved or a potential for harvest growth. Hispanics can be seen as a threat and inconvenience or as social and spiritual capital for future growth.

Unfortunately, much of the discussion today is referred to in terms of the "cultural wars" taking place in society. Today, for many, diversity or pluralism really involves the politicization of identity. A well-known process exists in American history, especially in politics, where various groups have followed the practice to balance the ticket with candidates. In 19th century leaders balanced the tickets with the Irish and the Italian. In the 20th century, they balanced tickets with African Americans. Now, in the 21st century, balance is sought with Hispanic Americans. As mentioned, the U.S. Census uses the term "Hispanic American" for the purpose of data collection.

Meanwhile, children and grand-children of Hispanics are wondering why society cannot "decide on a name and make up our minds if we are Hispanic, Latinos, Mexican American, Chicanos, Boricuas, or whatever." The younger generations continue to seek full participation in the life of their country in a time that *"America is moving backward rather than forward in its efforts to achieve the full participation of minority citizens in the life and prosperity of the nation." If we allow these disparities to continue, the United States will inevitably suffer a compromised quality of life and lower standard of living.*[211]

The new generation of Mexican Americans may not be as pessimistic about their history and culture as older generations. Still they are in desperate need of new information on some old issues and debilitating actions. Their generation, although not knowing the whole story, has an intense need to end the alienation that has denied them a full involvement in the society that rejected their parents. Yet I see this new generation wanting to honor the past efforts of their parents while wanting to forge a better future.

Already there are promising Mexican American young leaders in prominent positions of our nation who have "made it" in this society (e.g., Gaddi Vasquez, director of the Peace Corps). Hispanics serve as governors (e.g., Richardson in New Mexico), as mayors (e.g., Villaraigosa), as county supervisors (e.g., Gloria Molina), and as lawyers, educators, and business men and women. Thousands of young Hispanic leaders are beginning to make a difference in society.

Even so, this young generation is aware of the memories of seeing their parents struggle to make a living. Laura Diaz, anchor woman for an NBC affiliate, remembers spending the first four years of her life, not in pre-school or childcare, but on the vineyard labor camps in California. Comedian Paul Rodriquez remembers wondering as a child if God is fair. If so, why are all the workers stooped on the fields of brown skin and the owners that stood over them were of white skin?[212]This new generation has seen their parents' struggles on the fringes of society and has heard the engrossing stories of their elders. They wonder why their parents did not fight, as the African Americans. They question why their people decided to accept defeat and forget about it. The overall query that I hear from this younger generation is why did their parents accept the path of silent resignation?

If in the United States, where faith and life have always been integrated, they don't get answers, it will be less likely they will get the answers from Mexico. In Mexico people often express a concern about too strongly mixing faith and politics. The only education our America Hispanic youth have of their history and culture is the one articulated during the 60s from the Civil Rights era, which I will explain later. Reflecting on American ethnic cultures and political processes, Henry Nouwen, notable Christian author, makes this observation:

If any criticism can be made of the sixties (Civil Rights movement) it is not that protest was meaningless but that it was not deep enough, in the sense that it was not rooted in the solitude of the heart. When only our minds and hands work together we quickly become dependent on the results of our actions and tend to give up when they don't materialize. In the solitude of the heart we can truly listen to the pains of the world there we can feel that the cruel reality of history is indeed the reality of the human heart.[213]

In general, society continues to miss the fact that race and ethnicity are only the first step in understanding someone's deeper humanity. Race and ethnicity are not primary for humans to understand each other. Rather, their humanness is the primary level. It is not, however, always an easy task to cross the bridge into the primary level of our humanness.

## Crossing the River

Border crossing is part of the history and in the psyche of Mexican Americans. It was in the past, it is in the present, and it will be in the future. To understand this requires a different way of thinking about borders. It requires us to move away from merely considering boundaries between nations-states. Here we go deeper and highlight the several borders and boundaries - physical, political, social, and religious - in the pathway of Latinos. Boundaries define us. They define what is me and what is not me. Am I Mexican or am I American? The fact is we create a new identity and we are both. It is one of the challenges for both native born and immigrants living in the United States. This new identity comes with social and psychological challenges to overcome.

The story of Jephthah and the Gileadites in Judges 12:4-26 points out the subtleties of human discriminations. The Ephraimites could not be distinguished from the Gileadites by physical appearance and some tried to sneak through Jephthah's lines. Soon a clever test was devised. Those trying to cross the Jordan River were required to say the Hebrew word *shibboleth*. The word simply means "a torrent of water." Since the Ephraimites mispronounced the word as *sibboleth* , they were easily identified for their slight deviation of their accent and were killed.

*Shibboleth*, a word in our modern-day dictionary, relates to a single issue by which someone or something is distinguishable. Such words mark or distinguish a person, a characteristic, or an action. People in society love shibboleths; they love to find distinguishing features. It is a convenient way to separate and alienate others.

In this chapter, the heart of the matter lies in two simple terms: alienation and involvement. Here we deal with the cruel reality of history in the heart and soul of Mexican Americans. The theme of alienation permeates Latino literature. One of the challenges of diversity rests on integrating the goals of involvement into the fabric of our institutions. The Church, as we read in chapter 12, is challenged with reaching out to the heart of Hispanic Americans as they desperately search their socio-historical pilgrimage.

In this chapter we deal with reaching into the cosmic pain in the soul of Mexican Americans. In chapter 13 we saw a list of physical and psychological needs of Hispanic Americans. Here we will sense the plight and yearning of Mexican Americans. Our basic questions are:

- What is "deepest within the Mexican American?"
- "How do we reach deep enough with the gospel?"

My proposition in this chapter is that: *given the historical scars Mexican Americans carry and the sense of alienation in society, we can reach deep within this community's heart and yield a larger spiritual harvest in the 21st century by integrating culture and gospel and by relating the message of hope to their cosmic pain.* I have chosen the growing recognition of the "narrative" character of the Bible to help us frame the arguments of this chapter.

This emphasis includes narratives which explain how the people of God came into being and indicates the kind of behavior which is appropriate or inappropriate for their identity as the people of God. The two themes of this chapter, *alienation* and *involvement,* or in other words, *exclusion* and *inclusion,* can be found in a biblical narrative form.

The New Testament tells the story of Jesus, the story of the creation and expansion of the Church, and looks forward to the culmination of that story in the entry into the "New Jerusalem." In particular, we find in the Gospels, the story of Jesus who came to draw everyone unto himself by reaching out to the margins of society and centers of religion. He sought to bring the disenfranchised unto him with hope for their inner life and a transformation of their communities. The biblical focus is on the dignity and destiny of the human person which provides the moral cornerstone for social, economic, and spiritual life. The human person is not an impersonal individual but realizes his dignity only in community.

The efforts of Jesus to draw the disenfranchised and needy come into clear focus in the account of the Master and the Woman of Samaria (Jn. 4: 4-30). The story of the Samaritan woman is further described in chapter 17. The account of Jesus and the Samaritan woman is a story of exclusion and inclusion.

The Jews had alienated the Samaritans but Jesus chose to draw them into his fold. In this chapter we want to focus on the accent, the *Sibbolet* (*Shibboleth*), of the Samaritan people. Chapter 17 discusses the matter of reaching out to the heart of the Samaritan woman. Here it is about reaching into the soul of the Samaritan community of which she was a member. They were forced to live on the margins of society with their mixed linage (*mestisaje*), their isolation (barrio mentality), and their negative self-image.

That marginality marks the darker side of the Samaritan story. But there is a brighter side. There is the intersecting of culture and gospel where the gospel reached deep within and judges the culture according to its compatibility with the focus, values, and goals of the Kingdom of God.

From the outset, I compare the Mexican Americans to the Samaritans. To illustrate the depths of what lies within the souls of Mexican Americans, I have selected the biblical story of the Samaritans to describe anew their historical memory and social world. The Samaritan sense of personal and communal powerlessness repeats itself in Mexican Americans in their generation as well. Because it is important to know what shapes the behavior of Mexican Americans as a group and what drives their relations among themselves and with others, I intend to organize the principal ideas, contextual history, and collective identity, with those similar ideas in the life of the Samaritans in the Bible.

## The Self-Help Promise Land

Jews and Samaritans had been at war with each other since the year 444 BC. The conflict rested on the Jew's contentions concerning the history of the Samaritans and their ensuing behaviors and beliefs. Jews returned from captivity with a renewed loyalty to the Law and the Covenant with Jehovah which converged into a movement to purify the people of Israel of all foreign elements. The Samaritans, being a people of a mixed bloodline, were refused participation in the reconstruction of the wall of Jerusalem. A confrontation between the Jews and the Samaritans took place (Neh. 4-6). As a result, the Samaritans were expelled from the Holy City and stripped of their rights to worship in the Temple. Thereafter, the Samaritans were on their own to live in isolation with their own do-it-yourself religion.

For Mexican Americans, their history also consists of a legacy of conquests. There was the conquest of the Spanish over the indigenous population of Mexico. Then in 1848 the United States conquered of the northern territories of Mexico as a result of the Mexican-American War. The resulting annexation of what became the Southwest part of the United States laid the foundation for the tensions between Anglos and Mexicans.

My maternal great grandfather belonged to the annexation generation. He and his family lived in what is today the state of New Mexico. They did not cross the border rather the border crossed them. At which time they had to decide to remain on the United States side of the border as Americans or move further south as Mexican citizens.

In their understanding, the semi-feudal economic system of Mexico was one of the justifications Americans used for the war and subsequent appropriation of the Southwest. Americans, in favor of the war, argued that Mexicans had no right to the land because they were not using it to its full capacity. Americans described themselves as having a providential right to the land, a "manifest destiny." Anglo success in the war was interpreted as proof of Anglo economic and military superiority. Mexicans were viewed as representing the past and Anglo-Saxons the future. Among many, this view prevails to this day.

The Mexican-American War appears to have contributed to an inferiority complex and a sense of fatalism on the part of some in the Mexican American community. The war ended but the adage, "Mexico did not leave the Southwest it just learned English," is true in many ways. Los Angeles, for example, is the most populous Mexican city outside Mexico and as such it has a dual nature. LA is the great southwest frontier of Anglo culture but also the northwest frontier of the Mexican culture.

Many Mexican Americans could not help but notice that their experience of life in the U.S. and their belonging to contemporary society was unsatisfactory to them and to others. But they themselves were unaware of the underlying reasons for their failure to socialize and incorporate into society at large. That is until the crusade for Mexican American civil rights in the early 1960s when the country's long history of discrimination against and exclusion of their community was addressed.

Even this effort was largely limited to the rural struggles of farm workers led by Cesar Chavez. But then on March 1, 1968, *The Los Angeles Times* headlined the findings of the Kerner Commission report. The report highlighted the prevailing urban unrest across the nation and warned that racism was splitting the U.S. into two societies, "separate and unequal." On that day thousands of students from seven high schools walked out onto the streets of Los Angeles in a dramatic demonstration for better schools, protesting the under-representation at universities, and overrepresentation on the battlefields of Vietnam. This was the beginning of the *Chicano Movement*.

The Chicano Movement voiced the shared injury of Mexican Americans and reported their imposed social stigma in this country. The visions and values embraced in the term "*Chicanismo*," were reactions to the inconsistent U.S. policies and treatment against Mexicans. "Chicano studies" in universities in the Southwest focused their research on the status and condition of Mexican Americans, particularly those born in the U.S. A "*Chicano*," by the way, is short for "*Mexicano*," a native born or one who is Mexican born but acculturated in the U.S.

A Chicano is one who lives between Spanish and English, or "Spanglish." A Chicano is one who is looked upon as "Mexican" in the United States even though being a citizen, and considered an "*Americano*" in Mexico even though being of Mexican descent. A Chicano is one whose sense of identity, belonging, and potential has been profoundly influenced by a history and a social reputation which has greatly devalued the people and largely contributed to the social apartness exhibited in their life in the U.S.

During the notable waves of immigration from Mexico, the Chicano movement continued to explain to their people and others their social plight. This explanation became the voice from this side of the border on major issues between the U.S. and Mexico. These issues had existed for more than a century but no one was addressing them. The Chicano Movement served to highlight a neglected aspect of the U.S. immigration saga and mapped an essential territory of American cultural, social, economic, and political geography. This movement underlined the relationship between white and brown in the American Southwest. It transmitted the history and knowledge about the social and economic status of its community, a history about which parents had failed to inform the young.

Unfortunately, the Chicano Movement was part of the process of politicization of identity during the era. And much like other racial and ethnic groups, principally the African American, this movement also became primarily reactionary and militant. Its approach failed to give direction to the new generation of Mexican Americans whose context and political agendas had shifted. The Chicano generation became adult in their civil rights with the 1960s socio-political emphasis of victimization and its culture of blame failed to go deep enough into the humanness of Mexican Americans.

Not having strengthened the Hispanic social and political position in society, the movement weakened considerably. Some believe, however, the *Chicano* movement is being personified in the *new Latinos* in political power in California and increasingly in other states. Its spirit is resurrecting in Chicano literature per se. At this point the literature is scarce but young Latino authors continue to reflect and write on the subject of marginalization, a subject that does not go away.

What these young writers note is that the saga of new arrivals to this country makes up a significant part of the annuals of American history. The Mexican experience has not received the same treatment and does not compare to the European immigrant epics in the American historical experience. Nor does Chicano literature share the library shelves with the writings of an Upton Sinclair, the crusading writer who championed the downtrodden and persecuted. Also, Hispanic literature does not boast of a book such as John Steinbeck's book, "The Grapes of Wrath," that provides an explanation and acceptance of the border crossing of suffering masses from the South.

Even the U.S. policies for Hispanics vary significantly by country of origin. Puerto Rico is a commonwealth associated with the U.S. whose residents are naturalized citizens who have no border to cross. Cubans, as political exiles, have a much easier and more streamlined process for being granted citizenship. Persons seeking asylum from Central America and from other countries with whom the United States has good relations have shorter waiting periods in the U.S. citizenship line.

Stating that the Mexican-American War delineated more than geo-political boundaries, Lisa Garcia Bedolla, a young Latina author, for instance, believes:

> The analysis of the Hispanic experience in the United States must be situated at the intersection of power, collective identity (ies), and place. All affect where Latinos are positioned and where they end

up positioning themselves vis-á-vis the larger political community.[214]

Bedolla acknowledges that social, economic, and political power are the identity markers and modern-day currencies which can value or devalue, empower or disable the accommodation of the Mexican American culture to this country. But, she adds *"Because the accommodation of Mexican Americans in this country occurs in a stigmatized context, and includes processes not always under Latinos' control 'power' must be kept at the forefront of the analysis."*[215]

For Bedolla, the condition and sense of powerlessness is a key aspect of the experience of stigma. The dictionary defines a stigma as "blemish on one's record or reputation; a mark on the skin that bleeds during certain mental states." For Mexican Americans it is not as much suffering of discrimination which infers a concrete negative experience or denial of some benefit. She does not deny that racism and discrimination are factors in this community as in others. Rather most prevalent for Mexican Americans is being imposed with negative group devaluation. It is feeling of having a "thorn in the flesh" or a mark on one's reputation. To be "stigmatized" is to have a mark of disgrace on you; to be marked with a negative factor strong enough to limit your opportunities and choices.

Latinos' experience of powerlessness, both as individuals and as a group, influences both the internal and external aspects of their adjustment process in society. Internally, the feelings of powerlessness become a barrier for Latinos to feel positive about themselves and their larger group. Externally, their opportunities and choices are limited by the negative view of Latinos as a group. In most cases, the reason for the isolation and insulation of Mexican Americans and their lack of involvement with institutions as a whole.

Another young author, Martha Menchaca, conducted a recent study of Mexican Americans in California and found that Anglos and Latinos continue to be engaged in what she calls "social apartness" resulting in two distinct ethnic communities that interact only rarely.[216] The annexation experience and the feelings of stigma on Mexican American social identity have continued to affect the socialization of subsequent generations. Beginning with the native born of the annexation generation, Mexican Americans continue to socialize new immigrants using the memory of their contextual and social history to educate them regarding their place in U.S. society. Hispanic children quickly learn that they belong to an undigested minority, a smaller circle within the larger circle of society. The youth soon learn they are the product of the political and cultural borders that divide, but do not separate, the U.S. from its southern neighbors. Joined by other Latinos, they continue to remain not only geographically but socially separated from the Anglo majority in their barrios.

For generations the creation of barrios and maintaining of the Spanish language have ensured Mexican Americans survival in a hostile environment. What ghettos did for the early European immigrants and still do for some African Americans, and what reservations do for some Native Americans, presently is what barrios do for some Mexican Americans in today's society. Proximity of residence reinforces the language, social habits, and religion of many Mexican Americans and ensures the continuation of the distinctive culture. For the same reasons, ethnic-specific and storefront churches play a similar role.

## A Road Less Traveled

Demographic studies are being published and behaviors and beliefs are being analyzed. It is, however, time to go deeper. Traditionally, as Americans, we study our enemies more than we do our neighbors. The U.S. has lived for centuries in constant tension with Mexico, our closest neighbor to the south. Meanwhile, Mexican Americans continue to carry a social stigma that is still handed down from one generation to the next.

The Mexican American culture is not instinctual. Rather it consists of patterned learned behaviors acquired from historical and social circumstances. These behaviors and beliefs mark the point at which the two cultures often differ remarkably and clash. What is being portrayed thus far is an identity of Mexican American whose self-concept and self-esteem differs from other Hispanics and from mainstream Americans because of the affects of their historical and social experience.

A Samaritan complex isolated many Mexican Americans in their own world and insulated them in their own religion. First, the issue here is not if this self-concept is true or imagined, justified, or not. *What matters is that it is real to many in the Mexican American community*. What is important is the fact that, as in the case of the Samaritans, the manner in which group members see or *identify themselves* affects the ways in which they relate to each other and those outside their immediate social groupings. For this reason, it becomes important to understand the debilitating and conflicting tension in the soul of many Mexican Americans. Secondly, to what extent does group consciousness, group attachment, and perceptions of Mexican Americans affect their crossing of religious boundaries? Finally, what is the impact Hispanics have on religious, political, and civic engagement in the Latino community?

In 1999, as President of AMEN (*Alianza de Ministerios Evangélicos Nacionales*), I was approached by a national foundation, The Pew Charitable Trust, to do a major study on Hispanic Churches in American Public Life (HCAPL). A taskforce of co-director, Dr. Virgilio Elizondo, professor at Notre Dame University, and a project manager, Dr. Gaston Espinoza, assistant professor at Claremont McKenna College, conducted a national survey of 3,015 religious, political, and civic leaders and church members. We did what no one else had done before and that is to survey all Hispanic nationalities which included both Catholic and Protestant churches. The purpose of the three-year research project was to examine the impact of Hispanics in the United States society.

For the purposes of this chapter let me summarize just some of the many findings from our project and provide you with some indications of how Hispanics are moving out into the religious and public arena.

- First, we found that Latinos are much more interested in participating in educational, moral, social, and political issues than hitherto believed.
- Second, we found that religious organizations and groups can, in the future, serve as mobilization sites for political, civic, educational, and social participation.

- Third, we found that the Latino vote is volatile with a strong and growing tendency to be independents (37 percent) compared to alliance with Democrat (49 percent) or Republican (14 percent) political parties. Latinos are most sensitive to "bread and butter," that is, economic, immigration, and moral issues, and how the various political parties treat Latinos in the public arena.
- Fourth, we found that although Latinos tend to vote politically progressively, they clearly support traditionally and conservative pro-family, moral, and social issues such as school prayer, school vouchers, and the charitable choice initiative.
- Fifth, we found that despite the unique character of the Latino community, it shares many of the same goals, aspirations, and social political views as does a cross-section of American society.
- Sixth, we found in the midst of all the changes taking place among Latinos, our study found they occupy an "in between" space on the socio-political spectrum.[217]

On some issues, as mentioned above, Latinos lean to the right and on some issues and to the left of center other issues. This "in between" space may enable Latinos to help transform the liberal-conservative, black-white, and Republican-Democrat divide that has dominated American politics for the last half a century by forcing both parties to change and adapt to the growing needs of our increasingly diverse and multicultural society. Most encouraging, our study found that despite their reportedly marginal social status, Latinos believe that they can make a difference in American life and politics. Clearly, more research needs to be done before we can draw any definitive conclusions.

This Latino involvement in the political and civil life of the nation is not only encouraging but timely. Particularly in that the *"Generation —"* is being fed with the 1990s pop-psychology menu of empowerment and a self-help promised land." This philosophy can be summarized as:

> "Believe it, achieve it." For decades, Coors and Budweiser trumpeted the "Decade of the Hispanic" message in our communities with unfulfilled promises. Lost in the hyping of hope and adulation is the downside of being subjected to the problems of economic, social, and spiritual realities.

## Fluid Borders

Dr. John McKay, the former president of Princeton University and long-time missionary in Latin America, once said "Because Jesus is Lord he is to be followed on the road which is the place where life is lived in the midst of tension, where conflicts and concerns become the soil from which ideas are born."[218] Following our analogy with the Samaritans of Bible times, we must follow Jesus into Samaria with a God-idea. His idea was missional not political. Scripture says that *"Jesus had to go through Samaria"* (Jn. 4:4 NIV) and took the road less traveled in the region of the disenfranchised people of his day. The story of Jesus meeting the Samaritan woman perhaps epitomizes his commitment to revolutionizing the lot of the marginalized in society.

As we read in chapter 17 of this book, Jesus spoke to the woman in private despite strong cultural taboos against any social exchange between a Jewish holy man and a sexually promiscuous Samaritan woman. The underlying issues and barriers were social, political, and religious in nature. Jesus' desire was not just to cross the racial barriers between Jews and Samaritans but beyond that to have his disciples and Samaritans overcome the historical and spiritual barriers that prevailed in their rivalry.

More importantly, Dr. Isaac Canales believes that the presence of Jesus at the well in Samaria "marked the height and beginning of evangelization and world missions."[219] Other than the overly zealous patriotism of the Jews, which resulted in a narrow exclusiveness, little evidence exists that the Samaritans could not qualify as rightful participants in rebuilding the walls of Jerusalem. Yet this collective blindness ostracized the Samaritans, half-brothers, and stigmatized them into isolation. Because of this, Eugene Peterson says bluntly but probably accurately, "Jews wouldn't be caught dead talking to Samaritans."[220] So for the Jews, the notion of crossing the border to Samaria was sacrilegious. Jesus crossed over human boundaries to affirm the Samaritan woman's personhood and led her through the path of faith and revelation of an undivided God to a new crossing - from her religious ritualism to a spiritual experience.

Toward the end of his ministry, Jesus told the disciples that they were "to be witnesses in Jerusalem, Judea, Samaria, and the ends of the earth" (Acts 1:8). This was not intended as a list of regions but the progression of his program and mission. Here the notion of border crossing has not only geographical but also spiritual, social, and psychological significance. Whereas Jerusalem represents the place of religion and order, Judea represents the geographical place of incarnation and formation. Samaria represents the socio-political place of encounter and expansion to the outer border of religious engagement. Samaria marks the first step into the world.

Like Jesus' journey to the badlands of Samaria, the Church is compelled to go to this "new address" in a new way that is open to the spiritual (Jn. 4:24, 32) and the supernatural (Jn. 4: 35-38). Jesus confronted values and practices in society that needed to be changed. Changing or questioning practices and values that Christians have toward Hispanics must begin within the Church itself.

## Community without Borders

*"Neither on this Mountain
nor in Jerusalem" Jn.4:21*

As a Mexican American boy, I grew up in an environment where evangelical Hispanics were a mere two percent of the Hispanic population in this country which was predominantly Catholic. My father was Catholic, my mother Methodist, and I turned out Pentecostal. I came from both an ethnic and religious minority. I must confess, I did "cross myself" a few times when I came up to bat praying I would hit a home run.

I have been asked many times why I did not follow the religion *de tu gente* (of your people) or that of your mother. I have only been able to answer, because the Pentecostals crossed the street and knocked on my door. They picked me up for Sunday School. They had Vacation Bible School during the long, hot summers. For Christmas the Pentecostal Church was the only place where I received a toy and candy. And because the members cared for me, I, my brother and my sisters, and my parents later joined the church.

Today Hispanic *Evangélicos* are 23 percent of the Hispanic population, the largest growth having taken place in the past two decades. Our HCPLA research project findings found that when asked, do you consider yourself a born-again Christian, that is, have you personally had a conversion experience related to Jesus Christ, 37 percent gave a positive response. This statistic breaks down to 85 percent of Protestants and 22 percent of Catholics define themselves as born-again.[221] The following is the religious profile among Latinos:

- The Hispanic population is 70 percent Roman Catholic - This figure remains stable because of the influx of immigrants and the growing Charismatic (26 percent) movement.

- Protestant Hispanics have increased to an overall 23 percent in the past two to three decades.

- Of the Protestant Latinos responding to the survey, 88 percent are Evangelicals (of which 64 percent are Pentecostal) and the remaining 24 percent are in mainline denominations.

- Each generation Latinos are increasingly becoming Protestant—the first generation numbered 15 percent, the second generation numbered 20 percent and the third generation numbered 29 percent.

- Hispanics want their religious leaders, organizations, and traditions to become more proactively involved in trying to influence public officials on issues of morality, society, and politics.

- Despite all the genuine theological differences that have separated Latino Catholics and Protestants over the centuries, they do share enough in common to warrant working together on specific educational, social, and political issues for the betterment of the entire Latino community. They can achieve cooperation without having to water down or compromise their theological differences and traditions.[222]

In light of the above study, how can the *Iglesia Evangélica* in America continue to flourish in the lives of Mexican Americans and, for that matter, Hispanics as a whole? The study reveals a significant growth has taken place in the Hispanic evangelical church but did not inquire as to the reasons for this growth. I conclude the following.

- I believe Hispanic growth is God's sovereign move of the last days.
- Secondly, the Hispanic growth in the Church is a spiritual overflow of the evangelical church of Latin America.
- Thirdly, Hispanic growth is the increasing numbers of Hispanics sharing the gospel with fellow Latinos, "iron sharpening iron" as it were.
- Finally, Hispanic growth is allowing, by God's grace, the Church in America (Hispanics and non-Hispanics) to make converts serendipitously.

*But my argument here is that by speaking to that which is deepest within their life and bridging the elements between the gospel and culture to allow them to flourish according to God's purpose is how a spiritual revolution will take place among Mexican Americans and all Hispanics.*

To this end, the question is not how to extend an invitation to the gospel to this large group among Latinos but rather why Mexican Americans may or may not accept the invitation. What will enhance the group's acceptance is to address with the gospel the distinct contextual history of conquests and collective identity of Mexican Americans. The goal here is to position our Hispanic community to hear the gospel and come to the saving knowledge of Christ. This will require historical perspective, critical thinking of our present situation, and the understanding of God's truth and purpose for our growing Mexican American community in the United States.

More importantly, is for the Church to live its values in the world. This is more effective than any method I could list for you. In other words, the need is for the Church "to be" the Church. The Kingdom of God is best spread not by any methodology but by God's people who manifest the Kingdom of God on earth, a Kingdom that transcends national groupings or concerns. If the Cross means anything, it means the Kingdom of God is not realized through an exercise of power. God's people should demonstrate serving love, a love that prayed for the forgiveness of those sinners who put Jesus on the Cross.

## The Path for Evangelism Among Hispanics

How can the Christian movement overcome the barriers and achieve significant relationship with Mexican American cultures in the United States? What paths should the Church take to bring this people to Christ? I suggest several imperative paths.

## *Eliminate Destabilizing Forces*

First, the Church must eliminate destabilizing forces. Going back to the well in Samaria we have an example of such forces. The story says the disciples had "gone out to lunch" and left Jesus alone at the well with the Samaritan woman (Jn. 4:7). Few have given answers as to why the disciples would be absent for such an important occasion. I have three possible reasons.

- First, it was because of the religiously charged ethnocentrism that Jesus permitted or even required their absence. The disciples exhibited their Jewish culture rather than the values of the Kingdom and were not ready to let go of their prejudices (Lk. 9:54-56). By the time of the New Testament, Israel had become extremely exclusive and had forgotten her mission to the nations. The disciples were too Jewish and were in no condition to be "caught dead" speaking to a Samaritan woman. They were even less in a position to understand Jesus' global mission and vision.

- Secondly, it was because of their institutionalized Jewish dominance. Jesus was speaking about a "spirit and truth" they did not yet understand. The disciples would have taken exception when Jesus told the woman that true worship was "not on this mountain nor in Jerusalem."

- Finally, the rigid parochial mentality of the disciples disallowed them from the conversation at the well. Jesus was on a global mission that they still could not quite grasp.

The same destabilizing forces exhibited in the life of Jesus' disciples still prevail in the Church today. These forces do not create a positive environment where Mexican Americans can flourish. To these influences we can add a list of some other destabilizing forces.

1. *A lack of mission focus.* Americans have been so preoccupied with drawing boundaries between the races that religious boundaries have seemed less important.

2. *A consumer mentality.* The Church has been invaded by the market mentality, so that it has become in many instances another "consumer good." Consumer Christians shop for the church that is most convenient for their needs and switch, as casually as they change brands of dishwater detergent, if they think they can get a better package deal elsewhere.[223]

3. *A sociological shift.* "The Church has been all too willing to derive its theology from sociological assessments in the past: if we cannot overcome present sociological realities, we might as well adjust to them and make the best of it."[224]

4. *A political agenda.* "Our politics have determined our theology" caused by the over-mingling of religion and state and a neglect of the interior changes that bring transformation.[225]

5. *A growing nationalism.* "As history has proven, especially in times when church and state closely mingle, it is possible for the church to gain a nation and in the process lose the kingdom."[226] The Church could forget that it is global in nature and is called to serve all its neighbors, even those outside our boundaries of our nation.

6. *At a crossroads.* "Some Christians, anxious above all to be faithful to the revelation of God without compromise, ignore the challenges of the modern world and live in the past. Others, anxious to respond to the world around them, trim and twist God's revelation in their search for relevance."[227]

7. *An indictment.* "As the research data clearly shows, churches are not doing the job."[22]

## Become a Stabilizing Force

One thing is certain, the Church of Jesus Christ will not cease until the Marriage feast of the Lamb. Christ, the bridegroom himself, made a promise stating, "I will build my church." He spoke of the global Church, that body of believers who know no national boundaries, who do not depend on legislation or brand parties, and who serve every neighbor in need so that no one need perish. The Church is its own most stabilizing force by being itself and will affect our culture by living its unique core values and distinctive spiritual beliefs in a needy world. The Church will serve as the stabilizing force through the following elements.

### Stabilizing Force Number One

The first stabilizing force is *the theological basis for diversity in the Kingdom.* This element includes biblical truths relating to:

1. *The Father of all creation.* God is the God of creation and all human beings are His offspring. He is the God of history and holds in His hands the periods and boundaries of the nations.

2. *The Jesus Christ.* Jesus is the God of revelation through whom the Father made Himself known uniquely and decisively. He is the God of redemption our peace who has broken down the walls of hostility which divide human beings from one another.

3. *The Holy Spirit.* The Spirit of truth completes the revelation of Scripture and illumines God's people. The Spirit is the primary agent in creating and gathering His Church, in a world of disunity, alienation, and strife. The Spirit calls forth this community to bring glory to the Son, the Bridegroom.

4. *The Church.* The Church is a community in whose DNA is the diversity of God. The Church is the "called out ones." It is a pilgrim and resident much like the nation of Israel. The Church was meant to change its address and fulfill the purposes of the Father and of the Son through the Holy Spirit.

5. *The Gospel.* The Gospel is the broad invitation of the Good News to "whosoever" will.

6. *The Mission. The Mission is the Great Mandate to love God and neighbor and the Great Commission to go, make disciples of all nations and teach obedience to Jesus' Words.*

### Stabilizing Force Number Two

The second stabilizing force relates to a *process of spiritual enrichment and environments.* This spiritual enrichment and environment will involve the following elements:

1. *Proper Worship.* The chief end of God's diverse creation is to bring Him glory. The Father seeks only one kind of

worshipers, those who will worship Him in spirit and truth.

2. *Edifying Fellowship.* The Bible reflects a symbiotic relationship between God's people and others. Fellowship consists of a progression of God's people in cell, congregation, celebration, and communion.

3. *Go where God goes- A Dios.* The gospel must be repeatedly forwarded to a new address because the recipient is repeatedly changing places of residence. *"The wind blows wherever it pleases you cannot tell where it comes from or where it is going. So it is with everyone born of the Spirit."* (Jn.3:8)

3. *Be a change agent.* Transforming people and culture is at the center of evangelical identity. The Church's role is to make the existing society more Christian by being "salt and light," in obedience to the Lord not to design a perfect society.

4. *Discover what is truly human.* Reach deep within the real person that lies behind the "persona" of "ask" where the essence of human is hidden and look beyond the human situation to the uniqueness of that personhood created in the image of God. "Whereas Christology was the decisive issue for the early church, it may well be anthropology which is decisive for the church today."[229]

In a Quaker meeting in Philadelphia, one man broke the silence of the meeting to speak of the great experience of having met others across language, racial, and religious boundaries, the wonder of being able to reach across the barriers and touch another human being, and the turning of strangers into friends. Then Martin Buber, a great Jewish man of God who encountered and survived much enmity in his lifetime, stood up. Buber said that meeting another person was a great thing, but not the greatest thing. The greatest thing any person can do for another is to confirm the deepest thing in him/her. To take the time and have the discernment to see what's most deeply there, most fully that person, and then confirm it by recognizing and encouraging it.[230]

## My Prayer for a Sign of the Kingdom

Let me be, I humbly ask, a sign of Your Kingdom:

Where I celebrate and affirm the human unity You have created;
Where I acknowledge the colorful mosaic of human cultures, whose beauty will be brought into the glory of the New Jerusalem;

Where I preserve the riches of every culture, Your people, and renounce cultural imperialism;

Where I appreciate cultural achievement, at the same time resist the idolatry which lies at the heart of many cultures;

Where I proclaim that the God they worship as unknown has actually made Himself known in Jesus Christ;

Where I join the nucleus of the people of God, in which men, women, and children of all social, racial, and cultural origins are reconciled to each other; and

Where I joyfully join the singing around His throne that new song.

O Lord, I longingly anticipate the coming glory of the new community in Christ—a model of human harmony in divine destiny, the sign of Your Kingdom.

Forever and ever, AMEN!

---

Endnotes

[209] Carlos Fuentes, This I Believe, An A to Z of a Life, Random House.

[210] Craig Reem, "The Key to California's Future," The Metro Business Lifestyle Magazine, 12/22/05, **34-39**.

[211] data are supported by a 1988 report, *One Third of a Nation* (Commission on Minority Participation 1988), a joint undertaking of the American Council on Education and the Education Commission of the States and *The Challenge of Diversity*, Smith, Daryl. 1989 ASHE-ERIC Higher Education Report no. 5 Washington D.C., School of Education and Human Development. .George Washington University, 1989). When education leaders, such as former Secretary of Education, William Bennett, have called for a greater emphasis on academic studies stressing Western Civilization and for English-only education, this emphasis sends a symbolic message that the history and culture of others does not matter.

[212] KCET TV Special, Mexican Americans, 9/04.

[213] Henry Nouwen, *Reaching Out*, Intro. & 58.

[214] Lisa Garcia Bedolla, *Fluid Borders*, University of California, 2005, 4.

[215] Ibid.

[216] Martha Menchaca, *The Mexican Outsiders: A Community History of Marginalization and Discrimination in California, University of Texas Press, 1995.*

[217] Gastón Espinoza, Virgilio Elizondo, Jesse Miranda, Hispanic Churches in American Public Life: Summary Findings, Interim Reports, vol. 2003.2, 2d Edition, March 2003, 11-24.

[218] "Reflections," *Christianity Today*, 11/04.

[219] Isaac Canales, An Analysis of the Discourse in John 4: Unpublished exegetical paper-2003.

[220] Eugene Peterson, The Message, (see Jn. 4:4).

[221] Gastón Espinoza, Virgilio Elizondo, Jesse Miranda, Hispanic Churches in American Public Life: Summary Findings, Interim Reports, vol. 2003.2, 2d Edition, March 2003, 11-24.

[222] Gastón Espinoza, Virgilio Elizondo, Jesse Miranda, Hispanic Churches in American Public Life: Summary Findings, Interim Reports, vol. 2003.2, 2d Edition, March 2003, 11-24.

[223] Robert Bellah, ed. *The Good Society*, New York: Vintage Books,1991, 183

[224] Resident Alien, 39

[225] Ibid., 40.

[226] Phillip Yancey, CT 12/05, 128.

[227] John Stott, Involvement: Being a Responsible Christian in a Non-Christian society.

[228] George Barna, CT 1/06, 70.

[229] Ray Anderson, *The Shape of Practical Theology*, 137.

[230] Eugene Peterson, *Leap Over A Wall*, 54.

# CHAPTER 15

# THE HELLENISTIC ANALOGY

The Samaritan analogy posited by Dr. Jesse Miranda provides invaluable insights on the border crossings (geographical, social, psychological, and religious) of Hispanic Americans to areas north of the line between Mexico and the United States. The social stigma and adverse social structures associated with perpetual immigrant status and/or image continues to pose challenges and barriers beyond the first generation and into subsequent generations. Hispanic Americans facing these barriers will find comfort, instruction, and inspiration as they read Dr. Miranda's chapter.

This chapter attempts to find an analogy which is applicable to the more acculturated elements of Hispanic Americans, namely second, third, and fourth generations. While Miranda gave us a realistic picture of the struggles of an undigested and unaccepted minority in U.S. society, this chapter investigates the process of acculturation between the Jews and Greeks in the more positive light of the corporate culture of the Early Church.[231] The chapter also applies the insights of the process of assimilation to the Hispanic populations that are moving into the stream of the culture of the United States.

# Definition of the Term

A study of Scripture reveals that there was a segment in the Early Church that had experienced extensive assimilation into the Greek culture, the "Hellenists." The various usages of the term "Hellenist" make it imperative to define the term prior to engaging in this discussion. The word "Hellenism" refers to the Greek spirit, character, and culture of the ancient Hellenes.[232] "Hellenist" [Gk. *Hellenistas*], a derivative of "Hellenism," denotes a person who used the Greek language, ideals, or customs, especially a Jew, who after the conquest of Alexander the Great came under and accepted much of Greek influence.[233]

There are differences of opinion regarding the use of the term "Hellenist" in the Book of Acts (6:1; 9:29; 11:20).[234] Traditionally it has been held that the reference in 6:1 [*Hellenists*] is to Jews who were Greek-speaking, whereas "the Hebrews" were Jews who did not speak Greek. H. J. Cadbury, however, argues for the view that "Hellenists" here must be taken to mean "Greeks." He states, "'Hebrews' is used outside this passage mostly in the sense 'Jews' and we expect a corresponding meaning with 'Hellenists'."[235] A valid argument against this view is that up to this point Acts gives no indication that Gentiles had joined the Christian Church. [236] As Buttrick explains, the problem of the daily distribution implies a much larger group of complainants than that of a mere infiltration of "Greeks." [237]

Others have argued that the Hellenists were Jewish proselytes who had become Christians. At least one of the seven deacons was a proselyte. "A division between proselytes and those who were native-born Jews is held to be not unlikely. On the other hand, nowhere else do proselytes appear to be designated in this way." [238]

Some (e.g., F. F. Bruce, Mickelsen, Gentz, Buttrick)[239] favor the idea that the term is not used in any technical way but simply means "Greek speakers." Bruce explains that the context will determine precisely what kind of Greek-speakers is in mind on each occasion.[240] "In Acts 6:1 it will probably mean Greek-speaking Jewish Christians, in Acts 9:29 Greek-speaking Jews in the Synagogue, and in Acts 11:20 Gentiles."[241]

No one neat solution accounts for all the facts and excludes other views. The derivation of the word does make it look like "Greek-speaker." This fits all passages in Acts and takes into account that rather diverse groups spoke this language. This usage does not demand that on every occasion the Greek-speakers be of the same national group.[242] The term "Hellenist," therefore, will be used, in this chapter, to denote Greek-speaking persons. The context in which each usage is found will be examined to ascertain the cultural background of these persons.

The term "Greek-speaking," however, has implications beyond its linguistic dimensions. The process of Hellenization had social, political, economic, and philosophical as well as linguistic implications. The term "Hellenists" by itself, however, does not give an indication of the degree of Hellenization experienced by the group to whom it was applied or that it was a process at all (e.g., some were born into a Greek-speaking community). Perhaps one of the reasons why there is some confusion regarding the use of this term is that it is used in a broad sense encompassing several groups at different stages of Hellenization (or acculturation).

## Palestinian Hellenists

The fact that there were different stages of Hellenization was due in part to the various ways in which the Jews in Palestine reacted to the inroads of Hellenistic culture.

- The Essenes withdrew from the populated areas to the rural regions of Palestine in order to preserve their cultural and religious traditions. [243]

- The Zealots employed military force in an effort to regain political and cultural autonomy. [244]

- Galileans, who experienced prolonged contact with the Greek culture, were perhaps more influenced by it, yet they retained much of their Jewish cultural identity and religion.[245]

- There were apparently Jews in Jerusalem who were more influenced by the Greek language and culture than the groups mentioned above.[246] The region of Palestine, therefore, was influenced in varying degrees by the Greek culture.[247]

## Diaspora Hellenists

It was the Jews of the Diaspora, who were forced to live outside of Palestine, however, who experienced the greatest amount of acculturation into the Greek culture. For them acculturation was a strict necessity and not an option.[248] They adopted the Greek language and absorbed some of the customs of that culture, yet they managed to retain some elements of their cultural and religious traditions. The Septuagint, the translation of the Bible into Greek, was perhaps indicative of the process of acculturation which the Hellenists had experienced as a result of the Diaspora. [249] It represented a cultural adaptation not merely a translation from Hebrew.[250]

## Hellenistic Christians

The varying degrees of Hellenization (or acculturation) among the general Jewish population was evident in the early Christians. Due to the culturally pluralistic milieu of Galilee,[251] the Galilean disciples of Jesus were almost certainly exposed to some aspects of the Hellenistic culture.[252] The fact that they are often referred to as "Galileans" in the gospels and that at least some of them could be identified as such by their accents (e.g., Peter in Mk. 14:70) would appear to indicate that they had retained much of their native culture. They would quite likely be closer to the "Total Ethnic" category than to the other categories discussed in chapter 12[253] due to the fact that they had retained much of their culture.[254] For all practical purposes, therefore, they were not considered Hellenistic but Hebraic Christians.

A second group of early Jewish Christians experienced greater acculturation into the Greek culture than Galileans. Those in this group (which likely included Silas, Barnabas, and John Mark)[255] could perhaps be called "Median Hellenists" (cf. "Median Ethnic" in chapter 12)[256] in that they were bilingual and bicultural.

## The Apostle Paul

### His Cultural Background

Culturally, the apostle Paul is perhaps the clearest example of this Hellenistic Christian group. On the one hand he was a Hebrew Israelite. Although Paul was of non-Palestinian origin, his credentials in Judaism were beyond question, his ancestry was impeccable, and he had been sent from his homeland to Jerusalem to ensure a classical training in the Jewish faith (Acts 22:3).[257]

On the other hand, he was a Hellenistic Jew.[258] As E. A. Judge explains: "He was in full standing in the republican society of his homeland (Acts 21:39), belonging to the privileged group of Hellenistic families which had also been accorded Roman citizenship for services rendered (Acts 22:28)."[259]

Paul appears to give evidence of having a bicultural identity in the statements which he makes about himself. On the one hand he asserts that he is "a Jew" (Acts 22:3) while on the other, he states that he is a Roman (Acts 16:37; 22:25, 27). He appears to emphasize each side of this identity in keeping with the circumstance. On the one hand, his identification with the Israelites, his "brethren" and "kinsmen," is so strong that he is willing to be "accursed from Christ" for them (Rom. 9:3). On the other hand, he does not hesitate to claim the privilege of his Roman citizenship in order to have the freedom to preach the gospel (Acts 16:37; 22:28).

It cannot, of course, be assumed that Roman citizenship automatically indicated extensive Hellenization. The fact that Paul was born in a city which was Hellenized (Tarsus) in terms of its population and centers of learning culture,[260] that he apparently spoke Greek fluently, and that he was a Roman citizen would indicate that Paul's culture represented a blending of Hebrew and Greek influences.

There is a third dimension in Paul's cultural background which some highly reputable scholars such as E. Earl Ellis assert. That dimension is Paul's ability to function in the Latin world of the Roman Empire. In his book *The Making of the New Testament Documents*, Dr. Ellis affirms:

> Paul's release after two years detention in Rome (cf. Acts 28:30) is, as Harnack puts it 'a certain fact of history,' and his subsequent mission to Spain rests upon several items of evidence. (1) Paul himself anticipates it in Rom. 15:24, 28. (2) Paul's younger contemporary, Clement of Rome, implies it in I Clement 5:6f. (3) The Apocryphal Acts of Peter 1-3 (*Vercelli*), (*probably Asia Minor AD 160-180*) *and the Muratorian Canon (Rome AD 170-190) are two geographically separated and independent witnesses that reflect a widespread second-century tradition that Paul journeyed from Rome to Spain...*[261]

Dr. Ellis' assertion that Paul ministered in Spain is not only based on the sources cited above but on Paul's urban missionary strategy which is also articulated by Roland Allen.[262] Ellis Explains:

> Paul's mission to Gades (Cadiz, Spain) is not only attested by contemporary sources and implicitly confirmed by the second century apocryphal Acts of Peter and the Muratorian Canon but also accords with Paul's missionary strategy as it is known to us from Acts: Paul focused his labors on hub cities of well-traveled trade routes – Philippi, Thessalonica, Corinth, Ephesus – where he evangelized both residents and transients. For the Western reaches of the Roman Empire he could have regarded Gades a

prime site for Christian mission. A Roman *municipium*, Gades was second only to Rome in wealth and prestige and was the primary trading center both for sea commerce along the western coasts of Africa and or Europe and, with a 'splendid road system' (Albertini) for business intercourse with other cities in Spain.[263]

Dr. Ellis, supported by trustworthy historical documents, goes beyond the assertion that Paul actually carried on a mission to Spain and affirms that Paul was able to speak Latin which was the primary language in ancient Spain at the time.[264] He explains:

Released from prison in Rome in the spring of 63, we may conclude with some confidence that Paul (after a trip to Philippi and back?) sailed to Gades and established a Christian congregation there. That he was able to speak the language and knew the synagogue there can be inferred from his expressed intention to go there (Rom. 15:24, 28).[265]

The combination of social and cultural elements which formed a part of his background enabled Paul to reach a broad spectrum of society with the Christian message. Taking Dr. Ellis' assertions into account, it is quite possible that Paul might have been trilingual and related effectively to people representing three cultural basins. At the very least, we can affirm with certainty that Paul was bilingual and related in a positive and effective way to two cultures. Hengel states: "Thus intellectually Paul moved between two worlds: he lived in two different language-areas and cultures (Acts 22:2, 17:22). This dual cultural life is already evident from his double Hebrew-Latin name, Saul-Paul."[266]

Paul was able to bridge economic as well as cultural barriers. "Among his connections were, at Athens, a member of the Areopagus, the upper house of government (Acts 17:34); at Corinth, prominent religious (Acts 18:8) and civil (Rom. 16:32) leaders; at Ephesus, members of the titled aristocracy (Acts 19:31)."[267] Paul's biculturalism enabled him to cross cultural, linguistic, and economic barriers with the Christian message.[268]

## His Worldview Conversion

Despite Paul's biculturalism, he had to experience a worldview transformation before he could minister effectively to Gentiles. Donald Senior explains:

> As a Hellenistic Jew he could not be indifferent to the masses of his Gentile fellow citizens. As a Pharisaic Jew he maintained a strong conviction of Israel's elect status. Early Christianity's apparent relativizing of the law and its blunting of the sharp distinction between Jew and Gentile may have struck Paul as a dangerous slicing of the Gordian knot.[269]

The radical revision of worldview which Paul experienced changed him from one who was "zealous for the traditions of our fathers" to one who was an "apostle of the Gentiles."[270] While the principal thrust of this transformation was theological in nature,[271] it had significant cultural implications.[272]

This worldview transformation, however, did not cause Paul to lose sensitivity to the cultural characteristics of the various groups. He, for instance, does not advise Jewish Christians to abandon their traditions.[273] At the same time, he does not expect Gentiles to become Jews culturally and ceremonially in order to be considered fully Christian (e.g., Acts 15).

While it cannot be stated that Paul's primary purpose was to enunciate social theory, it can be said that Paul acknowledged cultural differences yet subordinated these to Christ in whom all believers have equal standing (Gal. 3:27-28).[274] It is quite likely that Paul's bicultural background and his worldview transformation contributed toward his sensitivity to the sociocultural ambience of his hearers as he preached the Christian message (1 Cor. 9:19-23).

## *The First Deacons*

A third group of early Jewish Christians perhaps fits the category of "Hellenists" (cf. "Marginal Ethnics")[275] more fully. These were persons who were perceived to be identified more closely with the Hellenistic culture than with the Hebrew culture and were called "Hellenists." Perhaps some examples of this group are some of the seven deacons who were chosen to deal with the distribution of food among the Hellenistic Jewish widows.[276]

Hengel states:

> With the exception of Philip and Nicanor, the list of the 'seven' in Acts 6:5 does not contain any typical Jewish names which are attested for, say, Egypt or Palestine. Simply from the exclusively Greek names, one might suppose that the 'seven' came from abroad; the last of them, the proselyte Nicholas, is said to have come from Antioch.[277]

Judge asserts that this body directly representing them was composed entirely of the Hellenists.[278] "The wise appointment of Greek-speaking Jews as deacons brought harmony and increased power." [279] Hellenists, therefore, were among the earliest converts to Christianity and among its first church leaders. They were selected as deacons to minister to everyone in the Jerusalem church, especially the Grecian widows who felt that they were being "neglected in the daily ministration" (Acts 6:1). Their bicultural background as well as their spiritual qualifications enabled them to address this problem sensitively and compassionately. Their ministry was so effective that "the word of God increased and the number of disciples multiplied in Jerusalem greatly; and a great company of the priests were obedient to the faith" (Acts 6:7).

These Hellenists were among the first to proclaim the message of Christ outside Jerusalem. Perhaps the better known of these was Philip the evangelist. Along with fellow Hellenists, Philip was forced to flee Jerusalem because of persecution (Acts 6:9; 8:1). As he went, Philip preached the gospel across cultural barriers to Samaritans (Acts 8:5), to an African national (Acts 8:35), and to Philistines (Acts 8:40). In so doing, Philip was a precursor in boundary-breaking missionary activity to the Apostles.[280]

It should be noted that it does not appear as though the Hebraic members of the early Christian community were implicated in this persecution.[281] Perhaps one of the reasons why the persecution was directed at the Hellenists is that they were not as bound by Jewish traditions as their more conservative Aramaic-speaking Jewish Christian brethren. Hellenistic Christians "called for the eschatological abolition of Temple worship and the revision of the law of Moses in the light of the true will of God."[282] The dispersion of the Hellenists resulted in the establishment of Christian groups in Phoenicia, Cyprus, and above all Antioch.[283] Hengel asserts:

> Whereas in Jerusalem they had turned to their Greek-speaking fellow countrymen in the Diaspora synagogues there, now - outside this heartland of Judea - new groups came into view which we might term the out posts of Judaism. To turn to the despised and second-rated marginal groups was also fully in accord with Jesus' preaching. Chief among them were the Samaritans, who were regarded as heretics; in addition were the Gentile 'God-fearers,' who were loosely associated with the Jewish synagogue and had not yet undergone circumcision or proselyte baptism: the boundaries between them, mere 'sympathizers' with Jewish customs, and real Gentiles was blurred.[284]

The Hellenists, driven out of Jewish Palestine, gradually went beyond the circle of full Jews and turned to Gentiles who were interested in Judaism; they were precursors of the mission to Gentiles.[285]

The Hellenistic freedom from Jewish traditions, which made them the object of persecution, helped them to reach the Gentile world with the Christian message. The "God fearers" who were "relatively uninterested in the ritual law and Temple worship"[286] were among those who responded more readily to the Christian message. To reach Gentiles, Hellenistic Christians employed the cultural, philosophical elements which they had in common with them.[287] "The original eschatological *kerugma* of the Jewish Christians had to be supplemented by elements from the Jewish-Hellenistic mission preaching.".[288]

# CHAPTER 15
*The Hellenistic Analogy*

The cultural pluralism of Hellenistic Christians was perhaps one of the elements which enabled them to transcend some of the cultural barriers to communicate the Christian message. Hengel describes early Christianity as a culturally pluralistic movement:

> One of the striking phenomena here, which they [scholars since B. F. Braun] often ignore, is the fact that the message of the crucified and risen Messiah Jesus of Nazareth also found its way particularly to the Greek-speaking Jews a few years, and perhaps only months, after the resurrection event which formed the foundation of the community. These Jews came from a wide variety of places in the Diaspora and had settled in Jerusalem. This astonishing influence on outsiders, transcending the boundaries of language and culture, distinguishes earliest Christianity from all other Palestinian Jewish movements, the Sadducees and Pharisees, the Essenes and the Baptist movement, the activity of which was largely confined to Palestine before the destruction of the temple.[289]

The influence on "outsiders" was due to a large extent to the fact that Hellenistic Christians were instrumental in reaching marginal groups (e.g., God-fearers, Samaritans, and Gentiles).[290] The selection of some from their ranks for positions of leadership enabled the Church to respond to the challenge of cultural pluralism which it was facing. Due to the fact that Hellenistic Christians were less bound to the Jewish traditions than their Aramaic-speaking counterparts, they experienced more severe persecution in Jerusalem. Their dispersion, in turn, made it possible for them to reach many marginal groups with the Christian message.

## Application to the Hispanic American Setting

Several concepts that emerge from the analysis of the experience of early Christians inform the Hispanic American search for identity.[291]

### *Acculturation Is Not Seen As a Negative Factor*

First, acculturation is not necessarily seen as a negative factor in the early Christian community. Each of the groups mentioned above contributed to the propagation of the Gospel. "Total Ethnics" such as the Galileans, who were the least influenced by the Greek culture, were instrumental in reaching not only their own group but Samaritans (e.g., Peter and John, Acts 8:14) and Gentiles (e.g., Cornelius, Acts 10). "Median Ethnics" such as Paul [292] and his co-workers were instrumental in planting churches in the various cultures represented in Asia Minor and Greece. "Marginal Ethnics" like Philip who were the most acculturated into the Greek culture were precursors of the apostles in preaching the Gospel in Samaria and in Gentile areas.

These Jewish Christian groups who had experienced varying degrees of acculturation into the Greek culture became an integral part of the Christian community and of its missionary effort. In their effort to stress the fact that Jesus had a deep and abiding concern for the marginal groups in society (e.g., Galileans) some writers give the impression that this concern was because of their cultural status. There does not appear to be in Scripture either a preference for or a bias against a group strictly because of its assimilation status.[293]

Some among the Hispanic American community view acculturation into the predominant society as a negative factor. These Hispanics repudiate the notion that Hispanic Americans should make cultural adaptations to the predominant society. This objection is either based on positive factors (affirmation of one's culture) or on negative factors (resentment toward the predominant society).

On the one hand, it needs to be stated that cultural groups have a prerogative to retain their cultural characteristics. As seen earlier, there are many reasons why a group would want to retain and express the richness of its culture. Likewise, it is true that such a decision is primarily a cultural and not a biblical one. It will be recalled that a study quoted in chapter 4 indicated that 78 percent of third generation Hispanic Americans speak "mostly English" to their children. The fact that these Hispanic Americans are choosing to encourage their children to adapt linguistically and culturally to the predominant society does not mean that they are violating a biblical principle. Acculturation, therefore, is not necessarily seen as a negative factor in Scripture.

The Marginal Hellenist and Median Hellenist Jewish Christians were an integral part of the Early Church. Their linguistic skills and cultural sensitivity were instrumental in addressing the question of cultural pluralism in the Church. They were among the first to reach across cultural barriers. Their experience provides a positive model for the Hispanic Americans who have experienced extensive assimilation into the predominant society. Their acculturation rather than being seen as a negative factor can be seen as an asset which enables them to make a distinct contribution to the Christian community by relating to a broad spectrum of society.

Hispanic Americans who have experienced the varying degrees of cultural assimilation need not feel inferior or superior to those who have retained more of their cultural heritage. They do not need to feel any longer that they are *"ni de aqu", ni de allá"* (neither from here, nor from there). Instead, they can have a positive feeling about the new cultural synthesis which they are forming which gives them the possibility of incorporating the best features of *both* cultures. Don C. Locke describes some of the Hispanics who have chosen to participate in both cultures:

> Many of the most acculturated Mexican Americans have become largely Anglo-American in their way of living, but retain fluent Spanish and a knowledge of their traditional culture. They maintain an identification with their own heritage while participating in the Anglo-American culture. Mexican-American culture represents the most constructive and effective means its members have of coping with their changed natural and social environment. They exchange old ways if the new ways appear to be more meaningful and rewarding than the old, and then only if they are given full opportunity to acquire and use the new ways.[294]

The Hellenistic paradigm, therefore, has the potential of inspiring the more acculturated Hispanic Americans to develop a positive self-image as persons whose linguistic skills and cross-cultural expertise can be valuable tools in their service to God and to others.

## Retention of Cultural Characteristics Is Permitted

Second, retention of certain cultural characteristics is permitted in the Christian community. Many Hebraic

Christians (e.g., Judeans, Galileans), for instance, retained characteristics (e.g., language, cultic practices of Judaism, and the celebration of its feasts) which distinguished them from the Gentile community.[295] The Jerusalem Council (Acts 15), for instance, sought to preserve that which was ceremonially and culturally significant for Jewish Christians and which was neither contrary to the gospel of the Kingdom nor offensive to fellow Christians. A principle which perhaps can be extracted from the writings of Paul is that cultural customs which are compatible with the gospel are permissible.[296] For instance, he applies the concept of freedom to the matter of food laws (1 Cor. 8). As long as the practices do not violate their conscience, Jews as well as Gentiles are free to observe or to refuse to observe food laws (1 Cor. 8:7).[297] For Paul cultural forms appear to be relative to given social settings.[298]

Hispanic American Christians, therefore, have the freedom to retain the cultural characteristics which are not incompatible with the gospel and which are not a stumbling block to fellow Christians of other cultural backgrounds. The exercise of this freedom does not make them inferior or superior to other segments of the Hispanic American community who are at different stages of acculturation.[299] At the same time, it must be stated that Hispanic Americans in more advanced stages of acculturation (Median Ethnics and Marginal Ethnics) should not view acculturation as a pre-requisite for full participation in the Christian community. Galilean Christians, for instance, made significant contributions to the cause of the kingdom without necessarily divesting themselves of their cultural heritage. There is room in the Christian life, therefore, for the joyful, free, and spontaneous celebration of one's cultural heritage in home life, liturgical gatherings, and in the commemoration of historical events.

## *Worldview Transformation Is Necessary*

Third, the transformation of a person's worldview is often necessary to bridge barriers between cultural groups and even between segments of a cultural group. Peter who was initially a "Total Ethnic" experienced a transformation in his worldview before he could include into the Christian community those whom he previously thought should be excluded (e.g., Cornelius).[300] Despite the fact that Paul (a Median Ethnic) was more acculturated into the Greek culture than Peter, he still had to work through the implications of his conversion experience and his calling to be a missionary to the Gentiles. When he came to the point that he was willing to be "all things to all people" (1 Cor. 9:22) he was a much more valuable instrument in the hand of the Lord.

This worldview transformation has implications for Hispanic Americans as well as for others. If it is true that throughout their sociohistorical pilgrimage some Hispanic Americans have been the object of prejudice on the part of the predominant society, it is also true that some Hispanic Americans have often had (reverse) prejudice toward the predominant society as well as toward other segments of the Hispanic American community (e.g., the newer arrivals).[301] In order to overcome an attitude of prejudice, Hispanic Americans (as well as others) need to experience a worldview transformation which has spiritual as well as social implications. As Harvie Conn explains:

> The impact of radical Kingdom rule of Christ will do more than merely "modify" a world-view or

accommodate itself to an existing one. If true transformational change (as opposed to merely external alteration) is to take place, the change must occur not merely at the behavioral edges of the world-view's manifestations but at its center. . . . Out of a world-view now Christ-possessed at its roots, the convert starts the lifelong habit of Christ-transformation. World-view reformation begins with the convert evaluating and interpreting each aspect of life in the Spirit in terms of the Kingdom claims of his new allegiance. From this comes "rehabituation," "changes in habitual behavior issuing from the new allegiance and the consequent reevaluation process."[302]

As Hispanic Americans experience this type of worldview transformation they will have the potential to be involved in a mission of reconciliation. By virtue of the fact that they are the product of several cultures, Hispanic Americans are in a privileged position to be instruments of reconciliation between cultural groups in the culturally pluralistic society of the United States as well as in other parts of the world. Their mission can be that of being a *gente puente* (a bridge people) which promotes better understanding, greater appreciation, and increased cooperation between the predominant society of the United States and the cultural groups of Latin America and marginalized groups around the world.[303]

## *The Hispanic Sense of Community Must Be Inclusive*

Fourth, the Hellenistic paradigm has implications for the Hispanic American sense of community. While many

Hispanic Americans are striving to promote a sense of brotherhood (*carnalismo*) there are significant differences in the manner in which this community is defined. Some Hispanic Americans have a concept of community which consists only of their particular group. Some, for instance, would exclude Hispanic Americans, who do not have the Chicano mentality, from this community.[304]

Other Hispanic Americans have espoused Vasconcelos's vision of the "cosmic race." Even though this race is perceived as being universal, it is limited to those who are the product of a biological *mestizaje* in Latin America and its immigrants to the United States.[305] Other Hispanic Americans have expanded the concept of the cosmic race to include the "colonized and oppressed" peoples of the world.[306]

The limitations of mentality, social status, and biological inheritance, imposed upon the concept of the cosmic race, cause it to fall short of the ideal of the new community described in Scripture. A transformation of worldview is needed to overcome these limitations. The new community described by Paul is one in which all human beings are included regardless of gender, culture, and economic status (Gal. 3:28).

The initial expression of this community was perhaps found in the church at Antioch which exhibited cultural pluralism in its membership and its leadership. Among the prophets and teachers listed in Acts 13 are: Barnabas (a Hellenistic Levite from Cyprus);[307] Simeon surnamed "Niger"[308] (probably a black person with close Roman ties);[309] Lucius (of Cyrene, a center of Greek culture and language);[310] Manean (who had close ties with Herod the tetrarch);[311] and Saul (bicultural, bilingual, Median

Hellenist). The variations of cultural (Hebrew, Hellenistic-Jewish, Greek, and Roman), economic (Barnabas and Lucius were quite possibly men of means),[312] and political backgrounds are evident in the leadership of the church of Antioch. This was a culturally pluralistic church which did not require its converts to fit into the Hebrew mould.[313] Yet, undoubtedly, it adhered to the admonition of the Jerusalem Council that sensitivity be shown to the cultural and religious values of fellow Christians (e.g., Acts 15).

The early Christian community, therefore, provides a model for the Hispanic American search for a sense of community (*carnalismo*). This model allows for acceptance of Hispanic Americans at the various stages of assimilation. It does not promote one stage to the exclusion of the others. It goes beyond this to include those of other cultural backgrounds. This model allows for each cultural group to contribute to the whole Christian community.[314] This model, therefore, makes it possible for Hispanic Americans to have a sense of appreciation for their cultural heritage and to experience a spirit of true Christian *carnalismo* which encompasses not only their group but those of other cultural backgrounds. Rene Padilla describes this spirit of *carnalismo* when he states:

> No one knows God in isolation from his neighbor. "He who does not love does not know God; for God is love" (1 John 4:8). The gospel includes God's purpose to wipe out division between men — the curse invoked at Babel — and to create a new man characterized by "the unity of the faith and of the knowledge of the Son of God" (Eph. 4:13 — the new unity prefigured in the church at Pentecost, composed of representatives "from every nation under heaven" (Acts 2:5).[315]

The Hellenistic paradigm posited here, therefore, has some very significant implications for the Hispanic American search for a sense of identity.

- First, acculturation is not necessarily seen as a negative factor in the early Christian community.
- Second, the retention of cultural characteristics is permitted in the early Christian community.
- Third, the transformation of worldview is at times necessary to bridge barriers between cultural groups and even segments of a cultural group.
- Finally, the early Christian community provides a model for Hispanic Americans in their search for a spirit of *carnalismo*.

## A Personal Testimony

As a fourth generation Hispanic American, I have found the study of Hellenists and particularly that of the Apostle Paul enlightening, inspiring, and most of all liberating. Having grown up in two cultures, Hispanic and Anglo, and feeling a need to relate to both effectively created in me an identity crisis when I was a young man. Who am I, Hispanic or Anglo? At home I felt Hispanic, but in school I felt the strong urge to relate to my teachers (most of whom were Anglo) and to some of my close friends (who were also Anglo).

From some in the Hispanic community I often felt the pressure to confine my social contacts to my Hispanic friends. Some would even comment that I was pretending to be Anglo. With regard to the Anglo community, there was much that attracted me as I saw the horizons of a larger world. Within me, on the one hand, I felt a sense of guilt that I might be denying my Hispanic heritage, but a sense of fear that I might limit myself if I restricted all of my social contacts to the Hispanic community.

The study of the life and ministry of the Apostle Paul has helped me to affirm the fact that I am the product of two cultures. This biculturalism is an asset and not a liability. There is a sense in which I have practiced "selective assimilation."[316] On the one hand I have retained many of the wonderful values of the Hispanic culture which stress the importance of family, personal relationships, respect for the elderly, and a sense of dignity among other things. On the other hand, from the Anglo culture I have learned a work ethic that values organization, punctuality, education, and teamwork among other things.

I feel blessed to have a blending of the best of these two cultures in my personality as a bicultural and bilingual minister. As stated above, Paul became an effective instrument in the hands of the Lord, precisely because he could move with effectiveness and ease within the context of two (and possibly three) cultures and speak their language in each setting. While, as a Christian, I need to affirm the life and ministry of those who like Peter serve in the context of one culture, I also need to celebrate the fact that the Lord in his wisdom has given me the privilege of preaching and teaching in two languages (now three) and serving in the context of two cultures. This actually has provided a foundation for me to function in many other cultures as I have been blessed to minister in over 40 countries.

As I reflect on my pilgrimage as a Hispanic American, I can honestly say that I thank the Lord from the bottom of my heart for who I am as a bilingual and bicultural person. The

Lord doesn't make mistakes. This sense of appreciation for who I am provides a foundation for me to have a deep appreciation for Hispanics at other stages of assimilation and for people of other cultures. To put it differently, *I believe in cultural identity, but not in cultural idolatry.* I thank the Lord for my cultural heritage, but I also celebrate the culture of those whose culture is different from mine.

# Conclusion

Several vital lessons that can be learned from the two analogies discussed in these two chapters.

- First, many Hispanic Americans find a sense of acceptance and identity based on the fact that Jesus accepted and identified with *mestizo* groups. This identity, however, is challenged and broadened by the example of the life and teachings of Jesus who did not confine himself to one group or one culture.[317]

- Second, while many Hispanic Americans find comfort in the fact that there is much in their culture which finds affirmation in Scripture, they need to be aware that there are elements in their culture which are condemned by Scripture.[318] There is, therefore, no romantic acceptance of any culture in Scripture. The fact that groups in the various stages of assimilation were a part of the early Christian community is perhaps illustrative of the principle of cultural relativity in Scripture.[319]

- Third, many of the marginalized segments of the Hispanic American culture find a sense of acceptance in the fact that they too can be a part of God's elect. This election, however, is not necessarily due to their marginalization but of God's good pleasure. Its purpose is not elitism but mission. This sense of acceptance can motivate them toward a mission of service, of reconciliation, and of conscientization.

- Fourth, there are some valid parallels between the experiences of Samaritans and those of some segments of the Hispanic American community. Through the use of his analogy, Dr. Miranda makes a valuable contribution by capturing the pathos of the alienation which many Hispanic Americans feel *vis-á-vis* the predominant society. The message of acceptance and election is indeed good news for these marginalized groups.

- Fifth, a new paradigm for the more acculturated segments of the Hispanic American community (Median and Marginal Ethnics) has been posited in this chapter: Hellenistic Jewish Christians. The example of these Hellenistic Jewish Christians who transcended cultural and linguistic boundaries and who were precursors in the mission to the Gentiles provides an inspiration for the more acculturated segments of the Hispanic American Community. Their bilingual and bicultural skills can be viewed as an *asset* rather than a *liability*. They can have a positive sense of identity knowing that they have inherent worth and that the capabilities which they have developed because of their unique sociocultural experience can be a blessing as they serve God and their fellow human beings.[320]

Gustavo Gutiérrez expresses this feeling when he states:

> Why are you searching for your identity? Why do you
> want to know that you are a people with value —
> values denied by the sowers of death but affirmed by
> people who know how to live with hope in the
> resurrection of the Lord? There can only be one
> answer, one that does not depend upon whether one
> is Hispanic American or Peruvian. The only reason
> why you need to affirm who you are is to be of
> service. If you are looking for identity for any other
> reason you are in danger of becoming egotistical and
> vain. Service should be at the core of our identity
> because it is at the core of our Christianity.[321]

Having reviewed the history of Hispanics in the U.S., the
diversity in the Hispanic community, the Samaritan analogy
and the Hellenistic analogy, we will now turn our attention
to the ministry that is needed among Hispanics.

---

**Endnotes**

[231] For a more in-depth treatment of this subject see Daniel R. Sanchez,
An Interdisciplinary Approach to Theological Contextualization with
special reference to Hispanic Americans, Ph. D. thesis, Oxford Centre
for Mission Studies, April 17, 1991.

[232] T*he Interpreter's Dictionary of the Bible,* 1962 ed., s.v. "Hellenism" by F.
C. Grant. The term "Hellenes" refers to all those who come under the
influence of Greek culture. *Baker's Dictionary of Theology,* 1960 ed., s.v.
"Hellenist, Hellenism" by A. Berkeley Mickelsen.

[233] *The World Book Dictionary,* 1978 ed., s.v. "Hellenist."

[234] Bromiley points out that the word "Hellenist" was apparently not used
before its occurrence in Acts. He also calls attention to the fact that
there is a textual problem in Acts 11:20 where MSS and the RSV, read
*Hellenas,* "Greeks" instead of *Hellenistas;* but most textual critics accept
*Hellenistas. The International Standard Bible Encyclopedia,* 1982 ed., s.v.
"Hellenist" by L. Morris.

[235] H. J. Cadbury cited in *International Standard Bible Encyclopedia,* 1982 ed., s.v. "Hellenist."

[236] Cadsbury, op. cit.

[237] *Interpreter's Dictionary,* 1962 ed., s.v. "Hellenism." He adds that the account of the conversion of the Gentiles (Acts 10:45; 15:3) relates to something new.

[238] *International Standard Bible Encyclopedia,* 1982 ed., s.v. "Hellenist."

[239] Bruce, cited in *International Standard Bible Encyclopedia,* 1982 ed., s.v. "Hellenist"; *Dictionary of Theology,* 1960 ed., s.v. "Hellenist, Hellenism"; *The Dictionary of Bible and Religion,* 1986 ed., s.v. "Hellenism, Hellenistic" by Ralph P. Martin; *Interpreter's Dictionary of the Bible,* 1962 ed., s.v. "Hellenism." Buttrick points out that Philo (in *Confusion of Tongues 26)* and Chrysostom (in *Homily* XIV, on Acts 6:1) used the term "Hellenist" to mean "Greek-speaking;" *Interpreter's Dictionary of the Bible,* 1962 ed., s.v. "Hellenism."

[240] Bruce, cited in *International Standard Bible Encyclopedia,* 1982 ed., s.v. "Hellenist."

[241] Ibid.

[242] Ibid.

[243] Theissen, op. cit., 31; Bornkamm, *Jesus of Nazareth, 33.*

[244] In so doing, they were seeking to escape the political domination of Rome and the Greek culture which the latter had adopted. See also Donald Senior and Carrol Stuhlmueller, *The Biblical Foundation for Mission,* Maryknoll, NY: Orbis Book, 1984, 30.

[245] Senior and Stuhlmueller, 217.

[246] See *Dictionary of Theology,* 1960 ed., s.v. "Hellenist, Hellenism." Buttrick points out that many languages were spoken by the Jews living in Jerusalem (e.g., Acts 2:9). *Interpreter's Dictionary of the Bible,* 1962 ed., s.v. "Hellenism."

[247] Harrison points out that even the most resistant groups could not remain untouched by Hellenism. *Baker's Dictionary of Theology,* 1960 ed., s.v. "Hellenists, Hellenism." Jeremias explains that relations between Jerusalem and Athens loomed large in the stories of Lam. R. I. I (Son. 74, 76f.) which mention people from Jerusalem journeying to Athens, and Athenians staying in Jerusalem. See Jeremias, 64.

[248] See Shorter,. 116.

[249] Ibid.

[250] Shorter points out that the Septuagint constituted a wider collection of books than the exclusively Hebrew selection used by Jews in Palestine and some of them had no Semitic original. Ibid., 116.

[251] "Portions of the Jewish population were interspersed with Greek and other foreign elements due to colonization in the period after Alexander's conquest of the Middle East." Senior Stuhlmueller, op. cit., 317. Cf. S. Freyne, *Galilee: From Alexander the Great to Hadrian, 323 B.C.E. to 135 C.E. (Wilmington, DE: Michael Glazier, 1980)* and E.

*Meyers and J. Strange, Archaeology: The Rabbis and Early Christianity (Nashville, TN: Abingdon, 1981), 31-47.*

[252] Shorter asserts that Galilee was particularly influenced by the Greco-Roman culture. Ibid., 119.

[253] The terminology employed in this section is that which is viewed from the perspective of the subordinate group. It outlines the progression away from the culture of the ethnic group: Total Ethnic, Median Ethnic, Marginal Ethnic and Alienated Ethnic. The terminology which shows progression toward the predominant society is: Passive Ethnic, Exposed Ethnic, Activated Ethnic, and Integrated Ethnic.

[254] In a stricter sense the Essenes fit the "Total Ethnic" category more completely. In terms of degrees, however, it can be stated that Galileans were closer to this category than to the "Median Ethnic" category which would signal greater assimilation into the Hellenistic culture.

[255] There is the possibility that Silas, Paul's co-worker had a similar background. His name is of Semitic origin, yet he was a Roman citizen. See *New Standard Bible Dictionary*, 1925 ed. s.v. "Paul." Barnabas is called a "Hellenist" yet his social and religious ties with Jerusalem appear to be very strong. *New Standard Bible Dictionary*, 1925 ed., s.v. "Barnabas." John Mark's Jewish-Greek name appears to reflect a degree of biculturalism. *New Standard Bible Dictionary*, 1925 ed. s.v., "John Mark."

[256] See chapter two, p. 121.

[257] E. A. Judge, *The Social Pattern of Christian Groups in the First Century* (London: The Tyndale Press, 1960), 58.

[258] See Theissen, op. cit., 49-50.

[259] Judge, op. cit., 58.

[260] *New Standard Bible Dictionary*, 1925 ed., s.v. "Paul."

[261] Ibid., 278-79.

[262] Rolland Allen, *Missionary Methods: St. Paul's or Ours?*, Grand Rapids: Wm. B. Eerdmans Publishing Co., 1962.

[263] Ibid., 282-83.

[264] M. Rostovtzeff, The Social and Economic History of the Hellenistic World, 3 vols., Oxford 1967 (1941), I, 80, 91.

[265] Ellis, op. cit., 282.

[266] Hengel, op. cit., 82.

[267] Judge, op. cit., 58. The members of the aristocracy were quite likely Roman Hellenists.

[268] For a discussion of Paul's rhetorical skills see Abraham J. Malherbe, *Social Aspects of Early Christianity* (Philadelphia, PA: Fortress Press, 1983), 57.

[269] Senior and Stuhlmueller, op. cit., 167.

[270] Rom. 11:13.

271 Paul had to work out the theological implications of his calling to be a missionary among the Gentiles. His tradition had led him to believe that God was the God of the people of Israel. His initial strategy was "to the Jew first."

272 Some have raised the question whether Paul gave evidence that he had not overcome his prejudices when he made the statement that "Cretans are always liars" (Titus 1:12). While it is clear that Paul was quoting one of their own prophets it is also true that he agrees with him (v. 13). There is no evidence that Paul was accusing all Cretans of being liars. Paul's observation seems to indicate that "the rebellious men, empty talkers, deceivers" (v. 10.) were living up to the reputation which Cretans had. See R. C. H. Lenski, *The Interpretation of St. Paul's Epistles to the Colossians, to the Thessalonians, to Timothy, to Titus and to Philemon (Minneapolis, MN: Augsburg Publishing House, 1937), 902-903.*

273 Roest, Crollius, A., *Bible and Inculturation.* Rome: Pontifical Gregorian University, 1983, 25. Shorter explains that Paul did not force Jewish converts to abandon circumcision and the Law but did not insist on them either. Shorter, op. cit., 128.

274 While actual changes (e.g., physical mutations) do not occur, "all (Jew, Greek) are alike in their spiritual standing, everyone has been baptized, declared righteous, etc., none are higher, none are lower, none are richer, none are poorer, none better, none worse, none with more, none with less, in every respect they are 'one person in Christ Jesus.'" R. C. H. Lenski, *The Interpretation of St. Paul's Epistles to the Galatians, Ephesians, and Philippians (Minneapolis, MN: Augsburg Publishing House, 1937), 89-90.*

275 See chapter 2.

276 Wagner suggests that the fact that the seven deacons selected had Greek names is a possible indication that they were Hellenistic and were better suited to deal with the problem. See C. Peter Wagner, *Our Kind Of People* (Atlanta, GA: John Knox Press, 1978), 122. See also Glenn W. Baker, William L. Lane, J. Ramsey Michaels, *The New Testament Speaks* (New York: Harper & Row, 1969), 134.

277 Hengel, op. cit., 71.

278 Judge, op. cit., 56.

279 *Baker's Dictionary of Theology*, 1960 ed., s.v., "Hellenist, Hellenism."

280 It falls his lot to take that first step in victory over Jewish prejudice and expansion of the Church, according to the Lord's command." *Dictionary of the Bible*, 1971 ed., s.v., "Philip the Evangelist" by William Smith. The fact that Hellenistic Christians were driven out by persecution, however, needs to be taken into account.

281 Judge, op. cit., 56.

282 Hengel, op. cit., 72-73.

283 See Judge, op. cit., 56.

[284] Hengel, op. cit., 75.

[285] Subsequently the Apostle Paul was instrumental in making even greater inroads into the Gentile world. Hengel, op. cit., 75.

[286] Hengel, op. cit., 89.

[287] Hengel explains that the message of Jesus had affinities with the universalist Greek-speaking world and perhaps even with some themes in Greek thought. Hengel, op. cit., 72.

[288] Hengel, op. cit., 72

[289] Hengel, op. cit., 71

[290] Hengel, op. cit., 75.

[291] The caveat made earlier perhaps needs to be repeated here. Due to the chronological, geographical, and cultural distances between the early Christian groups and modern Hispanic Americans, the analogies employed here quite possibly fit only in some respects and not in others. They are employed here with an understanding of their limitations.

[292] Larkin refers to Paul as a "Hellenistic Jew born in Tarsus." William J. Larkin, *Culture and Biblical Hermeneutics* (Grand Rapids, MI: Baker Book House, 1988), 199.

[293] Every cultural group has elements which come under the condemnation of Scripture. There are many elements, however, which are relative from a biblical perspective.

[294] Don C. Locke, *Increasing Multicultural Understanding*, Newbury Park: SAGE Publications, 1992, 130.

[295] See Senior and Stuhlmueller, op. cit., 273; Shorter, op. cit., 128.

[296] Thomas W. Ogletree, *The Use of the Bible in Christian Ethics* (Oxford: Basil Blackwell, 1983), 155.

[297] In order to keep from offending one another, however, Paul enunciates the principle of reciprocity. Christians are encouraged to exercise their freedom regarding practices which are not contrary to Scripture and do no violate their conscience. They are reminded, however, that they should avoid those practices (e.g., eating meat) which offend fellow Christians. Above all a spirit of fellow-ship should be maintained.

[298] These cultural forms, however, must be examined in the light of the Scriptures. See Paul Tillich, *Theology of Culture*, ed. Robert C. Kimball (New York: Oxford University Press, 1959), 51.

[299] See Daniel R. Sánchez, "Models for Practical Implementation," cited in C. Peter Wagner, op. cit., 163.

[300] See Acts 10. It is perhaps difficult to make a distinction between the religious and the cultural sources of Peter's reluctance to fellowship with Cornelius. Here we are addressing the cultural sources primarily.

[301] Vigil states that Hispanic Americans have often reacted to racism by becoming "reverse-racists," even toward other racial minorities. Vigil, op. cit., p. 181. In the Pew Hispanic Study, 83 percent of the Latinos

surveyed reported that Latinos discriminating against other Latinos is a problem. Pew Hispanic Center/Kaiser Family Foundation, 2002 National Survey of Latinos, 6

[302] Harvie Conn, "Conversion and Culture," *Down to Earth*, op. cit., p. 156.

[303] See Sandoval, op. cit., 56.

[304] Nieto, "Chicano Theology of Liberation," Mission Trends No. 4, Gerald Anderson, Thomas F. Stranski, eds, New York: Paulist Press, 1979, 278.

[305] Andrés G. Guerrero, *A Chicano Theology* (Maryknoll, NY: Orbis Books, 1987), p. 134.

[306] Guerrero, op. cit., 19.

[307] See *New Standard Bible Dictionary,* 1936 ed., s.v. "Barnabas." See also Acts 4:35-37.

[308] A Latin term meaning black, see C. Peter Wagner, op. cit., 125.

[309] Wagner, op. cit., 125.

[310] See *New Standard Bible Dictionary,* 1936 ed., s.v. "Lucius."

[311] C. Peter Wagner, op. cit., 136.

[312] See Acts 4:35-37.

[313] This is not to suggest that the culturally pluralistic church is the only model of a church in the New Testament. The Jerusalem church, for instance, was primarily a Jewish culture congregation. The mission entrusted to the church by Jesus Christ, however, did not permit this congregation to isolate itself from the other churches. This fellowship, however, does not obliterate cultural differences between the groups. Instead, as was manifested in the Jerusalem Council, there is a new sense of appreciation and sensitivity toward those of other cultural and religious backgrounds. While for some there may be some unanswered questions regarding the historical reliability of the book of Acts, there appears to be no major difficulty regarding the subject matter and the conclusions of the Jerusalem Council. See Senior and Stuhlmueller, op. cit., 273; Malherbe, op. cit., 73.

[314] The fact that they have experienced a degree of acculturation enables them to serve as bridges of understanding between cultural groups. See Guerrero, op. cit., 155.

[315] C. René Padilla, *Mission Between The Times (Grand Rapids, MI: William Eerdmans, 1985), 90.*

[316] For an extensive discussion on assimilation see Milton M. Gordon, Assimilation in American Life, Oxford University Press, 1964.

[317] While it can be stated that *mestizo* groups may find a sense of identity with Jesus, it also needs to be pointed out that the incarnation of Jesus has particular as well as universal dimensions. The incarnation took place in a particular context. Jesus was born a Jew, as a member of a particular race, yet it has universal meaning: Jesus came to save the world. See *Minutes and Report of the Meeting of the Assembly of the*

Commission on World Mission and Evangelism, Bangkok Thailand, December 31, 1972 and January 9-12, 1973 (Bangkok: n.p., 1973), 74.

[318] See Wilmer Villacorta, "Mentoring And Machismo," *Focus*, Fuller Theological Seminary, Fall 2005, 7.

[319] Crollius points out that the Bible meets many cultures holding with them a reciprocal relationship of receiving and giving. Yet the existence of a specifically biblical culture is neither expressedly stated nor denied. Crollius, op. cit., 5.

[320] It must be pointed out that each of these analogies is not sufficient to encompass the cultural variety represented in the groups which were a part of the early Christian community. Each of these analogies, therefore, can be of value to a different segment of the Hispanic American community in its search for a sense of identity. It is necessary, however, that these analogies continue to be examined in the light of Scripture

[321] Gustavo Gutiérrez, "Forward," *The Hispanic American Experience in the Church*, Moisés Sandoval, ed. (New York, NY: Sadlier, 1983), 11.

# CHAPTER 16

# RECONCILIATION AMONG CULTURAL GROUPS

A number of years ago I asked Dr. Don Larson what he thought of Dr. Donald McGravan's book, *Bridges of God*. Without batting an eye he responded: "The content is good, but the title is wrong. It should have been named, *Tunnels of God*." Aware of his extensive training in Cultural Anthropology, I immediately grasped what he was implying. By virtue of the fact that all human beings have God as their creator, they have infinitely more commonalities than they have differences.

If this is so, we might ask ourselves, "Why is there so much misunderstanding and discord between cultural groups?" Due to the complexity of human relationships, it is not easy to find a simple answer. It can be stated, however, that there are several clear cut factors that contribute to this discord. Numerous sociocultural studies indicate that lack of accurate knowledge is a major contributing factor.[322] This lack of accurate knowledge may be observed with regard to:

- the terms and concepts that are utilized
- the factors that contribute to the development of prejudice
- the factors that contribute to the reduction of prejudice

The objective of this chapter will be to address these three areas with the hope of contributing toward a greater degree of understanding and harmony between the various sociocultural groups in America today. It is our sincere desire that Hispanics needing to relate to other segments of the Hispanic population (different countries of origin and socioeconomic levels) will find this chapter helpful as well as compelling. Our hope is also that those wishing to be involved in Hispanic ministry will be challenged and inspired by the concepts in this chapter.

## Inaccurate Terms and Concepts

Often certain terms are utilized because they facilitate categorization. The positive value of these terms is that they serve as a shorthand that allows us to communicate quickly and efficiently. Without these, communication would be laborious and cumbersome. The potential negative value of some of the terms utilized, however, is that they communicate ideas that are contrary to reality or perpetuate concepts and stereotypes that foster suspicion and discord between sociocultural groups. With this in mind, we shall examine some of these terms.

### *The Concept of "Race"*

The term "race" is used today by the news media as well as by majority and minority groups. For society in general, this provides an easy way to categorize groups of people. Minority groups often use the concept of "race" as a rallying point of identity and common purpose.

A major problem with the utilization of the term "race," however, stems from the belief that the majority of the differences between sociocultural groups are biologically inherited. Racists, for instance, argue that certain races are naturally superior to others and this superiority entitles them to rule over "inferior peoples." The danger of "racial theory" is seen in the Nazi Holocaust, as Hitler systematically murdered six million Jews, just because he believed in the superiority of the "Aryan race." Even those who would never use the concept of race for sinister purposes run the danger of categorizing people on the basis of physical appearance.

The concept of "race" is being challenged today by many scientists. Recently, researchers who analyze the genetic threads of human diversity stated categorically that the concept of race has no basis in fundamental human biology. "Scientists should abandon it" they said at the American Association for the Advancement of Science. The conclusions of these groups grow out of a more precise understanding of the underlying genetics of the human species and how surface distinctions of skin, hair, and facial features, which may loom large in daily life, have nothing to do with the basic biology of human differences. "Biologically we are saying in essence that race is no longer a valid scientific distinction," said Solomon Kata, a University of Pennsylvania anthropologist. Lorin Brace, a biological anthropologist at the University of Michigan said:

> "Race is a social construct derived mainly from perceptions conditioned by events recorded in history and it has no basis in biological reality."[323]

Sociologist Gordon Allport expresses the same view when he states:

> Expert opinion holds that very few genes are involved in the transmission of pigmentation, and

that while color and other physical indications of race may run fairly true within a racial stock, they do not indicate the total inheritance of any given individual. It is said that not more than one percent of the genes involved in producing a person's inheritance are racially linked. Color is so linked, but there is no evidence that the genes determining skin color are tied to genes determining mental capacity and moral qualities.[324]

Racism couples the false assumption that race determines psychological and cultural traits with the belief that one race is superior to another. It is on these bases that racists justify discrimination against, segregating, and or scapegoating such groups.

Allport states:

There is a curious air of finality in the term 'racial.' One thinks of heredity as inexorable, as conferring an essence upon a group from which there is no escape.[325]

Most people do not know the difference between race and ethnic group, between race and social caste, or between nurture and nature.

Allport states:

It makes for an economy of thought to ascribe peculiarities of appearance, custom, and values, to race. It is simpler to attribute differences to heredity than to juggle all the complex social grounds for differentiation that exists.

When people confuse racial and cultural traits they are confusing what is given by nature and what is acquired through learning. This confusion has serious consequences, for it leads to an exaggerated belief in the fixity of human characteristics. Thinking in racial categories often leads to a caste-like approach to other cultural groups. Because they cannot change their physical appearance, members of certain sociocultural groups are expected to stay in "their place" forever.[326]

Two points stand out above all others from anthropological work on race:

- Except in remote parts of the earth, few human beings belong to pure stock, hence the concept has little utility.

- Most human characteristics ascribed to race are due to cultural diversity and should, therefore, be regarded as cultural, not racial.[327]

It is more accurate and more productive, therefore, to refer to these groups with varying characteristics as *sociocultural* rather than *racial* groups.

## *The Concept of Color*

Utilizing color is one of the most common types of categorization or stereotyping. As is true of most generalizations, the use of color provides a way to distinguish people quickly and conveniently. There are several inherent dangers, however, in resorting to this rubric.

First, color is generally not used as a neutral category simply to describe the pigmentation or hue of an individual or group. In many instances, color is connected in the mind of the person with social status.

Second, color is often utilized in such a way as to imply that all of the persons who have the same hue are of the same sociocultural group. Nothing could be further from the truth. Many cultures are represented among people who seemingly have the same skin color. To assume that all of the persons who have "black" skin have the same culture is as erroneous as making the same generalization for all of the people with "white," "yellow," "red," or "brown" pigmentation.

One example of this is the unfounded assumption that because there are physical similarities among Africans, Haitians, and African Americans, they must all be culturally similar. While there may be some physical similarities, their cultures, languages, and worldviews are vastly different. The same erroneous assumption can be made of the various groups within the Asian category (e.g., Chinese, Korean, Japanese, Vietnamese, etc.). In his article "What Color Is Black?" Tom Morganthau points out that among African Americans there is every conceivable hue from tan to ebony.[328]

Third, for many, color is erroneously connected with intellectual capacities. Despite the fact that numerous studies indicate that that is absolutely not the case, some believe that persons with certain skin colors work better "with their hands" while the tasks requiring "mental abilities" should be reserved for others.

Fourth, the utilization of color to categorize people implies certain finality. Because people cannot change their skin color, the implication is that there is nothing that they can do to change what some naively perceive to be their "negative characteristics."

Inaccurate terms, therefore, perpetuate prejudice instead of diminishing it. Referring to people as "white," "black," "yellow", "brown," and "red" puts people in such broad categories that allowances for cultural distinctions, let alone individual characteristics, are totally eliminated. A compounded error is to refer to these as races, such as the "white race" and the "black race."

There is a term that is currently being used that also fosters the perpetuation of stereotypes. The term is "people of color." The apparent implication is that there are the "white people" and all others are "people of color." The implication appears to be that "white" is the standard and the "people of color" are the deviation.

This term, even though it provides a quick shorthand, is detrimental because it categorizes people under such broad generalizations that it creates enormous chasms. Prior to the Civil Rights movement, African Americans were called "colored people." Now some call all non-Anglos "the people of color." This does not contribute to diminishing the utilization of stereotypes.

## *The Concept of Blood*

A subtle and attractive mystery surrounds the concept of "blood." There is definiteness, an intimacy, a symbolic importance hovering around this *shibboleth*. Both family and racial pride focus on "blood." While some may utilize this concept to promote cultural identity, this symbolism has no support from science. Allport states, "Strictly speaking all blood types are found in all races."[329]

The use of categories based on the concepts of "race," "color," or "blood," therefore, can lead to a type of *"pigmentocaracy."* As is true of the caste system in some countries, some people use the concept of race, color, and blood to justify and reinforce their prejudices. This, in turn, leads some to believe that people are inherently different and should be kept separate in accordance with these convenient categories. Viewing differences from a sociocultural perspective, on the other hand, will enable a person to have a greater understanding of individuals and groups. Understanding the development of prejudice and its harmful effects occupies an important factor in Christian ministry.

## Overcoming Prejudice and Discrimination As a Base for Missions

Christian workers on every level should recognize the adverse effects that prejudice and discrimination have on society at large and the Christian ministry in detail. One of the more imperative aims of Christians should be the recognition of prejudice and the overcoming of both prejudice and discrimination.

### *Factors That Contribute To The Development of Prejudice*

Due to the fact that relationships between sociocultural groups are complex, it is not an easy task to ascertain the factors that contribute to the development of prejudice. As a starting point, an effort will be made to define prejudice. This will be followed by a brief review of the various theories of prejudice, an analysis of the ways in which prejudice is acquired, and an examination of the ways in which prejudice is acted out.

## Definition of "Prejudice"

The word "prejudice" derives from the Latin noun *praejudictum*, which to ancients simply meant precedent or judgment based on previous decisions and experiences. In modern usage, however, it has come to mean *an unsupported judgment usually accompanied by disapproval.* James A. Banks defines prejudice as a "set of rigid and unfavorable attitudes toward a particular group or groups which is formed in disregard of the facts."[330] The net effect is to place people at a disadvantage, not because they have done anything wrong, but because the prejudiced person is predisposed to respond in a particular way, regardless of the facts. A distinction must be made between beliefs and attitudes which usually go together. Beliefs can be altered by rational argument and common sense, but doing so does not guarantee a change in attitude. Prejudiced people have a knack of adjusting beliefs to fit attitudes.

Allport states:

> Prejudice is a feeling, favorable or unfavorable, toward a person or thing, prior to or not based on actual experience. Thinking ill of others without sufficient warrant."[331]

Prejudice is an attitude in a closed mind which says: "Don't bother me with facts; I've already made up my mind." Ackerman states that "Prejudice is a pattern of hostility in interpersonal relations which is directed against an entire group, or against its individual members; it fulfills a specific irrational function for its bearer."[332]

195

## Theories of Prejudice

Gordon Allport lists six principal theories of prejudice:[333]

1. Historical. This theory claims that only by studying the total background of the conflict (e.g., Anglos and African Americans) can one fully understand it. While there is some truth to this theory, it fails to explain why some persons become prejudiced and others do not.

2. Sociocultural. This theory emphasizes the sociocultural context in which prejudiced attitudes develop. Some, for example, claim that prejudice develops as a part of the urbanization process. This fails to account, however, for the prejudice that is found in rural areas.

3. Situational. This theory stresses the effect that current forces have in the development of prejudice. Children that grow up surrounded by patterns of prejudice, simply conform to them. This, undoubtedly is a contributing factor, yet, one can find exceptions to this.

4. Psychodynamic. This is a psychological theory rooted in the "nature of man." This theory asserts that certain character structures (e.g., insecure, anxious personalities) develop prejudice as an important feature of their lives. A major weakness of this theory is that it fails to explain why such personalities express their prejudice only against certain groups or why all similar personalities are not prejudiced.

5. Phenomenological. This theory holds that a person's conduct is based on the way he or she perceives the world. While it is true that worldview influences a

person's perception, this theory does not demonstrate conclusively that all historical and historical forces converge into a final focus.

6. Earned reputation. This theory holds that there are ethnic, racial, or national traits that are menacing and invite disapproval, hostility, and prejudice. There are numerous instances, however, in which the target group has done nothing to earn that reputation.

No single, comprehensive theory completely explains the phenomenon of prejudice. While some of these theories may contain a kernel of truth, none is complete and multiple explanations of prejudice are necessary to account for its complexity.

## Ways in Which Prejudice Is Acquired

Prejudice is acquired through social interaction—in the home, society, and other sociocultural experiences.

1. The role of the home

Prejudice is not transmitted biologically; it is learned. The first place in which prejudice is learned is in the home. There are two ways in which the child acquires prejudice: (1) by adopting it and (2) by developing it.

A child adopts prejudice by taking over the attitudes and stereotypes from his family.

Another type of training does not transfer ideas and attitudes directly to the child, but rather creates an atmosphere in which the child develops prejudice as his lifestyle. Often the mode of bringing up the child (discipline, loving, threatening) is such that the child cannot help but acquire suspicions, fear, or hatreds that sooner of later may fix on minority groups.

2. The role of society

Whether actual prejudice or the predisposition for prejudice is acquired at home, it is reinforced in society. This happens when persons follow the customs of their society almost unconsciously. Wanting to be accepted within their own group, these persons, at times, follow its practices. It also happens when we develop ethnocentrism by considering our group to be superior and judging other cultural groups by the standards of our group.

Allport lists ten sociocultural conditions that seem to produce prejudice: 1) Heterogeneity in the population; 2) Ease of vertical mobility; 3) Rapid social change with attendant anomie; 4) Ignorance and barriers to communication; 5) Relative density of minority group population; 6) The existence of realistic rivalries and conflict; 7) Exploitation sustaining important interests in the community; 8) Sanctions given to aggressive scapegoating; 9) Legend and tradition that sustain hostility; 10) Unfavorable attitudes toward both assimilation and cultural pluralism.[334]

When these conditions, or a combination of them, are found in a sociocultural setting, the development of prejudice is more likely to occur.

**Ways in Which Prejudice Is Acted Out**

While prejudice is an inner attitude, it is expressed in a variety of ways. Allport lists the following ways:[335]

1. Antilocution -  speaking against or telling derogatory jokes about members of another cultural group with like-minded friends. Many people never go beyond this mild degree of antipathetic action.

2. Avoidance - avoiding members of the disliked group even at the cost of considerable inconvenience. In this case, the bearer of prejudice does not directly inflict harm on the group he dislikes but reacts by accommodation and withdrawal.

3. Discrimination - Here the prejudiced person makes detrimental distinctions of an active sort. This involves excluding persons from certain types of housing, employment, educational, recreational activities, opportunities, hospitals, and other social privileges. Segregation is an institutionalized form of discrimination enforced legally or by common custom.

4. Physical attack - conditions of heightened emotion prejudice may lead to acts of violence or semi violence.

5. Extermination - lynchings, pogroms, massacres, and Hitlerian programs of genocide mark the ultimate degree of violent expression of prejudice. The events currently being experienced in Dafur show the tendency of one cultural group to seek even the extermination of another group— even when the groups share religious affiliations.

It is important to understand that each stage of prejudiced behavior feeds the next and that extreme forms develop only when the more subtle forms are permitted to flourish. For example, racial slurs (e.g., "ethnic jokes") if unchecked may lead to discriminatory behavior (e.g., scrawling graffiti on synagogues, burning crosses) and that may lead to such violent behavior as lynchings, bombings, and other forms of scapegoating. Historians remind us that verbal abuse of Germany's Jews, though mild in Bismarck's time, became ferocious under Hitler, and led to the infamous Nuremburg laws which paved the way for the Holocaust.[336]

## The Relationship between Prejudice and Discrimination

When we act out our prejudices we engage in discrimination. Discrimination is differential treatment based on unfair racial, religious, or ethnic categorization. It is a denial of justice prompted by prejudice. People can be prejudiced without actually discriminating. Peter I. Rose employs four categories to illustrate the relationship between prejudice and discrimination.[337]

- **Unprejudiced Nondiscriminatory**—These individuals sincerely believe in the American creed of freedom and equality for all and practice it to the fullest extent. Some of them may have the firm belief that as Christians they must follow the teachings and example of Christ who affirmed the inherent value of all human beings.

- **Unprejudiced Discriminator**—These individuals are characterized by the homeowner, who denies any personal feelings against certain minorities, but keeps them out of his or her neighborhood for fear of altering the character of the community. One wonders if this is not a "subconsciously prejudiced discriminator." By not wanting to take the initiative to relate to other cultural groups or to pay the price of living in the same community with them, people,

200

who do not consider themselves to be prejudiced, can practice a subtle form of discrimination.

- **Prejudiced Nondiscriminatory**—These are the "timid prejudiced people" who feel definite hostility toward many groups and accept the stereotypes of others, but will not discriminate openly in defiance of the laws or customs.

- **Prejudiced Discriminator**—These are the "active prejudiced people" who neither believe in the American creed nor act in accordance with its precepts. They may engage in direct actions against certain groups. Some may even attempt to find biblical justification for their discriminatory practices.

It is important to note that prejudice, whether experienced covertly or overtly, has negative consequences. The fact that some people do not act out their prejudices does not mean that no harm is done. The goal, therefore, should be the elimination of prejudice. From a Christian perspective, if prejudice keeps us from understanding and loving people of other cultures, it is a serious obstacle to the implementation of the Great Commission.

## *Factors That Contribute To the Reduction of Prejudice*

Due to the fact that prejudice is learned and not biologically inherited, steps can be taken to reduce, and hopefully, to eliminate it.

Allport has documented the following approaches which have help reduce prejudice:[338]

- **Informational approach**—This approach imparts knowledge by lectures and textbook teaching. The more people develop an appreciation for the culture of others the greater will be the possibility for understanding and communication.

- **Vicarious experience approach**—This approach employs movies, dramas, fiction, and other devices to invite people to identify with the members of and out-group. This goes beyond the informational approach and involves the affective areas of a person's life.

- **Community study-action approach**—This approach calls for field trips, area surveys, work in social agencies, or community programs. Often as people serve others in community action programs on missionary projects, they have the opportunity of interacting with people of different cultural backgrounds.

- **Exhibits, festivals, and pageants**—This approach encourages a sympathetic regard for the customs of minority groups and our Old World heritage. Activities related to patriotic celebrations affirm the cultural heritage of the various cultural groups that participate.

- **Small group process**—This approach applies many principles of group dynamics including discussion, sociodrama, and group retraining. Often through games in which people of a majority culture are excluded from participation because of arbitrary rules, they can gain a new understanding of what it feels like to be excluded through no fault of their own.

- **Individual conference**—This approach allows for therapeutic interviewing and counseling. Talking with people about their cultural pilgrimage as they have sought to relate to the predominant culture in this country can be help a person to gain valuable information as well as establish meaningful relations.

While all of these approaches have the potential to contribute toward the reduction of prejudice, studies indicate that the approaches which lead toward *acquaintance* rather than *mere knowledge* obtain the greatest results. In other words it is not a matter of merely imparting knowledge (although this can be foundational) but one of enabling the prejudiced person to become personally acquainted with persons (and situations) of a different cultural group. In contrast with casual contacts, most studies show that true acquaintance lessens prejudice.

Direct demonstration of this point is contained in a research by J. S. Gary and H. A. Thompson.[339] They stress that to be maximally effective, contact, and acquaintance programs should:

- Lead to a sense of equality in social status between majority and minority groups;
- Occur in ordinary purposeful pursuit of common goals;
- Avoid artificiality;
- Be sanctioned by institutional supports (i.e. by law, custom or local atmosphere;

- Lead to perception of common interests and common humanity between members of the two groups. Goodwill contact without concrete goals accomplishes nothing. Minority groups gain nothing from artificially induced mutual admiration.

## How Christians Can Overcome Prejudice

### Recognition

Recognize that *all of us* have the tendency to be prejudiced. Because most of us have grown up in the context of an isolated cultural group, our natural tendency is to believe that ours is the only valid culture and that all cultures should be evaluated by our standards.

As was pointed out earlier, as children we pick up from our parents and the society that surrounds us ideas and attitudes before we have opportunites to critically evaluate them. The result is that even unconsciously we have prejudices related to cultural groups that are different from ours.

It is important to point out that this happens to people in all cultural groups. Ethnocentrism is often a *two way street*. If one group has negative attitudes toward another group, so does the other group. This is not exclusively a majority-minority issue. All of us need to recognize that there is much in the culture that surrounds us that fosters attitudes of prejudice.

### Repentance

Repent if our sin has been one of *pride*. There is the positive side of pride which causes us to feel good about ourselves.

The negative side is that of needing to look down on people so that we can feel superior. While it is helpful and necessary to have positive feelings about our own cultural group, the minute we start feeling *superior, judgmental,* and *negative* toward people in other cultures we dishonor God because He is the Father of all of us. In other words, we cannot call God "Father" if we are not willing to accept people of other cultures as our *brothers and sisters.* We, therefore, need to repent before God and ask him to forgive us of the sin of pride that has caused us to view others in a negative and judgmental way.

**Resolution**

Resolve to cultivate a friendship with at least *one person* of that particular cultural group. When you personalize, you demythologize. When you get to know someone from another culture personally you will find yourself getting rid of the myths that you had picked up from the people around you. Be intentional about developing a genuine friendship with a person of the group or population segment in which you are interested. Make sure that this is a friendship between equals in which you learn from each other and affirm one another.

**Resistance**

Resist efforts on the part of people in your cultural group to *put down* or *perpetuate* negative stereotypes (through jokes, snide remarks) of another cultural group. Some jokes are innocent and genuinely funny. Other jokes, however, seem to have the sole purpose of putting other cultural groups down.

## Realization

Realize that we have an opportunity to exert a positive Christian influence in building bridges between cultural groups. As Christians we must be willing to go against the non-Christian trends and attitudes in our society. We can do so when we choose to relate to people of other cultures and even bring about better understanding between the various cultural groups.

## Obedience

Obey the admonitions of the Word of God. The Bible condemns:

- Antipathy – "Love your neighbor as yourself." Who is my neighbor?  The Good Samaritan;
- Antilocution – "Thou shall not bear false witness";
- Discrimination – James speaks against "preferential treatment of the rich";
- Physical Attack – Jesus taught us to turn the cheek;
- Extermination – "Thou shalt not kill."

These practices are clearly unbiblical and should not be found in the lives of those who are genuine followers of Christ.

Allport makes the following sobering statement:

America, on the whole, has been a staunch defender of the right to be the same or different, although it has fallen short in many of its practices. The question before us is whether progress toward tolerance will continue, or whether, as in many regions of the world, a fatal retrogression will set in. Can citizens learn to seek their own welfare and growth not at the expense of their fellow men, but in concert with them? The human family does not yet know the answer, but hopes it will be affirmative.

If anyone should be in a position to give an affirmative answer to this challenge, it should be Christians who take the commandment of Jesus seriously: "Love your neighbor as yourself."

---

**Endnotes**

[322] Gordon  W. Allport, *The Nature of Prejudice*, Garden City, NY: Doubleday  Anchor Books, 1958, 405-407.

[323] *Fort Worth Star-Telegram*, "Researchers say race isn't base for scientific study," 1995.

[324] Allport, 107.

[325] Allport, 107.

[326] Allport, 108.

[327] Allport, 112.

[328] "What Color Is Black,?" *Newsweek*, Feb., 13, 1995.

[329] Allport ,108.

[330] James A. Banks, "Reducing Prejudice in Students: Theory, Research, and Strategies," in Kogla Adam Moodley, ed, *Race Relations and Multicultural Education* (Vancouver, BC: Center for the Study of Curriculum and Instruction, University of British Columbia, 1985), 65-88.

[331] Allport, 7.

[332] N.W.Ackerman and Marie Jacoba, *Anti-Semitism and Emotional Disorder*, New York: Harper, 1950,  4.

[333] Allport,  205-218.

[334] Allport,  233.

[335] Allport, 14-15.

[336] Ibid.

[337] Peter I. Rose, *They and We: Racial and Ethnic Relations in the United States, 3d ed. (New York: Random House, 1981)*, 91-94.

[338] Allport, 250.

[339] J. S. Gary and A. H. Thompson. "The ethnic prejudices of white and negro college students," *Journal of Abnormal and Social Psychology,* 1953, 48: 311-313. (Cited in Allport, 252).

# PART THREE
# MINISTERNIG
# AMONG HISPANICS

# CHAPTER 17

# REACHING HISPANICS FOR CHRIST

For Christians, the most loving thing and the greatest contribution we can make to the life of a fellow human being is to lead him or her to a personal experience of salvation in Jesus Christ. The admonition that Jesus gave to Nicodemus, "You must be born again," still holds true today. Nothing will make a greater impact on the life of an individual than to accept Jesus Christ as Savior and Lord. The assurance of the forgiveness of sin, of the presence of Christ, and of eternal life will give a person the sense of direction, the discipline, and the confidence to face the challenges of life with a positive and constructive attitude. Leading Hispanics to a personal experience of salvation in Jesus Christ, therefore, will give them an invaluable spiritual resource as they encounter transition and adaptation in this country. Two of the most effective ways to lead Hispanics to a personal experience with Christ are through ministry-based evangelism and through personal evangelism.

## Ministry-Based Evangelism

One of the best ways to reach people in any community is to discover their felt needs, to minister to them by addressing these needs, to build bridges of friendship and understanding, and to share the good news of salvation with an attitude of compassion and concern. By utilizing a holistic approach in ministry, the needs of many Hispanics can be met and their lives can be transformed as they become open to having a personal relationship with Jesus Christ.

A survey of Hispanic pastors, conducted by the Research Department of the North American Mission Board, revealed the following needs in the order of priority that the pastors established.[419] The percentages indicate the number of pastors who agreed that a certain need should be placed at a particular slot in the order of priorities.

1. Helping persons to get jobs or better jobs 68%
2. Helping new immigrants to establish themselves 60.8%
3. Helping persons to have better access to basic social services (health care, Social Security, Medicare) 60.8%
4. Counseling programs 60.8%
5. English or citizenship classes 58.3% 6.
6. Helping students to stay in school 53.3%
7. Church/community sports programs 51.7%
8. Job training 50.0%
9. After-school programs for teenagers 49.2%
10. Drug/ alcoholic rehabilitation programs 45.0%
11. Day-care or child care programs 45.0%
12. Reduce violence among the families 40.85
13. Food distribution 37.5%
14. Programs for the elderly 32.2%
15. Providing shelter for the homeless 30.8%
16. Reduce violence in the community (e.g., gangs) 29.2%
17. Adequate housing 25.5%
18. Voter registration 20.8%
19. Other community needs 15.8%

It is quite likely that the order of priority will vary from one community to another. On the other hand, the types of needs that are listed are found in every Hispanic community, especially those that are comprised of newer immigrants. It is important to note that many of the needs listed above relate to the adaptation of new Hispanic immigrants to life in this country. This is evident in the top five needs listed in the survey: Helping persons to get jobs or better jobs; Helping new immigrants to establish themselves; Helping persons to have better access to basic social services (health care, Social Security, Medicare); Counseling programs; and English or citizenship classes.

It is a given that as Christians we must minister to the needs of people in the name of Christ (Matt. 24:34-26). Compassionate ministries will alleviate the needs of people and will build the bridges of friendship and understanding that will facilitate the communication of the message of salvation. A young woman, who came from another country was greatly helped in her transition by a Christian lady, said of the lady: "She built a bridge from her heart to mine and Jesus walked across." That encapsulates ministry-based evangelism.

## Relational Evangelism

There is a sense in which ministry based evangelism and relational evangelism cannot be separated for one leads to another. In this segment, however, we are going to focus on constructive ways of building relationships with Hispanic persons. The purpose of this segment, therefore, will not be to help people discuss *religion* but to focus on a personal *relationship* with Jesus Christ as Savior and Lord. Jesus made it very clear that people need to be born again in order to enter the kingdom of God (Jn. 3:3). In this chapter we will focus on those Hispanics who have not experienced the new birth. Some of these are dear friends and very sincere people who do not have a clear understanding of the biblical teaching regarding salvation. They need to know about this personal experience with Jesus Christ which blesses people with *forgiveness of sin*, a *sense of purpose* in life, the *abiding presence of the Lord*, the *power* to live victorious lives, and a *steadfast hope* for this life and for eternity.

Some seek to witness to Hispanics by *arguing, attacking,* and *exposing* what they consider to be erroneous beliefs and practices. In all of my missionary experience, I have found that in most cases these approaches offend and alienate people who otherwise might have been willing to listen to the good news of salvation. The overriding theme of this chapter, therefore, is *"Tell the truth in love"* (Eph. 4:15). We need to tell the truth of the word of God, but we must do it in a spirit of love and compassion. We shall seek, therefore, to establish bridges of communication so that we can share the biblical teachings about salvation through personal faith in Jesus Christ in such a way that people will be receptive to the message.

This segment will focus on biblical teachings regarding the sharing of the good news of salvation. It will also provide instruction on how to witness in such a way that the attention of the listeners will be drawn to Jesus and not to peripheral matters that might distract them from coming to a personal experience of salvation in Jesus Christ.[342]

The dialogue that Jesus had with the Samaritan woman has valuable lessons which can help us as Evangelical Christians to know how to share our faith with those who have not experienced the new birth and who have questions regarding their relationship with God. As we study this marvelous dialogue we discover the things Jesus did to share very important spiritual lessons with a person who had a religious tradition but had very vague notions about God and how to relate to him. It was obvious from her lifestyle that she had serious spiritual needs that she did not know how to fulfill. As we study how Jesus related to this woman, we can learn how to relate to people who also have spiritual needs and are searching for purpose and meaning in their lives. The passage is found in Jn. 4:4-42.

## *Jesus Cultivated a Friendship (4:4-6)*

### By going out of His way geographically

John states that Jesus "had to go through Samaria." Actually, many Jews went around Samaria on their way to Galilee. The statement that Jesus "had to go through Samaria," says more about His commitment than about a geographical necessity. In other words, Jesus felt a strong desire to go and tell the Samaritans about God's love for them.

### By going out of His way socially

The Samaritan woman was startled that Jesus spoke to her. It was not customary for a Rabbi to speak to a woman in public. Furthermore, as John points out (Jn. 4:9), it was not customary for Jews to have social contact with Samaritans. John's comment borders on an understatement. Jews and Samaritans actually hated one another (Nehemiah 4; Ezra 4). A long history of hatred existed between these two groups. Despite this, Jesus was willing to go out of His way socially in order to tell the Samaritan woman that God

215

loved her, was willing to forgive her, and wanted to give her the spiritual resources so she could live a life full of joy and fellowship.

## Application

If we are to follow the example of Jesus and share with those who have serious questions about their relationship to God, we must cultivate friendships. Genuine friendship can become the bridge that overcomes suspicion, fear, and doubts. As we develop a friendship, we can also become more keenly aware of the spiritual needs of people and have a better understanding of how to share the good news of salvation with them.

Often to accomplish this, we need to be willing to go out of our way geographically and socially. We can become so comfortable with our circle of friends in church that we make little or no effort to get to know people who have not invited Jesus into their lives. We need to be intentional, therefore, about developing friendships, ministering to them in any way we can, and in the process, sharing with them what Jesus means to us and how they can also have a relationship with Him. We can do this by befriending people at work, at school, and in our neighborhood. Inviting them for a meal in our home, to a sports event, or other interesting activities can help build these friendships.

## *Jesus Created an Interest (4:7-15)*

### Jesus created an interest by beginning with a felt need.

The Samaritan woman came to the well to draw water. That was what was occupying her mind at that moment.

Jesus, therefore, started the conversation by asking her for a drink of water. In other words, Jesus did not just start talking about spiritual matters out of the clear blue sky. She came to draw water, so Jesus used that as the starting point of the conversation. Often people have material needs (food, clothing, shelter, etc.) that we might address through ministry. As we do so, this can be the starting point of our cultivation of a friendship.

**Jesus created an interest by relating to a spiritual need.**

The Samaritan woman asked Jesus, "Why is it that, being a Jew, you are asking me, a Samaritan, for a drink of water?" (v. 9). Jesus replied: "If you only knew the gift of God and who it is that is speaking with you, you would ask him and he would give you living water" (v. 10).

It was at this point that Jesus shifted the focus from material water to spiritual water. In other words, he was saying, you came to draw water for your physical thirst, but I have water that can quench the thirst of your soul. As he spoke to her about living water, a new possibility began to dawn on her: "How could this water Jesus was talking to her about quench the deep longings of her soul?" The more Jesus spoke, the more curious she became.

**Application:**

Like Jesus, we can often create an interest in the gospel by beginning with felt needs. Psychologists tell us that some of the basic needs of human beings are: (1) to love and be loved; (2) to feel secure; (3) to overcome a sense of guilt; and (4) to have assurance about the future. As we cultivate a friendship, we are in a better position to create an interest in spiritual matters by helping them see that Jesus can make a difference. One way to do this is to share our testimony of how Jesus has made a difference in our lives.

## *Jesus Comprehended Her Situation (4:16-19)*

### Jesus did not condemn the Samaritan woman.

As the conversation continued, Jesus told her, "Go call your husband. When she said that she had no husband, Jesus compassionately confronted her with the sad history of her life. Five times she had sought happiness only to end up in disappointment and despair. Jesus did not approve of her lifestyle, but there must have been a tone of compassion in His voice and an expression of concern on his face when he dealt with this delicate subject. It is obvious that she did not feel condemned or rejected by Jesus because she returned. When she went to the village, she said to the villagers that Jesus "told her every thing she ever did" (v. 39). The implication is that in spite of this, Jesus still showed compassion to her.

### Jesus found something positive to say about her

When she said "I don't have a husband," Jesus replied: "What you have just said is quite true" (Jn. 4:18). Having awakened in her an interest in a new lifestyle, Jesus maintained the dialogue on a positive note. She continued to listen as she sensed that He was willing to see the best in her. Jesus found a redeemable fragment in the life of the Samaritan woman and built upon it.

## Application

We can be in a better position to witness to people by avoiding a spirit of condemnation. Even though we may not agree with their lifestyle, we cannot expect them to act like born-again Christians until they actually are. Often persons who have not had a personal experience of salvation feel a sense of condemnation and rejection on the part of those who are trying to witness to them.

We need to remember that it is the role of the Holy Spirit to bring conviction. We need to avoid a spirit of judgment and condemnation as we share the good news of salvation with those who have not accepted Christ as their Savior. If they sense the love of Jesus in our hearts, they will be attracted to him.

## *Jesus concentrated on what was essential to Salvation (4:19-26)*

Jesus avoided discussing religion. The Samaritans were mistaken on several religious matters. They accepted only the first five books of the Old Testament. They also believed that Abraham had offered Isaac on their mountain (Gerizim) instead of Zion. That is why the Samaritan woman was asking where she should worship. While Jesus was very clear in explaining to her that "salvation comes from the Jews" (v. 22), he did not spend time trying to straighten out the Samaritan woman on every doctrinal point before he shared the gospel. In other words, Jesus did not get sidetracked by discussing religion with her.

**Jesus focused on relationship.**

The Samaritan woman asked in what religious tradition God should be worshipped—Zion's or Gerizim's? Jesus responded that *relationship* is more important than *tradition*: "true worshipers will worship the Father in *spirit* and in *truth*" (v. 23). True worshippers are those who know the truth about God and have a spiritual relationship with him.

**Application:**

If we are to follow the example of Jesus, we will not spend time discussing religion. We need to focus on relationship. Our question should not be "To what religion do you belong?" but rather "What is your personal relationship with Jesus?"

Many people operate under the false assumption that if they can just prove to people that they are wrong, they will automatically want to invite Jesus into their lives. Often the opposite is true. If they get into heated discussions about religious beliefs, they run the risk of alienating people or at the very least getting sidetracked and not focusing on Jesus at all. Later in the discipleship process there will be time to study what the Bible says about certain doctrines. While we are sharing our faith, we need to focus on Jesus. He said: "If I be lifted up, I will draw all men unto me." Let's focus on our relationship with Jesus.

## *Jesus Communicated Patiently (4:15-29)*

### As Jesus dialogued the woman's understanding grew

At first the Samaritan woman did not fully understand what Jesus was talking about. This is evident in verse 15 when she said "Sir, give me this water so that I won't get thirsty and have to keep coming here to draw water." She was still thinking about physical water. It was not until she said, "When he [Messiah] comes, he will explain everything to us," (v. 25) that Jesus said, "I who speak to you am he" (v. 28). The way the dialogue progressed is indicated in the terms she used to refer to Him.

**The way in which she referred
to Jesus showed this change**

First she called Him a "**(Jew)**," a member of the group she hated. He looked and sounded like a Jew. His appearance was the only thing she had to go by. For her, therefore, Jesus was a common ordinary Jew (v. 9).

Then she referred to Him as "**(Sir)**" a person who could be respected (v. 11). As she listened to him, she began to realize that this Jew was different. He was treating her with respect, so she reciprocated by seeing him as a respected person.

Then she stated "I can see that you are a "**(Prophet)**" (v. 19). In other words, "You are a man sent from God." When she realized that Jesus knew all about her, she concluded that this had to be a person who was in touch with God in an extraordinary manner. He was no ordinary man.

Finally she referred to Him as the "**(Messiah)**" (v. 29). Jesus communicated patiently until she was able to understand that he was the Messiah for whom people were waiting. It is obvious that her understanding of who Jesus was progressed as Jesus dialogued with her, answered her questions, and demonstrated an unusual type of compassion and love.

## Application

People who have not grown up in an evangelical setting often do not understand their need to have a personal relationship with Jesus Christ. We must communicate patiently until they are able to understand what the Bible teaches about a personal experience of salvation in Jesus Christ. It may take quite a long time for them to understand what salvation is all about and to make a decision to receive Christ. We, therefore, must be patient and allow the Holy Spirit to work in their hearts. It is, therefore, counter productive to pressure people and to expect them to make a decision to receive Christ when they still do not understand what this is all about or when they still questions and doubts in their minds.

## *Review*

◆ We must go out of our way geographically and socially if we are to lead Hispanics to a personal experience of salvation in Jesus Christ. This means that we need to be intentional in cultivating genuine friendships and establishing bridges of communication.

◆ We must create an interest in spiritual matters by relating to **felt** needs. When we are willing to listen to people as they speak about their problems, anxieties, and needs, we are in a better position to share with them about a personal faith in Jesus Christ that can give them peace, happiness, and hope, not only for this life, but for eternity.

◆ We must avoid a spirit of condemnation to help people see what they can become through the grace and power of Jesus Christ. When people are criticized and attacked, they feel offended and defensive. If they feel the love of Christ in our hearts, they will be attracted to him.

◆ We must concentrate on what is essential to salvation. There will be times when people have questions about the doctrines of the Catholic Church. At these times, we can point them to what the Bible says about these. We must, however, avoid the practice of trying to "straighten them out on every doctrine" before we lead them to a personal experience of salvation in Jesus Christ. When the Philippian Jailer asked Paul, "What must I do to be saved?" his answer was "Believe on the Lord Jesus Christ and you will be saved" (Acts 16:31). Paul did not deal with all of the doctrines at that point. He simply focused on leading the Jailer to Christ. He knew that later the time would come to disciple this man. The starting point was leading him to a personal faith in Christ.

◆ We must communicate patiently, allowing the Holy Spirit to work in the minds of the people. Often Evangelical Christians make the mistake of pressuring their friends and loved ones to make a decision for Christ. While we must admire them for their sense of urgency, we must caution them that this approach may get the opposite effect. People who feel pressured may become totally resistant and even antagonistic. Generally they are not resistant to Christ but to the methods that well meaning, but abrasive people, use. We need to communicate patiently as people gain a gradual understanding of the person and mission of Jesus Christ.

## Practical Suggestions

In light of the fact that many Hispanics have a Roman Catholic background, there are some things that Evangelical Christians should be aware of in seeking to lead them to a personal experience of salvation in Jesus Christ. We will begin with a list of the things Evangelicals should not do. Then we will deal with some things they should do. The goal is not to win arguments but to win people for Christ.

## *Things That We Should Not Do*

There are things that we simply should not do because they usually offend people, put them on the defensive, and distract us from focusing on their relationship with Christ.

**Do not criticize the Catholic Church,
its doctrines, practices, or people.**

Even if you feel you have a valid point, it is counter productive to criticize for two reason: (1) It is not in the Spirit of Christ; (2) It will only antagonize people. Many Hispanics will be open to conversing about the things that they know relating to God and Jesus. They will, however, not be responsive if they are criticized for their beliefs and practices. This will only cause them to become defensive or even to experience hurt feelings.

**Do not ridicule any of the practices
of the Catholic Church**

Some Evangelical Christians are too prone to make fun of catholic sacramentals (images, statues, crucifixes, etc.) and practices. These things are very dear to Hispanics Catholics. If they are hurt, they will turn a deaf ear to what we are saying and perhaps avoid out company. There is absolutely no excuse for showing lack of respect to Hispanic Catholics, their beliefs, and their practices. If we treat them with respect, they will in most cases respond in like manner. We do not necessarily need to agree with their beliefs to establish friendships and share with them what the Bible teaches about salvation in Jesus Christ.

**Do not be negative just because
you differ with someone**

You can disagree without being disagreeable. Just think, if you had grown up in the same environment, you would probably have the same beliefs that they do. You can prayerfully point them to what the word of God says instead of trying to win an argument. A negative attitude will evoke a negative response to the message of salvation.

## *Things That We Should Do*

These are the things that we should do to establish a bridge of respect, appreciation, and communication.

**Love our Hispanic friends**

Find opportunities to show your love in practical ways. Remember, each person you meet is one for whom Jesus died on the Cross. Pray that as you dialogue with them, they will feel the love of Christ in such a tangible way that they will turn to him.

**Pray with and for our Hispanic friends**

Many of them have never had the experience of someone praying for them by name. Mention specific needs. Say:

"Lord, I pray for (name). You know that he or she has this need (name the need) and you have promised to hear our prayers. Bless ___(name)___, help him or her." You may want to begin with the Lord's Prayer. This often provides a bridge because most Hispanic Catholics are familiar with this beautiful, biblical prayer.

### See the best in them

When someone says to you, "I'm a Catholic," be in a position both spiritually and emotionally to say to them, "I'm glad to meet you." Let the love of Christ flow through you. Remember, everyone you meet is a person for whom Christ died. Many of them are sincerely trying to draw near to God.

### Try to put ourselves in their places (1 Cor. 9:19-23)

Seek to reason, how would I move from a traditional to a biblical position? Many Hispanic Catholics have a very limited knowledge of the Bible. Some of the things you say to them about the Word of God may be entirely new. On other teachings they may have a limited understanding, but, it can serve as a bridge to lead them to a clearer understanding of God's Word.

## Preparation for Witnessing

### *Prepare testimony*

One of the most powerful tools in witnessing is to share our testimony. People will generally listen when we share the difference Jesus has made in our lives. When the Apostle

Paul (Acts 26) shared his testimony, he generally used the following outline:

1. What my life was like before knowing Jesus.

2. How I came to know Jesus.

3. How Jesus helps me face life today.

4. How you can know Jesus too.

## Practice testimony

Write a brief paragraph under each major heading telling how you came to know Jesus as your personal Savior. After you have prepared your testimony, take time to share it with someone in your group. When you share your testimony with a friend, speak about the doubts and fears that you had, then share with enthusiasm the difference that your personal faith in Christ has made in your life.

## Preparing to present the Gospel

Some guidelines that can help us lead our Catholic friends to experience personal salvation in Christ.

1. Do not discuss religion. Your main purpose is to lead the person to Christ.
2. Present the gospel with simplicity and sound logic.
3. As you study the Bible together, let your Hispanic friend discover what the Word of God says. Encourage him or her to read the verses, to think about their meaning, and let the Word of God speak to them.[343]

4. Concentrate only on issues essential to salvation. Don't discuss the wrong issues.

5. Don't ask: "Are you a Christian? or "Are you saved?" Your question should be: "What is your personal relationship with Jesus Christ?"

6. If necessary use a Catholic Bible or a version acceptable to Catholics such as a *Good News Bible.*

7. Emphasize that a gift is not a possession until it is received (Rom. 6:23; Jn. 1:12)

## *Marking the New Testament*

One of the best ways to present the plan of salvation to Hispanic Catholics is to use a marked New Testament. This helps them read the verses straight from the Word of God. It is also helpful to give the New Testament to the prospect. There have been numerous instances where the prospect has not understood the full meaning of the passages until he or she has read them several times over an extended period of time.

1. On the first page of your New Testament write the question: "What is your personal relationship to Christ?" Then put: "Turn to page __."

2. After you turn to page ___ where John 10:10 is found:
   a. Color the verse with a light yellow marker.
   b. Write on the top of the page the question #1: "Why did Christ come?"
   c. Write on the bottom of the page, "Turn to page__".

3. Repeat steps 1-3 for each verse used in the gospel presentation writing the appropriate questions of the gospel presentation (see next section).

4. Write on the last page of the New Testament:

Questions to Use
1. Why did Christ come? (John 10:10)
2. Why don't we have this gift? (Rom. 3:23)
3. What is the result of sin? (Rom. 6:23a)
4. What is God's gift? (Rom. 6:23b)
5. How did God make this possible? (Rom. 5:8)
6. Can we earn this gift? (Eph. 2:8-9)
7. How does this gift become ours? (Jn. 1:12)
8. How did the dying thief receive this gift? (Lk. 23:39-43)
9. Can we be sure we have this gift? (Jn. 5:24)
10. Will you open the door of your life to Christ? (Rev. 3:20)

## *Presenting the Gospel*

Begin with the question, "What is your relationship to Christ?" Explain, "We are not going to talk about religion; we just want to find out what the Bible says about our relationship to Christ." Lead from there to the questions found in your marked New Testament.

After you have gone through the plan of salvation with your Catholic friend, do the following:

◆ Ask your friend to pray the prayer of acceptance with you.

If your friend is not ready yet, do these things:

◆ Pray for your friend. Begin with the Lord's Prayer.

◆ Then ask God to help your friend learn the things that He wants your friend to know. Pray for any need he or she might have. (Suggestion: Make the prayer as personal as possible. You may want to hold hands with your friend.)

◆ Give your friend the New Testament as a gift. Suggest that he or she re-read these portions of Scripture. Ask them to sign his or her name when he or she has made a decision to accept Christ.

### MY DECISION TO RECEIVE CHRIST

I admit before God that I am a sinner and that Jesus died for my sins. I now open the door of my life to Christ and accept His gift of salvation.

Name _____

Date _____

The goal of this chapter has been to focus on the need to lead Hispanics to a personal experience of salvation in Jesus Christ. We have shared information provided by some Roman Catholic leaders regarding the number of Hispanics that are joining Evangelical churches. The aim, however, is not to get Hispanics to join Evangelical churches but to make sure that they have been born again. This is best accomplished by heeding the advice of Peter who said: "But sanctify the Lord in your hearts; always being ready to give an answer to everyone who asks of you a reason of the hope that is in you, yet with gentleness and reverence (1 Pet. 3:15).

**Endnotes**

[341] Survey conducted by Richie Stanley, Bob Sena, and Daniel R. Sanchez, in November of 2004.

[342] This material has been taken from Daniel R. Sanchez, Rudolf Gonzalez, *Sharing The Good News With Roman Catholic Friends*, 2004, Church Starting Network, .

[343] For an evangelistic Bible study series see Daniel R. Sanchez, *Gospel In The Rosary*, 2004, Church Starting Network. .

# Chapter 18

# Starting Hispanic Churches

The earlier statement (chapter 6), that said that "Hispanics are showing more receptivity to the Evangelical message than ever before in the history of this country"[344] holds significant implications for contemporary church planting.[345] More churches are currently being started among Hispanics than ever before in the history of this country.[346] In fact, the 21st century has potential to become the greatest Hispanic American church planting period in history. This fact encourages Evangelical Christians in light of the fact that Hispanics are the fastest growing ethnic group in America today.[347]

To maximize this opportunity that the Lord is giving us, we must approach the task of planting churches among Hispanics in the same way missionaries design strategies to reach target groups in other regions of the world.[348] This effort involves;

- establishing a solid biblical foundation,
- becoming thoroughly familiar with Hispanic cultural characteristics,
- designing culturally appropriate church planting strategies.

This chapter addresses these issues in an effort to inform and inspire us to respond to this challenge in a way that reaches and disciples unprecedented numbers of Hispanics in the context of biblically centered, culturally relevant, reproducing churches for the honor and glory of God.

# Biblical Basis for Hispanic Church Planting

The Bible clearly reveals that it is God's desire for every person on the face of this earth to have an opportunity to hear and to respond to the message of salvation in Jesus Christ. This is reflected in the Incarnation of Jesus, His missionary mandate, and the establishment of His Church. An examination of the cultural implications of these truths motivates us and guides us in the development of church planting strategies among Hispanics.

## *Biblical Mandate*

Before communicating the missionary mandate, Jesus provided a supreme example of cultural identification. "The word became flesh and dwelt among us ... full of grace and truth" (Jn. 1:14). Jesus "took on the form of a servant, and was made in the likeness of men" (Phil. 2:7). Charles Chaney points out the cultural implications of the incarnation of Jesus when he states:

> This intrusion of the Divine into the context of human history has meant the identification of Jesus with the needs, hurts, and hopes of men and women for almost two thousand years. Jesus responded to the needs of people within their cultural contexts and adapted his approach uniquely to them. He based his approach on his understanding of their values, attitudes, and conversations.[349]

234

In the Great Commission, Jesus said: "Make disciples of all nations." The word for "all nations" in Greek is "*ta ethne*" from which we get the word "ethnic." This term means "people group."[350] In order to implement this mandate, the followers of Christ are to cross linguistic, racial, cultural, religious, and geographical boundaries with the message of salvation. Every barrier to the gospel needs to be bridged by establishing churches that are near the unchurched, not only geographically but culturally. This applies to the Hispanic communities as well as all of the other socio-cultural groups.

## Biblical Models

The Bible directly addresses the importance of evangelism and church starting in the process of "making disciples" of all peoples. Two excellent examples are the Jerusalem Fellowship and the Church in Antioch.

### The Jerusalem Fellowship

The remarkable experiences among the Christians in Jerusalem in the beginning days of the Christian movement give an ample example of the life and witness of a Christian fellowship that reaches out to the lost (Acts 2:1-4:36). This fellowship demonstrated the functions of a church that is enabled to reach out to the world. The church engaged:
- in proclamation
- incorporation
- indoctrination
- worship
- confirmation that the Lord was in their midst
- cultural identification
- propagation that showed that people were being saved.[351]

Hispanic Church starters can learn from the Jerusalem Fellowship that the church is built on the foundation of believers joining together without any hierarchical power dictating or controlling. More importantly, this congregation indicates that congregations should be built on strong doctrinal foundations and should continue in fellowship, sharing, and witness (Acts 2:40-47). Hispanic churches that start and commit to carry out the functions of churches as seen in the Jerusalem example will grow strong and will naturally reproduce.

The Jerusalem Fellowship shared its people with other regions. The gospel moved from Jerusalem to Samaria, to Ethiopia, and to Antioch. From Antioch the Message spread to the entire Roman Empire. Evidences strongly suggest that from Jerusalem the Gospel spread to vast other regions of the world. The most important factor is the certain fact that the Jerusalem Fellowship was a reproducing church and Hispanic Churches today should emulate this practice.

**The Antioch Church**

As second biblical example, the Antioch Church, was started by refugees who "were scattered because of the persecution that rose in connection with Stephen" (Acts 11:19). These Jewish Christians had fled from Jerusalem but were not hesitant to preach the Gospel at Antioch. At first they were "speaking the word to no one except to Jews alone" (v. 19). It was a natural for them to concentrate on their own social group, for they understood their language and culture.

Their vision, however, was expanded by other Jewish Christian refugees (originally from Cyprus and Cyrene) who came to Antioch and "began speaking to the Greeks also, preaching the Lord Jesus" (Acts 11:20). It is evident that this pleased the Lord, for verse 21 states that the "hand of the Lord was with them, and a great number believed and turned to the Lord." As a result of this, Antioch became a multicultural congregation (Acts 13:1).[352]

This church was the first to send a missionary team (Barnabas and Saul) to plant churches in the Gentile world. This team had the freedom to start churches that were doctrinally sound, yet, culturally and linguistically different from the sending church. In addition to this, the Antioch Church shared its financial resources. When the members of this church received the report of a famine in Judea, they tool up an offering and sent it to their sister church in Jerusalem (Acts 11:28, 29). In addition to this, the Antioch church sent delegates to participate in the Jerusalem Council (Acts 15:2).

The Antioch Church is an inspiring example of a congregation that took the Great Commission seriously, reached out to its own group, expanded its vision to include other cultural groups within its own city, sent a missionary team to start culturally contextualized churches in Asia Minor and Europe, shared its financial resources with sister churches, and sent delegates to the Jerusalem Council to address the issue of the status of Gentile Christians. The Antioch congregation, therefore, was an evangelistic church, a missionary church, a generous church, and a cooperating church. This church did not exist in isolation but in a fraternal relationship with other churches that had the same task of fulfilling the Great Commission.

The Antioch Church provides a marvelous example for Hispanic Americans who find themselves in the midst of pervasive transition. These early Christians had fled persecution, uprooted themselves culturally and economically, and faced the daunting challenge of reestablishing themselves as a minority group in a new geographical region. These Christians however, did not spend all of their time feeling sorry for themselves or simply focusing on their social and economic recuperation. Instead, they went about the joyous task of sharing the Good News of salvation first with the members of their own cultural group, then with other local groups (Greeks), and finally sending out a missionary team to Asia Minor and Europe.

Following the example of the Antioch church, contemporary churches of every culture need to be open to reaching everyone they can through their existing congregations. At the same time, these congregations should make the strategic adaptations necessary to reach those who will respond better in congregations that utilize their heart language and reflect their culture. In addition, these congregations should take steps to go beyond to "the ends of the earth."

## Cultural Dimensions of Hispanic Church Planting

The most effective Hispanic church planting approaches being utilized today are those that take into account the cultural characteristics of their target group. Among the factors that need to be considered are religious background, personal relationships, family ties, emotional traits, and assimilation stages.

## *Religious Background*

Understanding the religious background of the Hispanic community has significant implications for the development of church planting strategies. Even though a large percentage of Hispanics are not actively involved in the Roman Catholic Church, they often experience pressures from their families and friends when they participate in Evangelical outreach activities. They may also go through periods of doubts and confusion when they begin to compare what they are learning from the Bible over against some of their religious traditions.

Evangelical efforts to lead Hispanics to a personal faith in Christ need to be accompanied by much prayer, study, love, and patience. An understanding of the Roman Catholic concept of salvation (through the Church and the sacraments) and an attitude that establishes bridges of communication (over against criticism, ridicule, and pressure) is absolutely essential.[353] Often, even after a person has indicated interest in a personal relationship with Jesus Christ, it may take months or even years for him or her to make the decision to be baptized and become a member of an Evangelical church. Many Hispanics go through a pilgrimage that involves discovery, deliberation, decision, dissonance, and discipleship.[354] This pilgrimage needs to be taken into account in designing evangelistic strategies and establishing time lines for church planting efforts among Hispanics.

## *Personal Relationships*

Because many Hispanics do not have an evangelical background, they often experience apprehension and pressure when they are invited to a "Protestant church." This obstacle can best be overcome through the establishment of genuine friendships and the utilization of cultivative evangelistic activities. On an individual basis, there are many things that can be done to establish bridges of communication. These include: having them as guests in our home for a meal, inviting them to join us in a sports or artistic event, and befriending them when they are in need, When it come to groups, activities such as; Block Parties; dramas; cantatas; (e.g., Christmas and Easter); Backyard Bible Clubs; Vacation Bible School, arts and handcraft festivals, film festivals (relating to marriage and the family), Jesus film showings (in a public place or in the homes) can go a long way toward establishing a bridge between the target persons and the church.[355] Home Bible Studies are proving to be some of the very best approaches for reaching Hispanics in this country and throughout the world.[356]

## *Family Ties*

Hispanics generally have strong family ties that go beyond the nuclear to the extended family. Alex D. Montoya explains the importance of the family:

> The family is the main unit in the Hispanic community, superseding the church, political parties, or any other group. Hispanics think and act as a family unit... In evangelizing them, this structure can either be a hindrance or a help. If we try to convert a member of the family, the family ties and pressure make it very difficult for that person to make a decision for Christ independent of the entire family. But a whole family may come to Christ when the elder member of the family is won first.[357]

In light of the role that the family plays in the Hispanic community, decision making styles need to be taken into account in church planting strategies. If children or young people make a decision for Christ, it may take a while for their parents to be reached. If a wife makes a decision for Christ it may take some time before her husband becomes a believer. During this time, the church family needs to surround the new believers with genuine love and fellowship. New converts will need to be trained to reach their loved ones without alienating them.[358]

## Emotional Traits

Another Hispanic cultural characteristic is the important role emotions play in their every day lives. Montoya describes this when he states:

> Hispanics are people of the heart... If something is not from the heart, *el corazón,* or for the heart, then it is hard to accept... All culture is permeated with what strikes the heart not the head alone... A truth wrapped in cold logic without warmth of life and emotions is not very well received.[359]

This characteristic has significant implications for church planting activities. The outreach approaches that are utilized and the type of congregations that are established need to reflect the affective as well as the cognitive dimensions of the Christian life. This was made very clear in a survey the response of Hispanics to Evangelical efforts. In describing what attracted Hispanics to Evangelical congregations Tapia makes the following assertions:

1. They have found a deep involvement with their faith and Scripture

2. Relevant worship services

3. Committed and understanding ministers

4. A laity that is as equally concerned with worship as it is with spiritual growth and a concern for others...

5. Freedom to pray and preach in the style true to their cultural background is also inviting Hispanics...

6. Sermons are practical, speaking to daily issues

7. Prayers focus on specific needs such as jobs or health...

8. The emphasis of evangelical churches on a personal relationship with God and on the fellowship of believers is an invitation for intimacy at a divine and human level.[360]

In light of these observations it is very important to make provision for cultural adaptations in the planting of Hispanic churches. Regarding worship services, the style of music and the instruments that are used should reflect the culture of the Hispanic congregation. In selecting these, a distinction should be made between the *meaning* and the *form*. The meaning of the songs should be theologically sound but there can be flexibility in the style (the form) of the music. In most instances the extent to which the worship service reflects the culture of the target group has a direct bearing on the way in which they respond to the Gospel in a church starting effort.

The sermon as well as the music in a Hispanic church should be felt as well as understood. People in Hispanic churches respond better if the sermons touch their emotions as well as their intellect. The minister, therefore, should not be afraid to show genuine emotion while he is preaching. Conveying joy, sorrow, compassion, and other emotions through the words that are utilized, facial expression, and tone of voice can help the listener feel as well as understand the thoughts that are being expressed.

The use of carefully selected illustrations can also help the listeners to comprehend and internalize the Gospel message. Sermons on key parables (e.g., the Prodigal Son), on persons whose lives were changed by Christ (e.g., the Samaritan woman), and on key events in the life of Christ (e.g., birth, miracles, death, resurrection and ascension) can establish bridges between the religious experience of Hispanics and what they need to know about a personal experience of salvation in Jesus Christ.[361]

## Hispanic Church Planting Strategies

There is a sense in which church planting in the Hispanic community has much in common with church planting in general. In all types of church planting there are basic steps to be followed. There are, however, some unique characteristics pertaining to the Hispanic community that need to be taken into account if church planting efforts are to be effective. To facilitate this discussion, we will utilize some of the key steps in David Hesselgrave's "Pauline Cycle"[362] and highlight the cultural adaptations that are needed.

## Commissioning Church Planters

In order for churches to be started, church planters need to be called by the Lord and set aside by the churches. This means that churches and potential church planters need to catch a vision of what the Lord wants them to do. Several things can contribute to this. A church can catch a vision as it studies the Bible and prays. Studying the New Testament (especially the book of Acts) will help a church arrive at the conviction that it is the will of God that new churches be started. When the church of Antioch "persevered in the study of the Word and in prayer" it caught a vision of God's will regarding its missionary work (Acts 13:2). A study of the Antioch Church itself can provide the motivation for congregations to reach out beyond their own group to other cultural groups in the community and as well as globally.

## Contacting the Target Group

Before an audience is contacted, there must be a clear understanding of its sociocultural characteristics. Some of the standard steps to accomplish this involve:

- a demographic analysis

- a religious survey

- a survey of the people in the community

### Analyzing the Target Group

A demographic analysis can be of great help to a church because it can give it an idea of the potential that there is in that community for starting a congregation. A complete analysis can include factors like: number of inhabitants; socioeconomic groups; types of housings; educational level; types of employment; and types of family structures. In addition to this, the church planter in an Hispanic setting needs to have information about the geographical origin of the various sub-cultural groups (e.g., Cuba, Puerto Rico, Mexico, Central or South America, etc), about their mode of entry into this country (annexation, immigration, refugee, etc), about their length of residence in this country (First, second, third, etc. generation), and about the language utilization of each group (Spanish, English, Bi-lingual). These factors have significant implications for the decisions that are made regarding pastoral leadership, worship styles, outreach methodologies, and congregational models.

### Finding a Person of Peace

One of the most important things to keep in mind in determining where to start a Hispanic church is the discovery of people who are receptive to the idea of starting a new church in their community. In Matthew 10 Jesus instructed his disciples to go into a city and focus on finding "a man of peace." Once they had found that person they were to remain in his home and utilize it as a base for the evangelization of the city.

Finding a person (or persons) of peace in the Hispanic community is a crucial in the strategy. The surveys that are typically utilized can provide the church planter with vital information about the community. Often, however, it is not a matter of focusing on the area with the greatest numerical concentration but on the one with the greatest spiritual receptivity. Since Hispanics place a strong emphasis on kinship and friendship ties, finding a person of peace in a community can open the door for key networks that can be very helpful in reaching people with the gospel and starting new congregations.

Church members can also catch a vision by participating in prayer walks. When they see children playing in the streets without supervision, senior adults sitting in front of their houses just passing the time of day, and young people hanging out in street corners, they return with a new vision of what their church should be doing to reach these people with the gospel. Visiting ministry points in the community can also help church members catch a vision for church planting. A church that has established hundreds of units (home Bible studies, ministry centers, and missions, especially in apartment communities) has the practice of taking key church members every Sunday to visit the house churches during the Sunday School hour.[363] They are invariably touched when they see children, young people, and adults participating in worship and Bible study and giving testimonies of how these ministries have changed their lives.

## Communicating the Gospel

Communicating the message of salvation in a way that relates to the target group is of utmost importance. The strategy church planters need to employ in Hispanic communities should be one that cultivates friendship and sows the seed of the gospel. For children and youth, Vacation Bible School, Backyard Bible Clubs, activities for recreational groups; voluntary tutors, musical and arts festivals and handcrafts can be very effective. For adults video series (especially on marriage and the family, the Jesus

Film (or video) in the homes or a public building, English as a second language, specialized classes (e.g. cooking, sewing, job training), dramas (especially on Christmas and Easter), and prayer surveys can help establish bridges for the communication of the gospel.

A personal touch is also needed in media efforts. A Hispanic church planter, for example, tried to use some of the media approaches that innovative Anglo church planters have successfully employed. He discovered that the recommended methods (direct mail, newspaper advertising, radio, TV), personalized telephone calls, home visitation, and other cultivative activities were helpful. In addition to these means, however, additional practices were needed in order to get Hispanics to respond to attend the first public service. All of these methods had been preceded by six months of Home Bible studies. Culturally appropriate communication methodologies (and the sponsoring church's patience and understanding) have contributed to the growth of this church.

## *Leading the Hearers to Conversion*

One of the most difficult concepts for non-evangelical Hispanics to understand is that of a personal relationship with Jesus Christ by grace through faith alone. This doctrine needs to be the focus of witnessing efforts in Hispanic church planting. It must be kept in mind, however, that even after they come to have an experience of salvation in Christ, due to their religious traditions, social pressures, and often limited knowledge of the Bible, it may take a while for them to understand the implications of their conversion for the vocational, financial, domestic, social, and spiritual aspects of their lives.

This fact means that discipleship must be viewed as an integral part of evangelism in Hispanic church planting efforts. Culturally relevant discipleship needs to deal with the "putting off" (previous un-biblical cultural and religious practices) as well as the "putting on" (the new Christian lifestyle) aspects of their new walk with the Lord (Col. 3:8-0). Helping Hispanics understand the implications of their conversion is essential as the group moves on toward the congregational phase.

## *Congregating the Believers*

Paul was aware that in order to disciple the converts adequately he needed to gather them together in congregations. A question that church planters ask is: What model should we follow in establishing this new congregation? In chapter 12, Dr, Bob Sena outlined the different types of churches that are needed for Hispanics in the various stages of assimilation into the dominant culture. In addition to the socio-linguistic considerations, the church planting model that is employed will have significant implications on the effectiveness of the church starting efforts. There are several models that are being utilized in the establishment of new churches.[364] There are some traditional approaches that have been utilized with a great deal of success. There are also some innovative approaches that are being employed to start the largest number of congregations possible. In this segment we shall discuss both traditional and innovative approaches.

## Traditional Church Planting Approaches

In the ministry of starting new congregations, church leaders have discovered and employed several models or approaches—all with effectives. Some models will provide inroads to some groups and other approaches will prove more effective in different circumstances. Among the more effective models for starting churches in general and among Hispanics in particular are the following.

## Model One: "Mother Church

The "Mother church — Daughter Congregation" model is a frequently used approach. A congregation can be started within the building of the Mother church or at another building. In this model the Mother church assumes responsibility for a new congregation and it watches over its financial development and doctrinal soundness. The Mother Church can be Anglo, Hispanic, or another culture and the Daughter congregation can also be among any of these cultures.[365] A weakness in this approach, however, develops if leaders insist that this is the only way and new churches cannot be started without a Mother church.

## Model Two: "Multiple Sponsorship"

The model of several churches sponsoring to a new congregation is helpful where there are few established churches that do not have sufficient finances to sponsor a congregation on their own. A possible application of this model is that of establishing a partnership between a Sponsoring Church (Anglo or other culture) and a Hispanic congregation to start a new Hispanic congregation. This has the advantage of combining financial and personnel resources in the establishment of the new congregation. Combining their resources with the expertise and personnel of an existing Hispanic church can result in the formation of an excellent church planting team.

## Innovative Church Planting Approaches

### Model Three: "Multi-Congregational"

The multi-congregational model (one church, several congregations) is especially suited for urban areas in which property is extremely expensive. These congregations, bound by a consortium agreement, can share resources (e.g., financial, personnel, building, equipment), make provision for worship services in the different languages, and plan joint activities (e.g., fellowship, Lord's supper) to stress unity in the midst of their diversity.

An adaptation of this model can be utilized in areas where Anglo (or other culture) churches come to the realization that their community is almost totally Hispanic.[366] If there is still sufficient Anglo (or other culture) membership committed to ministry in that community, starting a Hispanic congregation within the building of the existing church may be an excellent option. The degree of Hispanic assimilation and utilization of the English language will need to be considered in deciding the type of church that is needed.

### Model Four: Church Planting Movements

In his book, *Church Planting Movements: How God is Redeeming a Lost World*, David Garrison reports that a missionary strategist assigned to a North Indian people group found just 28 churches among them in 1989. By the year 2000, a church planting movement had erupted catapulting the number of churches to more than 4,500 with an estimated 300,000 believers.[367] "Each month," David Garrison asserts, "an estimated 1,200 new churches are started in Africa.[368] During the past decade in a Latin American country, despite relentless government persecution, Baptists grew from 235 churches to more than 4,000 churches with more than 30,000 converts awaiting baptism.[369] Even among "the last of the giants" (the Muslim World), amazing things are happening. Garrison reports that in an Asian Muslim country, more than 150,000 have embraced Jesus and gather in more than 3,000 locally led Jesus Groups.[370] He explains that through contextualized evangelism and the utilization of house churches "more Muslims have come to Christ in the past two decades than at any other time in history."[371]

Garrison defines a Church Planting Movement as *"A rapid and exponential increase of indigenous churches planting churches within a given people group or population segment.[372]* He explains that these are not revivals, mass evangelism, people movements, or just church planting. He states that Church Planting Movements are characterized by ten essential elements:[373]

1.. **Prayer.** Prayer is fundamental to every Church Planting Movement. It is typically the first element in a master strategy plan, and it is the vitality of the missionary's prayer life that leads to its imitation in the life of the new church and its leader.

2. **Abundant Gospel Sowing.** A Church Planting Movement does not emerge where evangelism is rare or absent. The law of the harvest applies well: *"If you sow abundantly you will also reap abundantly."*

3. **Intentional Church Planting.** In every Church Planting Movement someone implements a strategy of

deliberate church planting before the movement can get underway.

4.  **Spiritual Authority.** Church Planting Movements rest solidly on the authority of the Word of God. Even when the Bible hasn't yet been translated into the heart language, its authority is unquestioned.

5.  **Local Leaders.** In Church Planting Movements, missionaries walk alongside local believers cultivating and establishing local leadership rather than doing it themselves.

6.  **Lay Leadership.** Church Planting Movements are driven by lay leaders. These leaders are sometimes bi-vocational and always come from the general profile of the people being reached. Reliance upon lay leadership ensures the largest possible pool of potential church planters and cell church leaders.

7.  **Cell or House Churches.** In a Church Planting Movement churches begin as small reproducible cell churches of 10-30 members meeting in homes or storefronts. There are distinct advantages to utilizing house churches: 1) They help to overcomes Fears/Biases; 2) They are close by; 3) They employ a simple structure; 4) They are culturally relevant; 5) They encourages participation; 6) They develops leadership; and 7) They are easily reproduced.

8.  **Churches Planting Churches.** As CPMs enter a multiplicative phase of reproduction, the churches themselves plant new churches. Nothing disqualifies

local lay believers from winning the lost and planting new churches.

9. **Rapid Reproduction.** Rapid reproduction is evidence that the churches are unencumbered by non-essential elements and the laity are fully empowered to participate in this work of God.

10. **Healthy Churches.** Church Planting Movements consist of healthy churches carrying out the five purposes of: 1) worship 2) evangelism and missions, 3) education and discipleship, 4) ministry, and 5) fellowship.

In addition to discussing the essential elements, Garrison provides valuable information about church planting movements as he discusses common factors and gives practical advice on ways to be instrumental in starting and encouraging these movements.

In his book, *House Church Networks: A Church for a New Generation*, Larry Kreider describes what is beginning to take place in North America:

> It is happening again. A new species of church is emerging throughout North America. In major cities as well as rural areas, a unique kind of church life is peeking through like fresh growth of new crops through the surface of the soil. Hungry for community and relationships, people are learning the values of the kingdom by first-hand participation... Within the next ten to fifteen years, I believe these new house church networks will dot the landscape of North America just as they already do in other nations of the world.[374]

Daniel Sanchez, in his edited volume, *Church Planting Movements in North America,* suggests that Church Multiplication Movements might be the better term for these advances in evangelism and church starting. Sanchez has gathered information that indicates that such movements are possible, desirable, and indeed happening.

Brent S. Ray and Ebbie C. Smith concur in the use of the term, Church Multiplication Movements. These writers stress that the methods that lead to House churches, they prefer the term Basic Churches and Church Multiplication Movements, are not the only possible means of evangelism and church planting. They do call for the Christian movement to accept these practices as valid and acceptable means of furthering the Gospel.[375]

The Lord can use church planting movements here in America as well as around the world. Understanding the basic principles that contribute toward the initiation and development of church planting movements is the starting point.[376]

## *Model Six: Cell Group Churches*

The largest Hispanic churches in Latin America and in the United States are cell group churches. Several factors contribute to this. First, when it comes to the first visit, Hispanics are generally much more comfortable with the idea of going to the home of a relative or close friend than to an Evangelical church. In this sense the home becomes a bridge for the church. Second, the strong emphasis in the Hispanic culture on social relationships centering on the family and close friends lends itself for the establishment of cell groups. Third, Hispanics who have not grown up in

Evangelical homes are less accustomed to the idea of speaking in large groups of people. The home, therefore, provides a safe environment for them to ask questions and express opinions. This often leads to the development of leadership skills which are helpful in the growth and multiplication of home cell groups. Fourth, the cell group necessitates that local lay people assume leadership positions. This contributes to the involvement of more lay leaders than in other congregational models. Fifth, the cell based model does not require that significant sums of money be spent in large educational buildings. This makes it possible for congregations to experience exponential growth even if they have limited financial resources or are in settings where government authorities do not permit the construction of church buildings.

## Definition

There is a difference between churches that have cells and cell churches. Churches that have cells are essentially churches that utilize cell groups as one of its methods for evangelism and discipleship. The cell approach is just one of the methods it employs to carry out its ministry. Some of these are to some extent program-based churches. This means that they carry out their ministries through a variety of programs that have been established, such as: Sunday School, Men's programs, Women's programs, Youth programs, Children's programs, etc. In one sense, the cell is principally another one of the programs that the church employs. The cell church, on the other hand, is not a church that uses cells but the cells are the church. While they have times in which all the cells gather for celebration, the main functions of the church are carried out in the cells.

## Proponents of Cell Group Strategies

*Paul Yonggi Cho*

Perhaps one of the earliest modern day proponents of cell group strategies was Dr. Paul Yonggi Cho, pastor of the Full Gospel Central Church in Seoul, Korea. In his book, *Successful Home Cell Groups*, Dr. Cho shares his spiritual pilgrimage of being seriously ill, intensely studying the book of Acts, and arriving at a strategy that involved utilizing the laity in their homes for evangelistic, discipleship, and nurturing ministries. He states:

> Generally the idea began to form in my mind: Suppose I release my deacons to open their homes as house churches. Suppose they taught the people, prayed for them to be healed and helped them, and suppose the people helped one another in the same way in those home cell groups. The church would flourish in the homes, and the members could even evangelize by inviting their friends and neighbors to the meetings. Then on Sunday they could bring them to the church building for the worship service. That would exempt me from laboring in visiting and counseling, and other such time-consuming work. I would be free to be the pastor – to teach and preach and equip the lay leaders for ministry.[377]

In this brief paragraph Dr. Cho encapsulates the principal concepts related to cell groups. These are small groups that meet in homes (or other places) for the purpose of evangelizing, discipling, nurturing, ministering, mutual accountability, and prayer. The manner in which these groups carry out their activities will vary significantly from one culture to another. The important thing is to focus on the principles that are employed and to apply them in a contextualized manner to the different cultural settings.

*Ralph Neighbour*

On the American scene, one of the most effective and enthusiastic cell group proponents is Ralph Neighbor. He affirms that here is a radical difference between a church that uses small groups and a cell church. The first incorporates cells into its programs, drawn from its tradition. The second builds its ecclesiology on New Testament principles. In a church that has cells, the cells are just one of its programs. In a cell church, the cell is the church.[378]

He explains that there are three functions and three structures that characterize cell churches: 1) Community: the cell group; 2) Celebration: all the cell groups; 3) Coordination: cell groups clustered by "congregations," or "sub-zones."

Neighbour explains that every task of the church is realized through the basic Christian community, the cell. All the church does, it does through these units. He then describes the characteristics of cell life: 1) Intimate: helping one another; 2) Mouth to ear, modeling, personal values shaped; 3) Used to build up others in the cell group gathering; 4) Models the life of the believers; 5) Servants are developed in cells; 6) They are tested and set apart; 7) There is heavy emphasis on prayer & fasting; 8) They apply Scriptures to needs and relationships; 9) Cell members build up one another and people are placed in communities ministering to others which results in total servanthood and stewardship. Neighbor concludes that the key phrase of cell groups is "go and make disciples."

Neighbour basis his cell group strategy on the theological conviction that there are always those who are called out to serve in a more radical way as well as to lead and "rule" (Scripture's word) in the assemblies of the believers, *but we are all capable of having a full relationship with God and of passing that on to others"* (Italics mine).

*Other Proponents*

Other proponents of the cell group approach include such persons as Rick Warren with his Purpose Driven Church approach Dale E Galloway who designed his 20/20 Vision[379] strategy and numerous others in different parts of the world.

In reviewing the various models for implementing cell group approaches, a word of caution is warranted. Those who are tempted to transplant exact replicas of models that have been used elsewhere are usually going to fail in their attempts. The reason for this is that cultural, doctrinal, leadership style, and even personality differences must be taken into account.

For example, many who tried to transplant Dr. Cho's model to America found out that there are significant differences between the Korean and the American cultures which militate against a total acceptance by the people in America. Contextualized models, therefore, need to be designed for the various cultural settings in which cell group strategies are going to be utilizes.

# Methodological Implications of Hispanic Church Planting

Due to the continued influx from Latin America, Spanish speaking churches will continue to be needed in the future. We need to remember that half of the population increase of Hispanic Americans was due to immigration. We also need to be aware that as soon as their children start watching television and going to school they will begin to experience the acculturation process.

The fact that Hispanic Americans are becoming more culturally pluralistic does not mean that they are abandoning their cultural values. Hispanic churches will need to take this into account in their worship, fellowship, leadership, and organizational patterns. In other words these churches will need to reflect the cultural blends of their members.

Hispanic churches will need to be cross-generational churches. Due to the fact that the family continues to be such an important factor in the lives of Hispanic Americans, the churches they attend will need to make provision for the parents, the children, and for the grandparents who may not be fluent in English. Some churches have opted for having two services, one in English the other in Spanish.

Anglo churches wishing to reach Hispanic Americans in large numbers will need to adapt some of their worship, fellowship, and leadership patterns. They will need to be willing to incorporate some of the cultural elements of Hispanic Americans in the life of the church, thus enriching the fellowship and helping everyone to feel culturally as well as spiritually at home.

Due to the explosive growth and unprecedented expansion of the Hispanic population in America strategies for exponential church multiplication are needed. While we want to affirm any type of biblically-sound church start among Hispanics, it stands to reason that unless we use rapidly multiplying church planting strategies, we are going to fall further and further behind in leading Hispanics to a personal faith in Christ and discipling them in biblically-sound culturally-contextualized congregations.

In a *Christianity Today* entitled: *"Viva Los Evangélicos,"* Andres Tapia states that "U. S. Hispanics are the fastest growing segment of the Protestant Church."[380] It adds that if it had not been for Hispanic growth some denominations would not have shown any growth in the past decade.[381] While we thank the Lord that many Hispanics are coming to have a personal experience of salvation in Jesus Christ, we can obviously do *much more* to reach the millions who have not been born again.

Hispanic church planting is one of the greatest and most exciting challenges Evangelicals face today. In this chapter we have discussed the importance of establishing a solid biblical foundation, the need to understand the cultural characteristics and the value of utilizing culturally relevant strategies in starting churches among Hispanics. The explosive growth of the Hispanic community gives us an unprecedented opportunity to start thousands of churches among them in this new century. May God help us to respond to this challenge? In the next chapter we are going to discuss how to enable Hispanic churches to grow and become more effective in ministering to their communities.

# CHAPTER 18
*Starting Hispanic Churches*

## Endnotes

[344] The Reverend Andrew M. Greeley, "Defection Among Hispanics" (Updated), *America, (September, 27, 1997), 12-13.*

[345] This chapter is an expansion of a chapter I wrote entitled, "Starting Churches in the Hispanic Community," in Richard H. Harris, ed., *Reaching a Nation Through Church Planting*, Alpharetta: North American Mission Board, 2002.

[346] See, Andrés Tapia, "Viva Los Evangélicos," *Christianity Today* (October 28, 1991),18, and Rodolpho Carrasco, "Reaching out to Latinos," *Christianity Today,* (September 6, 1999), 32-36.

[347] Brook Larmer, "Society," *Newsweek,* (July 12, 1999), 48.

[348] See Paul G. Hiebert, *Anthropological Insights for Missionaries* (Grand Rapids: Baker Book House, 1985). Tom A. Steffen, *Passing The Baton* (La Habra: Center for Organizational & Ministry Development, 1993).

[349] Charles L. Chaney, *Church Planting at the End of the Twentieth Century* (Wheaton: Tyndale house Publishers, Inc., 1991), 133-34.

[350] R.C.H. Lenski, *The Interpretation Of St. Matthew's Gospel* (Minneapolis: Augsburg Publishing House, 1961), 1173.

[351] Daniel R. Sanchez, Ebbie C. Smith, and Curtis E. Watke, *Starting Reproduction Congregation: A Gudebook for Contextual New Church Development* (Ft. Worth: Church Starting Network, 2001), 28-30.

352Thom Hopler, *A World of Difference* (Downers Grove: Inter Varsity Press, 1981), 109, points  out that Simeon was Black, Lucius was Greek and Manaen was Jewish.

[353] For more information see Daniel R. Sanchez, Rudolf Gonzalez, *Sharing The Good News With Roman Catholic Friends*, 2004, Church Starting Network, , The Spanish version is *Cómo Testificar a Sus Amigos Católicos* (El Paso:Casa Bautista de Publicaciones, 1998).

[354] See Daniel R. Sanchez, Rudolf Gonzalez, *Sharing The Good News With Roman Catholic Friends*, 2004, Church Starting Network, This an adaptation of the process described by David Hesselgrave, in *Planting Churches Cross-culturally* (Grand Rapids: Baker Books, 2000).

[355] For other cultivative ideas see Steve Sjogren, *Conspiracy of Kindness (Ann Arbor: Servant  Publications, 1993).*

[356] David Garrison, *Church Planting Movements,* (Richmond: International Mission Board, n,d,), 11-16. . For especially designed Bible Studies in Spanish see, Daniel R. Sanchez and Jorge Pastor, *Evangelicemos a Nuestros Amigos* (Birmingham: Woman's Missionary Union, 2000). For bi-lingual materials see Ted Lindwall, *ROCks and Friendship Groups,* (Church Starts International, P.O. Box, 177, Henrietta, Texas, 76365). Also see Charles Brock, *I Have Been Born Again, What Next?* Church Growth International, P. O. Box 428C, Neosho, Missouri.

[357] Alex D. Montoya, *Hispanic Ministry in North America (Grand Rapids: Zondervan, 1987),* 14,15.

[358] Don Wilkerson, *Bring Your Loved Ones To Christ (*Old Tappan: Fleming

261

H. Revell, 1979).

[359] Alex D. Montoya, *Hispanic Ministry in North America* (Grand Rapids: Zondervan Publishing House, 1987), 18.

[360] Andrés Tapia, "Viva Los Evangélicos," *Christianity Today* (October 28, 1991),19-21.

[361] For a more complete discussion see Daniel R. Sanchez, "Preparing for a Revival Meeting in an Hispanic Church,@ in Dan R. Crawford, *Before Revival Begins,* (Fort Worth: Scripta Publishing Inc., 1996), 111-121.

[362] David Hesselgrave, *Planting Churches Cross-Culturally* (Grand Rapids: Baker Book House, 1980).

[363] Erma Holt Mathis, *The Mission Arlington Story: Tillie's Vision* (Forth Worth: Scripta Publishing Inc., 1996).

[364] For a more extensive discussion on church planting models see, Daniel R. Sanchez, Curt Watke, Ebbie Smith, *Starting Reproducing Congregations* (ChurchStartingDotCom: Forthcoming Publication).

[365] See J Timothy Ahlen and J.V. Thomas, *One Church, Many Congregations (Nashville: Abingdon Press, 1999).*

[366] For more information see, 444. Harvey Kneisel, *New Life for Declining Churches* (Houston: Macedonian Call Foundation, 1995).

[367] David Garrison, *Church Planting Movements: How God is Redeeming a Lost World,* Richmond: WIG Take Resources, 2004, 17

[368] Ibid.,

[369] Ibid.,

[370] Ibid.,

[371] Ibid.,

[372] David Garrison, *Church Planting Movements* (Richmond: International Mission Board, n.d.), 7.

[373] Ibid., 33-36.

[374] Larry Krieder, *House Church Networks: A church for a new generation, Ephrata, PA: House to House Publications, 2001, 2.*

[375] Brent S. Ray and Ebbie C. Smith, Basic Churches are Real Churches: Biblical Support for Simple Churches, Organic Churches, House Churches and Congregations That Grow Out Of Church Multiplication Movements (Ft. Worth: Church Starting Network, 2006), 14.

[376] See Rad Zdero, *The Global House Church Movement, Pasadena: William Carey Library, 2004.*

[377] Paul Yonggi Cho, *Successful Home Cell Groups*, South Plainfield, NJ: Bridge Publishing Inc., 1981, 19

[378] Ralph Neighbour, TOUCH Outreach Ministries Inc., Power Point presentations, 2003.

[379] Dale E. Galloway, *20/20 Vision: How To Create A Successful Church With Lay Pastors and Cell Groups,* Portland: Scott Publishing Company, 1986,

[380] Tapia, op. cit., p. 18.

[381] Ibid., p. 20.

# Chapter 19

# Church Growth Among Hispanics

After a church has been established, one of the most challenging tasks is to lead the congregation to continue to grow. Since this book focuses on Hispanic church starting, it is instructive to study the growth factors of existing Hispanic churches. Recently a study of ten of the fastest growing Hispanic churches in Texas was conducted by two of the authors of this book, Drs. Daniel Sanchez and Ebbie Smith. The study utilized four sources of information: (1) a demographic analysis; (2) a statistical analysis (from the Associational Annual Letter); (3) a survey of the pastor and key members; and (4) an on-site visit by a staff member of Scarborough Institute.[382]

The comparative analysis of the reports, the interviews, and the findings of the on-site visits to the churches revealed several commonalities in these congregations that seem to have contributed to their growth. In addition to the growth criterion, attention was given to geographical areas in the selection of these churches. The authors of this report fully understand that church growth is solely the result of the Holy Spirit's action. They also understand that the Spirit works through various strategies, circumstances, and methods. While many different growth-enhancing factors surfaced in this study, we include in this report the most significant factors which appeared to contribute more directly to the growth of these congregations.

## Pastoral Leadership

This survey confirmed a long-standing principle of church growth: "Pastoral leadership is the key, or at least a key, to the growth of any church." This survey confirmed the importance of pastoral leadership for church growth and indicted that this general church-growth principle operates in Hispanic churches as well as others. It was obvious that these pastors of growing Hispanic churches have several characteristics in common.

## *Pastors Have a Vision for Growth*

Invariably, these pastors, in one way or another, gave evidence of having a clear vision for the growth of the church and a willingness to pay the price for realizing this growth. Each of them, while expressing gratitude for the growth he is experiencing, also indicated that present growth was only scratching the surface of what could be done. No one among these pastors was satisfied with the present accomplishments of the church.

The pastors' visions are clearly recognized and expressed through the church membership. The church that featured the goal of 1000 by 2000 demonstrates the overriding presence of and importance for such expressed vision. Further, the pastor's vision has been shared with the congregation and adopted by the people.

All of the pastors clearly demonstrated a burden for Hispanics in their communities and dreamed of the day when many more of them can be reached and discipled with the Gospel in Hispanic congregations. Several of them have a vision for reaching their entire communities (all of the cultural groups) and are making provision for this by having English as well as Spanish-speaking services

All of the pastors want their churches to grow but are convinced that they will grow with the Lord's help. They demonstrate extreme optimism about the future of the churches that they are pastoring. They are aware of the challenges and obstacles that they face. These leaders do not, however, spend time lamenting these obstacles, but center on the opportunities before them and their congregations.

These convictions of optimism and vision were clearly stated by the pastors. One pastor said: "We want our church to impact our city with the Gospel of Jesus Christ. When Anglos ask what should be done to prepare our city for the future, we want them to look at our church and use it as a model." Another pastor stated: "We don't want to be important but we want to have a Christian influence in our city and our state." Further, another leader exclaimed, "We, I mean the members and myself, believe the Lord will continue to bless us with growth among the Hispanic population of our city." One member said of his pastor: "Our pastor is always setting goals. He is never satisfied with what we have accomplished in the past."

Vision held, expressed, and shared was almost universally evidenced by the pastors of these growing churches.

## *Pastors Are Willing to Exercise Leadership*

The pastors of these growing churches shared their basic convictions that it is *the pastor's responsibility to provide strong leadership in order for the church to reach its full potential.* They see aggressive, servant leadership as the divinely intended method for leading churches. When given the choice of the type of leadership that the pastor should exercise, all of them selected "very strong and direct" over "by persuasion" or "simply following the will of the church."

It is important to note that these pastors do not see themselves as being autocratic and dictatorial. Instead, they see themselves as motivators. Once they have received a vision, they concentrate on communicating it to the membership and challenging the people to become a part of this vision. They believe in this way the vision will become a reality in their church.

While holding to the necessity of strong pastoral leadership, these pastors provide, in one form or another, opportunity for the leaders of the church to be involved in the decision-making process. They believe this shared leadership strategy to be the primary pattern of pastoral leadership.

## Pastors Have a Commitment to Stay With the Church A Long Time

All of the pastors indicated that they had made a commitment to stay with the church an extended time. They stated their commitment to stay in their churches in the following manner: "until the Lord says," "this is the only church I plan to pastor," "until the Lord comes," "I have no plans elsewhere." One pastor declared his intention to remain with his church until the year 2000 AD. It is important to note that none of the pastors interviewed saw their present church as a stepping stone for pastoring larger churches. Each of them felt his present place of service to be the place the Lord wants him and are excited and challenged by the opportunity to serve that particular congregation. While some of the pastors are relatively new in their present pastorates (their average length of tenure is 8 years), they all voice a desire to remain in their present position for many years to come.

## *Pastors Have Learned Managerial Skills*

Another quality that was evident in the pastors of the congregations studied was their ability to manage the work of the church. While some of them had received studies in leadership methods in connection with their theological training, most of them developed their managerial skills in connection with their secular jobs. Some have extensive experience in military service, others in the business world, and still others through individual study and personal experience. These managerial skills are evident in the way in which they organize and manage the activities of the church. This involves the utilization of training and materials that are available through the denomination and the willingness and creativity to develop new structures and new approaches to carry on the work of the church. In the interviews with these pastors it became evident that they had a clear understanding of the goals of the church and also the abilities to organize, train, and lead the members to reach these goals. The importance of their experience in the work-a-day world seems to have enhanced these leadership and management skills now used in the leadership of the church.

## *Pastors Are Willing To Take Risks*

In the pastor's surveys, most of the men indicated that they were willing to take either moderate or major risks in seeking to carry out the work of the church. In the interviews with these pastors, it became evident that these pastors did not take risks for the sake of doing it. Instead, they sought the leadership of the Lord and then were willing to venture out in faith to do what they felt the Lord wanted their church to accomplish. Some risks related to their own personal lives such as quitting a part-time job and dedicating their full time to the work of the church even when it was not completely clear that the finances for their support would be there. Other risks involved leading their congregations to adopt seemingly unattainable plans for outreach and growth. Still other risks involved changing the structure and programs of the church in order to become more effective. This risk can be seen in the willingness to change the style of worship and in the willingness to merge with another church to strengthen the ministry of both congregations. Several of the pastors are implementing far-reaching plans for buildings and other needed equipment. In the opinion of the survey team, this willingness to venture out in faith stimulates the growth of these congregations.

## Positive Response to Change

A second factor in the growth of these ten churches indicates that these churches have positive responses to change. Instead of feeling threatened by the social, economic, and political changes that surround them or spending all of their time trying to hold on to "the way we used to do things," these churches have found ways to accept the challenge of change and design approaches to help them reach and disciple people in new ways. The changes to which these churches have and are responding include the following:

## *Change: From Surviving To Thriving*

Many Hispanics have climbed from the lower rungs of the economic ladder. Some have experienced the Great Depression. These and other experiences have caused some Hispanics, especially the middle-aged, to develop a survival mind-set. Having paid for their homes at great sacrifice, they have dedicated themselves to maintaining the gains they have made. Some carry this attitude to the church. If their church building is paid for or within reach, they resist plans to assume the risk of branching out and enlarging their building, building another one, or moving to another geographical location.

The same is true of their attitude toward the budgeting of outreach programs for the church and the addition of other church staff positions. If they are reaching the budget and staying out of debt, they opt to play it safe and not take risks. This unwillingness to take risk greatly inhibits the growth potential of their churches. It leads to a maintenance ministry rather than to an aggressive outreach strategy.

Pastors who are able to challenge and guide their people to move from a surviving to a thriving mentality usually experience significant growth in the congregations. Achieving this paradigm change is, however, a major challenge. One pastor who led his congregation to sell their small, paid-up building and purchase a larger building in a more accessible location stated: "The Lord doesn't think of minimums. Filling the building is not enough; you have to change the mindset of the people." Another pastor said: "I try to convince my people that we can be as effective as the best Anglo churches and this includes buildings, programs, and staff." One church actually both moved and merged with an Anglo congregation—showing the willingness of both pastor and people to take risks.

Churches that are growing, therefore, are those that have a mindset (a vision) of what the Lord wants them to do in their communities and are willing to live in the faith dimension as they make the necessary commitments, sacrifices, and changes to turn their vision into reality.

## *Change:  From Mono-cultural To Multi-cultural*

All of the churches that were studied are aware of the sociological changes that are taking place within the Hispanic community and are willing to make the necessary changes to reach as many segments of this community as possible. Interviews with the pastors and church leaders revealed that these churches understand that Hispanics are now found in several stages of assimilation. Some of these Hispanics are recent arrivals and need to hear the Gospel and to worship in Spanish. Some, however, have been here for at least two generations and are bilingual. Still others have been here longer and hardly understand Spanish but are fully fluent in English. All of the churches studied showed an awareness of this cultural diversity as well as a willingness to adapt their approach in order to reach these cultures.

*Church Growth Among Hispanics*

The approaches utilized by the churches in this study varied significantly. All churches have bilingual Sunday Schools in which some classes are taught in Spanish, others in English, and still others in both languages. The differences between these churches were more marked in their worship services. Some churches hold bilingual worship services in which the songs, announcements, testimonies, etc. were done bilingually. When it came to the sermon, some pastors preached bilingually (interpreting for themselves). Other pastors preached in either English or Spanish but had made provision for the people to hear a translation of the sermon through the use of head-sets. This saved the amount of time that otherwise it would take for the pastor (or someone else) to interpret the message from the pulpit. Other churches are bilingual in the sense that they have two Sunday morning services (one in English, the other in Spanish). Some of the churches that do this have a bilingual service on Sunday and nights to keep from developing two distinct congregations.

The different stages of cultural assimilation at which people find themselves and the linguistic capabilities of the pastor (and the staff) are factors which need to be taken into account in determining the approach that a particular church needs to take. The most important factor, however, is that *the pastor and the members of the church need to be committed to the fact that the primary purpose of the church is to communicate the Gospel and not to preserve the culture.* In most instances culture is an instrument for the communication of the Gospel, but churches that refuse to make changes in order to reach the various segments of the Hispanic community (especially the young people), end up being one-generation churches. In other words, these churches lose their young people.

## Dynamic Worship Services

A third factor in the growth of these churches relates to the worship services involving the entire persons of the members. Significant variety exists in the format of the growing churches studied. There was one common denominator: *The worship services involve the total personality of the members.* This is seen in the fact that these worship services are culturally relevant and that they lean toward being innovative instead of being strictly traditional.

## *Culturally Relevant Worship Service*

A factor that appears to be constant is that these services engage the total personality of the worshipers. There is a strong cognitive element (focusing on content) in that the format is well planned, attention is given to Bible reading, and the sermons convey biblical concepts clearly. At the same time there is a deep emotional quality in their singing, preaching, testimonies, prayers, and fellowship. In other words, people in these churches cultivate a strong sense of the presence of the Lord in the worship service and express it in a way that people feel comfortable.

Some of the expressions that are used to describe these services are: "dynamic, exciting, enthusiastic, great expectation, a service where healing takes place, genuine praise, much prayer, people sense the presence of God in a special way, genuine fellowship is experienced, people are not in a hurry to conclude the service and leave and we seek to meet the needs of all the people."

## *Innovative Worship*

Growing Hispanic churches in general demonstrated a positive willingness to engage in innovative worship. Traditional elements were not totally replaced but innovative means began to predominate. Innovative worship certainly had a central place in growing Hispanic Churches. The worship patterns are clearly visible in several areas.

### Music

Significant variety in the music is utilized in the churches that were studied. The format ranges from moderately blended (which utilizes hymns as well as choruses) to significantly innovative (which utilizes mainly choruses). One of the surprises that the survey team encountered was that the music was not necessarily typically Latin (or Hispanic). While some of the songs did have a Latin flavor, by and large, most of the songs (especially the choruses) were of the *contemporary praise type*. This may be indicative of a degree of assimilation into the Anglo culture or perhaps of greater availability of this type of music to these congregations.

### Instruments

In keeping with the utilization of praise music, more than half of the churches studied utilized guitars, drums, keyboards, and other instruments in addition to the piano and the organ. The volume of the music was not excessively loud as in the case of some charismatic churches. The utilization of additional instruments seems to contribute to the involvement of the people in the worship service. In most instances there was a joyful, celebrative mood during the worship service.

## Praise Teams

The majority of the churches studied did not have a choir. Instead, these churches had a praise team which assisted the Music Director in leading the music. These praise teams usually consist of 4 to 8 persons who stand with the music leader and sing the congregational songs as well as the special music.

As was true of the instruments, the praise team seemed to contribute to a greater degree of involvement on the part of the congregation. Some of the pastors indicated that often it is difficult to have a choir in their churches due to the multiplicity of activities that they have. A praise team appears to give them the option of having a group that contributes to the worship service without involving a large number of people or needing to have an almost professionally trained music director.

## Preaching

A wide variety of preaching styles can be found in the churches that were studied. Some pastors utilized an expository (verse by verse) approach to preaching. Most of them, however, utilized a more topical approach. In most cases, however, the sermons focused on the needs of the people. This was evident not only in the application of the biblical material but also in the illustrations that were used.

While a wide variety of preaching styles was utilized, there appeared to be one constant factor: *the sermons had a redemptive, positive note.* Instead of focusing on what people have done wrong or how bad things are, these sermons focused on the positive ways in which people can live their Christian lives, achieve effectiveness in their work, and make a contribution to the work of the Lord. In other words, people were encouraged and inspired to keep growing in their Christian faith. One member explained, "The authoritative Word of God is being preached in a clear manner and we are being nurtured by it."

Another factor that these sermons had in common was that they were inspiring and emotional. This was especially evident in the illustrations that were utilized and the way in which the pastors communicated. Many of the illustrations were taken from the daily lives of the people and this helped the people to identify with the message.

## Perennial Evangelism

A fourth factor in the activities of these growing churches relates to a sustained program of evangelism. Even though the methods which are utilized vary extensively, they have one thing in common: *The members are trained and utilized in a consistent program of evangelism.* In other words, there is a commitment to be involved in evangelism on the part of both the *pastor* and the *members*. These churches invest time, personnel, and money in their evangelistic outreach. They give evangelism a high priority. Evangelism is not left up to chance; it is an *intentional activity* of the church. Some methods are more fruitful in one community than in another, and perhaps better fit the lifestyles of the members. But a major factor for their success is the *continuous involvement of the members.*

The following were some of the evangelism methods most used by the churches that were surveyed.

## *Personal Evangelism*

All of the churches that were surveyed have a sustained program of personal evangelism. The methods that they employ for personal evangelism, however, vary significantly. Perhaps the primary factor here is the concept of sustained rather than from time-to-time.

## *Door-To-Door Witnessing*

Some but not all the churches employed the method of door-to-door visitation and witnessing. One church, for instance, engages in door-to-door witnessing every Saturday morning. They have carried out this method consistently for close to 20 years. The church experiences public professions of faith almost every Sunday. This church has often led the Hispanic churches in the state in baptisms. A group of people gets together in the church building every Saturday morning, spends time in prayer, and then goes out to a targeted neighborhood to visit. The members of the team basically knock on doors, talk with the people, share their testimonies, read a brief track, invite people to receive Christ, and then pray with them. The team visits the same neighborhood for three Saturdays in a row. First, they talk with those who made a decision for Christ the previous Saturday. Second, they visit those who were receptive but did not make a profession of faith. Finally, they visit people that they missed on the previous visits. On each visit the people are invited to church and efforts are made to develop friendships with the people. The pastor told the survey team that a large percentage of the professions of faith and baptisms come from the people that they visit on Saturdays.

## *Friendship (Relational) Evangelism*

Another church, on the other hand, involves its members in Friendship (relationship) Evangelism. The members of this church go out of their way to make friends at work and in their communities. This is done on a consistent basis as a life style. The members are then encouraged to involve their friends in cultivative activities such as picnics, viewing special sports events on television, and establishing support groups in their homes. This foundation then leads to the establishment of Home Bible Fellowships. Many of the people who are reached are professional and white collar workers. Quite likely this higher socioeconomic group responds more favorably to friendship evangelism than to house-to-house visitation. The pastor of one church explains: "Ours is known as a 'fun church' more of a family church. We try to be a fun people away from the church building and this attracts people to the Gospel."

## *Ministry Evangelism*

Under girding all of the evangelism of the churches that were studied in this survey is a commitment to practice ministry evangelism. This type of evangelism takes many forms. One church, for example, has a group of women on call to prepare meals for people who have lost loved ones. Upon hearing of the death of a person in their community, the women immediately call one another and decide who is going to take the food. This often has led the families of the deceased to request that the funeral be conducted in the church offering them this ministry. As a result of this, many people have been converted to the Lord.

Other ministries include a food pantry, a clothing closet, and referrals to helping agencies. One church has a well-developed food distribution program for people who live in the immediate neighborhood of the church building. Some churches have highly organized ministries such as an Academy (elementary through high school). The significant thing about these ministries is that they not only target physical or educational needs but seek to lead people to Christ. Many professions of faith are reported in these churches annually as a result of these types of ministry evangelism.

## Public Evangelism

### *Cultivative Events*

Most of the churches that were surveyed utilize cultivative events as a form of public evangelism. Many of these have dramas, musical presentations, and social gatherings. These churches also utilize the major Christian celebrations as outreach events. Celebrations related to Christmas, Easter, and Thanksgiving are times in which they invite many of their friends and neighbors. Other churches also utilize some of the cultural events as a means of outreach. Special celebrations such as the 15th birthday of the young ladies are times in which family and friends are invited. One church does a banquet for all of the graduating Hispanic students in their city. These are seen as excellent outreach opportunities.

Some churches utilize recreational events such as baseball, football, and volleyball to get acquainted with new people.

The pastor of one church states: "We have men that really care and are willing to serve as coaches. They spend time with the kids and young people and share the Gospel with them."

## Revival Meetings

The majority of the churches that were surveyed utilized revival meetings more as a time of harvest than a time for seed sowing. In other words, these churches utilize their cultivative events to establish friendships and sow the seed of the gospel. By the time friends and neighbors are invited to a revival meeting they have already had an opportunity to hear a Christian testimony and perhaps a Gospel presentation.

## The Persons Evangelized

An important factor in the evangelistic efforts of these churches relates to the persons evangelized. The survey team found that for close to 30% (29.85%) of the members their current church was their only church experience, 27.16% came from other Baptist churches and 42.98% converted from another denomination. Of the members who converted, 58.87% were previously Catholic.

## Provision for Small Groups

A fifth factor in the growth of these churches involves the tendency to provide for small group ministries. A significant number of the churches in this survey have in one way or another made provision for small groups. These are groups that meet not only during Sunday School or Church Training but during the week in the communities where the members live.

## *Small Group Evangelism*

Evangelism is conducted in small groups. Some of these groups are Home Bible Fellowships which the churches use for evangelistic outreach. The pastors and members of these churches stated that often people with a Roman Catholic background are reluctant to attend a "Protestant Church," but are willing to attend a neighborhood Bible Study. Often this small group experience becomes the bridge to relate the people to Evangelical churches.

## *Small Group Discipleship*

Most of the churches studied also use Small Groups for discipleship. Some churches are using small groups for new convert training in preparation for baptism. The pastor of one of the churches surveyed stated that their church is reaching so many new people that he is having to supplement his Wednesday night discipleship training with Home Cell Discipleship under the direction of the deacons whom he has trained for this purpose. Whether it is at church, in the homes, or at work, the churches studied in this survey are setting aside time, financial resources, and personnel to train new converts and lead church members to a deeper form of discipleship.

## Assimilation of New Members

A sixth factor in the growth of these ten churches includes plans to welcome guests and assimilate new members. A great deal of attention is given to guests from among the unchurched in these congregations. In addition to having a special place for guests' parking and greeting them in the services, members go out of their way to visit guests and encourage them to return. In one church, the pastor and the members try to make one contact a day with each of the guests for the first week after they have visited the church. In another church the pastor does not call them "visitors" in the worship service but "guests." He encourages church members to get acquainted before the service and to sit with them and to introduce them as "guests" during the service. Often in follow up, the members will visit the homes of the "guests" and take cookies as an expression of their gratitude for attending the worship service. *A recent publication indicates that Mainline churches will decline unless they welcome strangers.*[383]

In addition to making guests welcome, these churches make an effort to incorporate the new comers into the life of the church. Some do it through the New Converts' class, others through one-on-one discipleship, still others through home cell groups. The important thing is that they take an interest in making sure that new comers become a part of at least one of the fellowship groups of the church. This involves not just receiving them into the fellowship of the church but finding a place of ministry for them as soon as possible.

One pastor stated: "Our fellowship groups have helped us to close the back door of our church. We were getting many persons who visited our church, made a profession of faith, and then were gone after a brief period of time. They were just not becoming a part of the fellowship of the church even though they were a part of the membership." One member explained: "The love and warmth of the fellowship of our church is very real and people who visit want to become a part of it."

This is supported by a study done by Patrick Chaffered which indicates growing churches invite strangers, make strangers feel welcome, and find ways to include outsiders in the activities of the church. He explains that churches cannot include strangers unless they recognize that the church is not their private family property "but God's house, where God is the host and we are all strangers together."[384] This may be one clue as to why some small Hispanic churches appear to be composed of one family or a small group of families for long periods of time. A feeling that a church is a "private family property" may keep many others from attending and joining. Growing Hispanic churches, therefore, work constantly at the task of inviting guests, helping them to feel welcome, and making every effort to incorporate them into the life of the church.

## A Clear Discipleship Plan

These growing churches demonstrate a strong emphasis on discipleship. One church utilizes Sunday School and Church Training for discipleship. They supplement existing Sunday School and Church Training quarterlies with special materials such as Experiencing God, Parenting, etc. This strong commitment to discipleship is carried out in several ways: (1) one on one discipleship, (2) discipleship in home cell groups, and (3) discipleship through mid-week Bible studies.

One pastor stated that the need to disciple new converts was so great that he was using all three methods simultaneously. Yet another discipleship method that is being used is that of putting new members to work immediately under the guidance of a mature Christian. A lay person commented: "It is amazing how quickly people learn when they have an opportunity to be involved in a ministry of the church." They introduced us to a couple that had previously been very active in the Roman Catholic church. Upon their conversion, they were immediately asked to help with the audio-cassette ministry of the church. This couple has grown spiritually and has found a great deal of satisfaction in being involved in such an important ministry. One thing was evident in these churches: *they did not simply depend on an outside source to supply their discipleship materials. They determined what the needs were and set out to get the training and the materials to start an effective discipleship program.*

The survey of the members of the churches revealed a very high level of satisfaction registered in connection with the Bible Study Programs. The members indicated they are very satisfied with Bible study to the degree of 56.53% and satisfied to the degree of 42.25%. These data indicate a high level of satisfaction but the percentages are a little lower than seen for worship services, preaching, and music. Do these data indicate an area of possible improvement in the ministries of these rapidly growing churches?

## A Workable Approach to Church Governance

The growing churches demonstrate a workable approach to church planning, organization, and governance. The study revealed some variation in the way these churches are governed. This was evident in leadership styles, organization, and frequency of business meetings.

### Leadership Style

In the surveys as well as in the interviews, it became very evident that the members of these growing churches were very convinced that *the pastor needs to provide strong leadership if the church is going to grow.* At first sight it might appear as though this meant that these pastors utilized an autocratic leadership style, but this was not necessarily the case. All of the pastors involve a group of leaders in the church (deacons, church council, other) in developing the vision for growth and in implementing it through their participation in the various ministries of the church.

It was evident in the interviews of the church leaders that they had a *high degree of confidence in the pastor's leadership abilities.* This confidence is the result of the way in which the pastors related to the people and the manner in which they have led them. The deacons in one church told us: "There is nothing we would not do for our pastor. He has shown us that he is truly committed to the Lord, is willing to sacrifice, and is committed to our spiritual development." Another way of saying this is that *the pastors of these churches have been able to communicate their vision for growth and have involved the leadership in developing a sense of ownership of this vision and a commitment to implementing it in their communities, for the glory of God.*

## *Business Meetings*

Several things became evident as a result of this study. *These churches have found a way of avoiding over attention to maintenance details of church governance and have focused on the activities that will help them to grow.* Patrick Chaffered points out that in non-growing churches, 35-40% of the time is given to governance and mediating structures while growing churches give only 10 to 20% of their programs to "mediating structures," that is, to committees and business meetings.[385] This was seen in several ways.

The majority of these churches have a quarterly, not a monthly, business meeting. While they keep the church members informed at all times, the pastors of these churches believe that it is too time consuming and distracting to dedicate an entire mid-week service every month to a business meeting attended by a small minority of the members of the congregation. One pastor commented, "We have so much in terms of discipline our people that we do not want to spend an excessive amount of time giving attention to minute details and short-term reports."

Many of these pastors meet and plan with the Church Council on a monthly basis. The Church Council, in turn, reports to the church in regular quarterly business meetings. A few of these churches have only an annual business meeting in which they give detailed reports to the church and seek a vote of confidence from the church for the following year. *It appears that these churches do not focus on how all of the individual organizations are doing on a monthly basis. Instead, their focus is on their overall goals and how the organizations are contributing to the attainment of these goals.*

When it comes to describing the organization of these churches, it can be stated that they are more centered on *ministry* than on *administration*. The deacons and the church council members are viewed as ministers and not as administrators.

Another thing that is apparent in these churches is that, while they are significantly loyal to their denomination, they do not confine their activities to those sponsored by the official organizations (e.g., Lifeway). In other words, these churches are willing to utilize all that is useful to them from these organizations but they are willing to find (or develop) additional approaches and materials to help them to accomplish their evangelistic, discipleship and missionary goals.

## A Vibrant Prayer Ministry

Most of the growing churches have a vibrant prayer ministry. They hold prayer meetings in homes during the week in addition to the regular prayer meeting at the church on Wednesdays. Many churches utilize prayer partners. "People pray every day." One of the churches that is experiencing the greatest growth opens its doors for prayer every morning. Many of the members stop to pray on their way to work. The pastor says that prayer is the greatest key to their success in reaching people with the Gospel of Jesus Christ.

In order to enhance their prayer ministry and discipleship, several of the churches surveyed are using studies such as "Experiencing God" (*Mi Experiencia Con Dios*), "Master Life" (*El Plan Maestro*) and other materials that are helping their people to have a closer walk with the Lord.

## Adequate Facilities

These growing congregations have ventured in faith and have obtained, or look toward, facilities that will enable them to grow. Some have inherited buildings from other churches, bought used buildings, built their own, or in one instance, merged with an Anglo church, but somehow they have found a way to get adequate facilities.

One congregation's willingness to sell their previous building which was almost paid for and to branch out in faith to purchase a large, attractive building represented a clear step of faith. This faith has been demonstrated in many other ways and has contributed to the growth of this promising, exciting congregation.

Several of the churches have definite plans for upgrading their facilities. The plans are long-range and show the forward looking spirit of the congregations and their leaders.

A related factor is that the church buildings are easily accessible to the majority of the members. The study of the travel time shows that many of these church buildings are in locations that are easily accessible.

Few members live as much as 30 minutes travel time from the church facility (3.88%). Over 9% (9.55%) live 20 minutes or more from the facility. This is indicative of the fact that those who live 20 to 30 minutes away believe that it is worth the effort and the expense to come to this church. Almost one-half, (49.85%) live between 5 and 15 minutes travel time from the church building. The somewhat revealing statistic is, however, that only 16.12% live less than five minutes from the church building. Does this fact indicate that the churches may not be reaching their immediate neighborhoods? While 86.57% of the members live within 15-20 minutes of the church facility, only 16.12% are within five minutes of the building. These indications might direct the attention of the churches to means of reaching the immediate areas around the church buildings.

## Commitment to Stewardship

The churches studied in this survey have secured a high degree of commitment from their members in the area of giving. Some use denominational programs while others do not. The main factor is that the members have developed a deep sense of responsibility in this area. The giving on the part of the members appears to be directly tied with three things: (1) Their understanding of biblical principles for stewardship; (2) An understanding of and commitment to the goals that the church is trying to reach; and (3) A profound sense of confidence in the ministry and leadership of the pastor. Several pastors described instances in which large sums of money were needed to make a down payment on land or on a building or to pay off the mortgage of an existing building. These pastors basically called on their congregations to pray and to seek the leadership of the Lord in giving. To the amazement of the pastors, the people gave far beyond what appeared to have been possible. This made it possible for the congregations to move forward in addressing their building needs and expanding their outreach ministries.

In addition to the principles found in the survey that we have just discussed, it is helpful to focus attention on the organizational structure of the new congregation in order to enhance its continued growth. When the church is small it has a simple structure. As the church grows from a small church, to a medium church, and to a large church, it needs to adapt its structure to facilitate growth.

## Conclusion

The explosive growth of the Hispanic population (25.7 million in the last 3 decades) and the astounding projections regarding future growth (triple in the next four and a half decades) present all of us with an awesome challenge.

The fact that the immigrant generation is now the largest segment of the Hispanic population (40%) and that the vast majority of them (72%) are primarily Spanish speakers cause us to re-examine the perception that most Hispanics have assimilated and that specialized programs are no longer needed. Together we face the dual challenge of dealing with *immigration* and *assimilation* simultaneously.

As we look at the astounding task of reaching unprecedented numbers of Hispanics for Christ, we must challenge and encourage one another to work together more closely, to try new approaches, to make the necessary structural changes, to call on mission agencies to assist, and to do whatever it takes to get the job done. In light of the explosive growth of the Hispanic population incremental strategies will not suffice. What is needed is strategies that facilitate exponential growth in evangelism and church planting.

In August of 2002 the Fox News Agency gave the following report: "Kmart Corp, which is reconstructing from bankruptcy protection, said Wednesday that it will publish its weekly circular in Spanish for the first time, in a bid to reach out to the growing Hispanic market. The discount retailer said the advertising circular will be translated into Spanish starting August 29. The circular will be available in 160 stores located in large Hispanic populations and appear in 10 Spanish-language newspapers throughout the U.S., K-Mart is expanding its effort to reach this influential group. More than 55 percent of all Hispanics living in the United States are within 15 minutes of one of its stores."[386]

Valuable lessons can be learned from the business world. It is regrettable that a business firm that had 55 percent of the Hispanic population within 15 minutes of one of its stores had to experience bankruptcy before it recognized the necessity of contextualizing its marketing strategies. Our hope is that this will not happen to missionary and denominational agencies. Since Hispanics are now the largest minority group in America today and are projected to become a fourth of the population within the next four and a half decades, all of us who are interested in leading Hispanics to a personal experience of salvation in Christ must pray earnestly that the Lord may guide us to develop the necessary strategies to gather the crops that are white unto the harvest.

At the turn of the previous century, thousands of Latin Americans fled revolutions and persecutions in their lands to come to North America. Upon their arrival, they were as shepherds without sheep. Spanish-speaking priests and ministers were in very short supply, and the new comers were receptive to the Evangelical message. While heroic measures were taken by a limited number of Baptists, Methodists, and Presbyterian missionaries, the fact remains that many fields were not harvested because the laborers were few, the vision was limited, and the resources were scarce. What a difference it would have made if Evangelicals had had the vision, the resources, and the personnel to respond to this challenge.

Today, at the outset of the 21st Century we face a similar challenge. The Hispanic population has exploded, their receptivity to the Gospel is unprecedented, and they are now found in every region of the country. What will future generations say of us? "If they had only..." or "Thank God that they had the vision, the passion, and the willingness to make whatever changes were necessary to lead untold numbers of Hispanics to a personal faith in Christ for the glory of God!"

---

**Endnotes**

[382] The Scarborough Institute for Church Growth under the direction of Drs. Daniel Sanchez and Ebbie Smith undertook a study of ten Hispanic Texas Baptist churches that have shown signs of healthy growth during the past five years.

[383] Patrick Chaffered, Church Innovations Institute, St. Paul Minn., cited by Andy Lang in UCC ONE NEWS, Nov. 6, 1995.

[384] Ibid.

[385] Patrick Chaffered, Church Innovations Institute, St. Paul Minn., cited by Andy Lang in UCC ONE NEWS, Nov. 6, 1995.

[386] Fox News, "Kmart Reaches Out to Hispanic Customers, August 28, 2002.

# Chapter 20

# Hispanics Involved In Missions

Diana Barrera

"It is time for us as Hispanics to begin to move from being a mission field to becoming a missionary force." Key Hispanic Evangelical leaders across America are expressing this sentiment.[387]

For many years Hispanics have been the object of Evangelical missionary efforts on the part of numerous religious organizations. Many of the missionaries sent by these agencies are to be commended for their sacrificial spirit as they sought to lead Hispanics to an experience of salvation in Jesus Christ, to start churches, and to establish institutions (e.g., hospitals, schools, theological seminaries) that contributed to their training and development in Latin America as well as North America. In light of the explosive growth of the Hispanic population in North America, evangelistic and church planting efforts on the part of all Evangelicals are desperately needed today. This, however, needs to be coupled with a new vision on the part of Hispanic Evangelicals to both reach Hispanics for Christ in this country as well as to respond to the call to be missionaries in highly strategic parts of the world.

For more than five decades dedicated Hispanics have responded to the missionary call and have served in numerous countries throughout the world. In recent years, some of the leaders have caught the vision of challenging Hispanics to seek to discern God's purpose in their pilgrimage and to work cooperatively to become much more actively involved in taking the gospel to the ends of the earth.

## A New Vision

A video entitled, *"Somos Su Pueblo,"* (We Are His People) vividly describes the feelings of key Hispanic Evangelical leaders who have caught a new vision and have a passion to participate actively in the implementation of the Great Commission of our Lord Jesus Christ.[388] In order to communicate the vision and the passion encapsulated in *"Somos Su Pueblo,"* I will quote portions of the transcript and comment on their significance.[389] The narrator of the video describes the predicament in which Israel found itself:

> Egypt, 1446 years before Christ; the people of Israel were suffering under Pharaoh. Slavery and oppression were asphyxiating them. But what was it that took them to Egypt? Was it hunger, natural disasters, the desire to progress, or the politics of Pharaoh? We know that beyond the circumstances God was forming a people to bless the nations.

God's people have reached a degree of maturity when they are able to see His hand in the events that have impacted their lives. Joseph provides a dramatic biblical analogy of this truth. He was cast down into a well, sold into slavery, falsely accused of immorality, locked in prison, forgotten by those whom he had helped, and finally taken to the palace and exalted to be second in command in the land of Egypt.

In spite of all of this, when Joseph saw his brothers once again, he said: "As for you, you meant evil against me, but God meant it for good in order to bring about this present result, to preserve many people alive" (Gen. 50:20).

In "*Somos Su Pueblo,*" the authors describe the events that led Jacob and his clan to go to Egypt. They are convinced that beyond the hunger, natural disasters, oppression, and the politics of Pharaoh, God was "forming a people to bless the nations." They explain:

> Our Hispanic people groups have also lived these realities. The political struggles, corruption, natural disasters, and hunger overwhelmed them and caused many to migrate. And now we ask ourselves, why are we here? Why did we have to abandon our land, our people, and our customs? Was it only to improve our economic situation, to give our children more opportunities, or to escape violence? These are worthy goals. But God's goals are much bigger. As he did with Israel in Egypt, God is forming here a people to bless the nations.

These Hispanic leaders are to be commended for seeking to discern the hand of God in their pilgrimage. Roger E. Hedlund also sees a clear and profound connection between election and service. He states:

> The election of Abraham (and implicitly of Israel) coincides with the promise or prospect of being a blessing to the nations.[390] "In you all the families of the earth shall bless themselves" (Gen. 12:3). This means that election has a missionary dimension. Why did God choose Abraham? God's choice of

Abraham was an act of pure grace. There was nothing in Abraham to merit God's favor. There were others, for example, Melchizedek and Job, who knew the true and living God in that day. Yet God chose Abraham, "a wondering Armenian" (Deut. 26:5) from an idolatrous family (Josh. 24:2), a true representative of the fallen human race, to be the recipient of his revelation... God's election of Abraham was to bring into being a vehicle for his unique work (Gen. 12:2)... "It was his purpose to reveal himself and his will through his people... Israel was to be Yahweh's representative among the peoples..."[391] Her election set Israel apart from the nations so that she might in a particular way serve God and reveal his glory and lordship upon the earth.[392]

While we acknowledge that in salvation history, Israel was elected in a unique way, there is also a sense in which all followers of Jesus Christ are called to be missionaries (Matt. 28:19, 20). In light of this, Hispanic Christians are called upon today to look beyond the political struggles, corruption, natural disasters, and scarcity that may have caused them to leave their native lands and see themselves as a people whom God is forming to bless the nations. This type of perception can enable Hispanics to find new meaning and purpose in life as a people with a mission to share the message of salvation in the nations of the world. Instead of considering themselves victims of the social, economic, and political circumstances that have impacted their lives, they seek to discern God's purpose and design in their lives. Why is it that Hispanic Americans live in a nation that has so many resources (financial, educational, religious, media, diplomatic, etc.) that facilitate the fulfillment of missionary task? Is this just an accident of history, or is the hand of God behind all of the events and circumstances that have made Hispanics a part of this nation?

"*Somos Su Pueblo*," continues by pointing out that there are mission fields in highly strategic parts of the world for which Hispanics are uniquely suited as a missionary force:

> Today, God is preparing a missionary people to rise up and help with the missionary task. God has designed us perfectly for this mission. Our children are bicultural; they know how to live in the midst of cultural diversity. Our physical appearance opens doors for us around the world, in India, in North Africa, and in East Asia. In addition to the family, friendship, and hospitality, our idiosyncrasies distinguish us. Our idiosyncrasy tells us that "there is more time than life." But these same idiosyncrasies have built a bridge to the unreached. Every day, in the most remote places, millions follow the Argentine, Mexican, and Venezuelan soap operas. Latin music is heard throughout the world. Our soccer players are known the world over. Do you realize that God has prepared us for this time in the history of the nations?

It is important for Hispanic Evangelical Christians to be aware of the fact that there are parts of the world in which by divine wisdom they are specifically designed to make an impact with the gospel of Jesus Christ. The authors of the video presentation point out four factors that make it possible for Hispanics to be missionaries in politically and religiously sensitive parts of the world.

The first factor that is an asset for Hispanic missionaries is their bi-lingual, bi-cultural experience. "Our children are bicultural; they know how to live in the midst of cultural diversity." Many Hispanic Americans have had the experience of relating to two cultures throughout their lives. Many of them know what it is like to speak Spanish at home in order to communicate with their parents and grandparents. They have also faced the challenge of learning English in order to get their education and communicate in school as well as in the market place. The challenge, therefore, of going to another part of the world, learning an additional language, and functioning in another culture is not new to them. They already have many of the adaptive and cooping skills. Furthermore, based on their own pilgrimage, many Hispanic missionaries have an instinctive empathy with minority groups in different parts of the world. This empathy often leads to the type of heart to heart communication that facilitates the communication of the gospel message cross-culturally.

The second of these factors is physical appearance. While it is true that there is significant variety in the physical appearance among Hispanic Americans, it can be acknowledged that many of them would be able to blend in easily in such regions as India, North Africa, East Asia, and the Middle East, to name but a few. After serving in an Arabic country for two years, a Hispanic missionary was asked by a local man, "You mean to tell me that you are not Arabic?" He added: "You look so much like us, that I assumed you were Arabic." During that time the Hispanic missionary and his wife were able to build many friendships, lead numerous Arabic persons to a personal faith in Christ, and enable them to start a congregation in their community. There is a sense in which some of the cultural and political barriers were overcome simply because the Hispanic missionary couple looked like the Arabic people they were trying to reach with the gospel.

The third factor that can be a plus for Hispanic missionaries is their cultural characteristics. Many Hispanics have a worldview which places great emphasis on family, friendships, and hospitality. The fact that there are numerous cultures in the world that have very similar worldviews makes it possible for Hispanic missionaries to adapt rapidly to the culture and establish meaningful personal relationships in those settings. While there are some significant cultural and linguistic differences, the values that Hispanics have in common with many people groups serve as a bridge that enhances empathy and communication. The concept of time ("there is more time than life") which many Hispanics have also resonates with many people groups in the two-thirds world where most of the unreached are found. This people-centered approach that many Hispanics have enables them to adjust easily to cultures that are not very time conscious.

The fourth factor mentioned in the *"Somos Su Pueblo"* is the appreciation that many of the people in the world have for the art forms (e.g., soap operas and the music), that are produced in Latin America. In addition to this is the admiration that many cultures have for Latin American sport heroes (especially soccer stars). As is true of the cultural values mentioned above, the commonalities that Hispanic missionaries have with other people groups regarding art forms and sports personalities provide valuable bridges for the establishment of meaningful friendships and the communication of the gospel.

*"Somos Su Pueblo"* ends with a passionate missionary appeal:

There is no reason for us to feel diminished because of our appearance or our Hispanic culture. These are the same characteristics that enable us to fulfill God's purpose. God used the people of Israel in a powerful way. Today, He wants to use us. He calls us today to rise up and bless the nations. The future of millions depends on us. Now is the time and we are His people. There is not time to lose.

It is a wonderful moment when people of any culture begin to look at themselves in the light of God's purpose and design. In Chapter 14 of this book, Dr. Miranda calls on "Modern-Day Samaritans" to stop viewing themselves as others would view them and start viewing themselves through the eyes of our Master, Jesus Christ. He explains:

Jesus spoke to the woman in private despite strong cultural taboos against any social exchange between a Jewish holy man and a sexually promiscuous Samaritan woman. The underlying issues and barriers were social, political, and religious in nature. Jesus' desire was not just to cross the racial barriers between Jews and Samaritans but beyond that to have his disciples and Samaritans overcome the historical and spiritual barriers that prevailed in their rivalry. More importantly, as Dr. Isaac Canales says, "the divine encounter in Samaria at the well marked the height and beginning of evangelization and world missions."[393]

In Chapter 15 of this book, Dr. Sánchez describes "Modern-Day Hellenists" among Hispanics who have learned how to live and function effectively in two cultures. They, like the Apostle Paul, can be valuable instruments in the hands of God for the communication of the Gospel among people of many different cultures. Having the mind set of being "all things to all people" (1 Cor. 9:19-22), they can be trailblazers in some of the most politically sensitive and culturally diverse populations of the world.

As a result of their own pilgrimage they have quite naturally learned to be bicultural bridges. Learning another language and relating to another culture comes naturally to them for that is what they have done all their lives. Bilingual Hispanics speak the second and the third top ten languages of the world. The first is Mandarin which is spoken by 885 million people. English comes in second with 322 million speakers. Spanish comes in third with 266 million speakers.[394] Combined, 588 million people speak either English or Spanish. Being bi-lingual and bi-cultural, therefore, can be a marvelous asset in the work of the Kingdom of God as it was for the Apostle Paul who was the product of two cultures and was fluent in Greek and Aramaic.

It is obvious that Dr. Miranda and Dr. Sánchez agree wholeheartedly with the authors of "*Somos Su Pueblo*" in their statement:

> There is no reason for us to feel diminished because of our appearance or our Hispanic culture. These are the same characteristics that enable us to fulfill God's purpose. God used the people of Israel in a powerful way."

The truth of the matter is that as Hispanics we ought to feel privileged that God in his divine wisdom has fashioned us for a time such as this (Esther 4:14). While on the one hand we want to avoid the sin of *cultural idolatry,* placing our culture above all others, or *cultural isolationism,* focusing only on our people we on the other hand, can have a healthy sense of *cultural identity* discerning the hand of God in our pilgrimage and responding to his call to be *"gente puente,"* (bridge people) to the unreached people groups of the world.

# New Initiatives

It is truly inspiring to see that many Hispanics are not just talking about capturing a new vision; they are responding to the missionary call. The International Mission Board of the Southern Baptist Convention reports that over 150 Hispanics are serving as missionaries in numerous countries throughout the world.

Another example of this is the missions mobilization network organization called "COMHINA" which stands for *"Cooperación Misionera de los Hispanos de Norte América"* (Missionary Cooperation of North American Hispanics). COMHINA was started in 1991 for the purpose of encouraging Hispanic Americans to be involved in sharing the gospel with unreached people groups throughout the world. COMHINA is a network of churches from all denominations including Assemblies of God, American Baptists, Southern Baptists, Church of God. Mennonites, and other denominational groups.

During the past thirteen years under the leadership of it's executive director, Diana Barrera, this missionary organization has focused on awakening the hearts of thousands of Hispanics who have been interceding, giving, going, and sending missionaries to unreached people groups. In accord with the principles of the COMIBAM network throughout the Americas, though it supports the efforts of Hispanic missionaries throughout the Spanish Speaking world, COMHINA's focus is on the unreached people groups of the world.

In the last 3 years volunteer teams sparked by COMHINA have participated in mission projects in China, India, Banda Aceh, and others. The theme for the present thrust is *"Ahora es el Tiempo"*, made popular by the now famous music video and CD featuring all the greats of Hispanic and Latino Christian music. With offices in Orlando, Los Angeles, and New York, this organization has matured into a powerful instrument to awaken Hispanics to interpret their pilgrimage from God's perspective and to respond to the challenge of becoming a missionary force in today's world. In the words of Dr. Paul McGaughan, president of EFMA for years, "COMHINA is the only national organizations challenging all Hispanic churches to fulfill the Great Commission"

The results of COMHINA's tireless work can be seen in individual churches, denominations and strategic alliances. The "El Calvario" Assemblies of God church in Orlando has taken very consistent strong stands for world evangelization. It's pastors have served as key leaders over the years. Under it's present pastor, Saturnino González, the church has adopted many Latin American missionaries, hosted innumerable mobilization events, and sent dozens of volunteers to Cameroun, China, India, and to Indonesia after the Tsunami.

It is inspiring to note also that in the last three years the Southeastern division of the Iglesia de Dios Pentecostal Movimiento Internacional under the leadership of it's superintendent, Edgar Nazorio, has initiated the bold mobilization of all it's member churches in prayer, giving and going. Their willingness to go beyond their "comfort zone" and stretching their traditional paradigms for the sake of the unreached is an inspiration.

In the west coast we are also seeing another Hispanic church sending a couple of missionaries to Cameron , Africa to work in church planting among the Baka pygmy. Jose & Liliana Castillo were send by Esmirna Church AG, Los Angeles to work among this unreached group in 1996. In 2004, when they left Cameron a church had been started among the Baka pygmy.

Interestingly God has also used sensitive Anglo-Americans and "traditionally western" organizations to feed the movement. One organization is Conexion 1040 which appeared on the scene in 2004. This organization was started by a former missionary to Kolkata who recognized the advantages of Brazilian, Argentine, and Mexican missionaries in reaching his city. Conexion 1040 task is to accelerate the sending of Latin American and Hispanic missionaries while helping them be as effective as possible by training them in the principles of strategy coordination and church planting movements

Meanwhile, the humility displayed by western missionaries in Indonesia some years back set the stage for the latest strategic alliance. In 2004 on the campus of Wycliffe in Orlando, God forged an alliance to help reach the Indonesian peoples. Comhina convened representatives of Pioneers and IMB to forge an agreement to field a missionary from the Iglesia Cristiana to set up a receiving context for Hispanic missionaries. Trained by Pioneers she will work with support of the broad missionary alliance in

Indonesia. Humbly these same groups years ago sensed that God was telling them that Latin Americans had to be a part of reaching Indonesia if the task were to be completed.

One of the most dramatic examples of Hispanics responding to the missionary call is a couple in their mid 50s who was willing to resign from their ministry positions, sell their belongings (including their homes), and go to a north African country to serve as missionaries. Due to the sensitive nature of the context in which they serve it is not wise to publish their names nor the location of their works. Early reports indicate that this missionary couple, after just a short time on the mission field, is finding extraordinary opportunities to share the gospel of Jesus Christ in an area that has traditionally been very resistant to missionary work.

Another example of the new vision that some Hispanics are capturing is that of a volunteer group from Iglesia Bautista Horeb (Horeb Baptist Church) in Houston who went to a country in Northern Africa to "seek to know people, make friends, and share the story of Jesus with those willing to listen."[395] In a post 911 world, this effort required some courage. But this volunteer group was unique. In addition to having the prayers and support of their church, family, and friends, they had the advantage of being Hispanic.

Campo Elías Londoño, the leader of the group said: "Some people thought I was an Arab. I bought a tarbush (a hat) and when they saw me and heard me speak they thought I was one of them."[396] Londoño explains that his group was able to use a cultural bridge that had existed for centuries: "Since before the advance of Islam, Spain and North Africa have had cultural, economic, and religious ties. The Iberian language and culture are established in many homes in

North Africa and this has made all the difference to our volunteers."[397] In addition to the similarities in physical appearance, the cultural similarities facilitated the cultivation of friendships that otherwise would have taken years to establish or might have been almost impossible to form.

Londoño and his group had studiously obtained information on the political, cultural, and religious characteristics of their ministry focus group. He explains:

> Sharing the gospel in North Africa should be done with care and discretion. Suspicion and fear abound. Hostility toward the West and the Christian faith is very evident. In many places it is totally illegal to try to convert a Muslim. But the words of Jesus carry a mandate; a mandate that supersedes the laws of nations and of men. For that reason, this team, inspired by the love of Christ and in obedience to his mandate, has found a way to do it.[398]

María Velásquez, a member of the team gives valuable insights on the manner on which she, as a Hispanic woman, was able to build communication bridges with Muslim women: "The women that were willing to talk with us were very friendly and open. They talked about the restrictions they have as Muslim women."[399] This type of deeply personal conversation would not have taken place had the Muslim women not felt a bond between them and the Hispanic women. The fact that this level of communication was achieved within a two-week missions project is indicative of the cultural ties that exist between these two groups.

Londoño described the challenges that his team encountered among some of the more resistant groups. Despite the fact that there were some physical and cultural similarities, some groups were not very receptive to the evangelistic efforts of this team. Yet the approach that this group used and their perseverance enabled them to plant the seed of the gospel in many places. Londoño explains:

> The gentle and patient way of our team builds bridges of confidence and friendship with many North Africans. Having established friendships, some of the members of our team found opportunities to share their faith. Other friendships will be nurtured by the missionaries and volunteers with the hope that these will also lead to opportunities to share the gospel. In a culture restricted by fear and suspicion, even a respectful contact without confrontation on the part of the volunteers was not always received with smiles and friendships. In some cases our team encountered open hostility. But these circumstances did not discourage the team. Instead they strengthened their decision and deepened their faith.[400]

Gloria Londoño, a team member, said: "I felt God's presence. In the moments when we felt fear, we were able to have the assurance that everything was going to turn out well."[401] Like all other cross-cultural missionaries, Gloria had anxious moments. It was during these moments that she was able to feel the presence of God in tangible ways. This point vividly to the fact that the missionary task goes beyond the establishment of cultural bridges. While missionaries must do all they can to bridge cultural gaps, they must continuously rely upon the Lord to do His work in the hearts of the recipients.

Another team member, Lolly Orquera, shared insights on what it was like to be involved in this missionary venture: "To discover that even with all of my fears God uses me. With all of my defects and virtues God has permitted me to have this experience so that I can see the love He has for all of the people of the world."[402] Her experience undoubtedly taught her that the Lord can use Hispanics in missionary efforts in highly strategic countries. There is evidence also that this experience helped Lolly to broaden her horizons as she felt God's love flowing through her to people of another cultural in another part of the world.

Through this experience Campo Elías Londoño came to a clearer understanding of the radical commitment that some Muslims have to their faith. While not condoning their actions, Londoño sees a parallel between them and his team's commitment to Christ. He adds:

> In a world where hate and violence are the fruit of a radical faith, these volunteers have chosen a different path. Their radical faith, their obedience, has brought them here not as terrorists or soldiers but as ambassadors; ambassadors in the name of Jesus Christ, the prince of peace. For this reason, their world, and the world of those whom they were able to touch will never be the same.

It is truly instructive and inspiring to receive such positive reports from ordinary church members who took the risk of going to North Africa to share the good news of salvation in Jesus Christ. Out of their experience they concluded that being Hispanic was marvelous asset for them. The fact that they "looked Arabic" and had innate cultural sensitivities opened opportunities to build bridges of friendship that they would not have had otherwise.

# Sacrificial Giving

As more and more Hispanic churches declare a passion for overseas missions, some congregations are putting their money where their mouths are.[403] Casa de Vida para las Naciones[404], a Hispanic Baptist congregation in Greenacres, Fla., posted a greater than 10-fold increase in their Lottie Moon Christmas Offering giving (the annual offering to support missionaries). With about 90 members, this church gave more than $18,000 for the 2004 offering. The previous year's total was $1,200. The pastor, Mauricio Alvarez, said:

> One man at the church earned his Lottie Moon Christmas Offering by driving an ice cream truck. We're talking about someone who works with pennies and quarters. [This church] has a heart for God and a heart for missions.

Members of the congregation increased their goal after Alvarez challenged them to examine their spending. He urged them to pray about how much God would have them give to the offering. Alvarez explained:

> They realized how much they gave for Christmas gifts, and they decided they needed to change their priorities. [The congregation] realizes the importance of sacrificial giving. We feel we can change the lives of people by a giving heart.

The church recently attended the annual Iniciativa 21 Missions Conference -a major force in shaping the new boldness in Hispanic mission to learn more about missions and how they can impact their world for Christ. Their goal is to give $30,000 to missions this year. "This type of commitment takes both passion and leadership," said Jason Carlisle, the International Mission Board's director of Hispanic church strategies. He explained:

> First, the people have to be burdened for the lost or no one is going to give up their comfort and the pastor [at Central Baptist Church] has given them a constant vision of global responsibility. I think there is a sense of this being the time for Hispanics to take a serious role in world missions.[405]

"Even a small church collecting 'pennies and quarters' can make a difference with missions," Alvarez said. "We must believe that God can really provide."

Another inspiring example of sacrificial giving by Hispanics is that of Iglesia Bautista Glenview in Ponce, Puerto Rico. Under the leadership of its pastor, Rev. Rene Pereira, this congregation gave close to $100,000 to mission causes last year. Because of their commitment to missions, they chose to keep meeting in their remodeled warehouse rather than cut their missions offering. In the last six years this church has bought parcels of land in China, India, and Bangladesh and donated them for the establishment of institutes to train Christian leaders. This church has also donated funds for the establishment of churches in the Ukraine and Russia. A church that started with a few people in a living room in a house in Ponce, Puerto Rico, Iglesia Bautista Glenview now has over 2,500 members, has started nine churches in their beautiful island and is praying that the Lord will enable them to be instrumental in reaching one million people for Christ in the 10/40 window in the next ten years.

# Conclusion

In his book, *Evangelism in the Early Church,*[406] Michael Green points out that a convergence of factors (or pathways) contributed toward the rapid expansion of the gospel in the 1st Century. He states that pax Romana (Roman Peace) made it possible for Christians (e.g., Paul) to move safely and rapidly (through the road systems of the Empire) in order to communicate the gospel. The Greek culture with a widely used language, highly respected thought patterns, and even the contributions of the Greek philosophers contributed toward a preparatio evangelica (preparation for the gospel) upon which Christians could build in order to evangelize people. In addition to this, there was the Jewish religion with its monotheistic emphasis, ethical values, synagogue worship, Scripture reading, and zeal to gain adherents. All of these factors paved the way for the rapid, breath-taking expansion of the gospel in Jerusalem, Judea, Samaria, and to the ends of the earth.

As we prayerfully analyze our Hispanic pilgrimage we also see the convergence of providentially ordered factors (pathways) that have the potential of making us a powerful missionary force in our day for the salvation of untold numbers of persons for the glory of God. Again we ask, are the biculturalism, the physical appearance, the cultural characteristics, and the appreciation for Hispanic art forms the world over simply accidents of history or are they God-ordained pathways that can contribute to making Hispanics a powerful and effective missionary force in our day?

The passionate plea of the authors of *"Somos Su Pueblo"* is ours also:

He calls us today to rise up and bless the nations.
The future of millions depends on us.
Now is the time
We are His people.
There is no time to lose.

---

### Endnotes

[387] One example of this is found in the mission statement articulated by Diana Barrera, Executive Director of COMIHNA - Cooperación Misionera de Hispanos de Norte América (Missionary Cooperation of Hispanics in North America.

[388] Jason Carlisle, *Somos Su Pueblo*, International Mission Board, 2004.

[389] The transcript was originally produced in Spanish. For the purpose of this book, I have translated it into English and assume responsibility for any variation that might occur due to the translation. Daniel R. Sánchez.

[390] Roger E. Hedlund, *The Mission of the Church in the World*, Grand Rapids: Baker Book House, 1985, 37. Citing J. Blauw, *The Missionary Nature of the Church*, New York: McGraw-Hill, 1962, 22.

[391] Roger E. Hedlund, *The Mission of the Church in the World*, , 37, citing R.R. De Ridder, Discipling the Nations, Grand Rapids: Baker Book House, 1975, 32.

[392] Roger E. Hedlund, *The Mission of the Church in the World*, , 37

[393] An Analysis of the Discourse in John 4: Unpublished exegetical paper-2003)

[394] Barbara F. Grimes, Ethnologue Languages of the World, ed., Summer Institute of Linguistics,

[395] Jason Carlisle, Video: *Hispanics*, International Mission Board, 2004.

[396] Campo El"as Londoño, in Video: Hispanics, International Mission Board, 2004.

[397] Ibid,

[398] Ibid.

[399] Ibid.

[400] Ibid.

[401] Ibid.

[402] Ibid.

# CHAPTER 20
*Hispanics Involved in Missions*

---

[403] This is an adaptation of an article entitled "Hispanic church demonstrates  sacrificial giving to Lottie Moon Christmas Offering," written by Shawn Hendricks, RICHMOND, VA (Baptist Press)

[404] The church changed it's name from Iglesia Bautista Central in 2005.

[405] For more information about Hispanic missions opportunities, contact Jason Carlisle at (866)407 9597 or go to . To learn more about the Lottie Moon Christmas Offering, visit .

[406] Michael Green, *Evangelism in the Early Church* (Grand Rapids: William Eerdmans, 1970), pp. 13-28.

# CONCLUSION

In this book we have discussed ten startling Hispanic realities that are impacting America's social, economic, and religious life. The growth of the Hispanic population is surpassing even the boldest projections of demographic experts. **The explosive growth of the Hispanic population (25.7 million in the last 3 decades) and the astounding projections regarding future growth (triple in the next four and a half decades) present all of us with an awesome challenge.**

Hispanics have spread throughout the country faster than any previous immigrant group. The first generation (the immigrants) now constitutes the largest segment of the Hispanic population. The use of the Spanish language in America has increased dramatically in the past two decades. Second and third generation Hispanics have made significant strides in educational attainment, yet the first generation lags behind.

Hispanics are showing more receptivity to the evangelical message than ever before in the history of this country. They are typically very conservative regarding social values. Second and third generation Hispanics have made significant strides financially yet typically newly arrived Hispanics have the most difficult time financially. **The fact that the immigrant generation is now the largest segment of the Hispanic population (40%) and that the vast majority of them (72%) are primarily Spanish speakers cause us to re-examine the perception that most Hispanics have assimilated and that specialized programs are no longer needed. Together we face the dual challenge of dealing with *immigration* and *assimilation* simultaneously.**

Hispanic Americans are the group with the largest number of children and young people. Hispanics have much in common with one another yet there is significant diversity among them. Few evangelistic opportunities surpass that of the Hispanic populations in the United States.

Understanding these realities is crucial for individuals, churches, missionary organizations, and educational institutions who want to be more effective in leading Hispanics to a personal relationship of salvation in Jesus Christ, encouraging the establishment of congregations, enabling these congregations to grow, and challenging Hispanics to view their pilgrimage in light of God's purpose and to respond to His call to take the gospel message to the ends of the earth.

While originally addressed to government and education policy makers, the observations made by researchers of the Brookings Institution's Center on Urban and Metropolitan Policy, the Pew Hispanic Center, and Kaiser Family Foundation have significant application for mission strategists seeking to respond to the challenge presented by the astounding growth, dispersion, and diversification of the Hispanic population in this country.

Part I expresses some of these realities of Hispanic populations today and suggests how these realities relate to Christian evangelistic and church development efforts. Among these findings are:

- *Overall findings suggest the need for new ways of thinking about the Hispanic population in this country;*[407]

# Conclusion

- *Newly arrived immigrants are bringing new energy to the Spanish language and to attitudes shaped in Latin America;[408]*

- *Two processes – assimilation and immigration – are taking place side-by-side in the Hispanic communities, often within a single family;[409]*

- *The vast and widespread growth of America's Hispanic population also signals new forms of growth and new areas of settlement across the nation's metropolitan landscape;[410]*

- *These Hispanic population trends seem to follow discernable pathways likely to carry into the future; [411]*

- *The need for policy makers (and mission strategists) to adapt quickly to vast change presents special challenges in metro areas that started with miniscule Hispanic populations and that experienced sudden, substantial growth;[412]*

- *Public officials (and mission strategists) responsible for planning the allocation of services and resources need to tailor their decision-making to the particular growth variation in their service area;[413]*

- *Due to the explosive growth of the Hispanic population, unprecedented cooperative efforts are going to be needed between international mission agencies, national mission agencies, state missions organizations, local mission groups and existing Hispanic churches.[414]*

After discussing the Hispanic realities, in Part One, we focus attention, in Part Two, on the factors that contribute to an understanding Hispanic American pilgrimage. A review of the history of Hispanics reveals that while some are descendents of the Spanish colonists, others have arrived in this country in recent years or even months. The diversity among Hispanics is due to the wide variety of countries of origin as well as the various stages of assimilation in which they find themselves.

Dr. Jesse Miranda explains that the pilgrimage of some Hispanics can be compared to that of the first century Samaritans. Dr. Daniel Sánchez, points out that the more assimilated Hispanics can be compared with first century Hellenists who served as *"gente puente"* (bridge people) between the various cultures. An understanding of the pilgrimage of both types of groups is vital for ministry among Hispanics in our day. The chapter on "Reconciliation among Cultural Groups, seeks to help all of the cultural groups in America to understand the nature and the effects of prejudice and to establish new bridges of love, respect, friendship, and cooperation to be worthy followers to Christ who broke down the walls of partition.

In Part Three we seek to provide information and insights for effective ministry among Hispanics. Reaching Hispanics for Christ must be done in the spirit of Christ. The way in which Jesus related to the Samaritan woman and patiently led her to receive Him as her Messiah is instructive as well as inspiring for us in our day.

Encouraging the starting of culturally relevant churches among Hispanics is absolutely essential. While numerous church planting models were presented, it must be kept in mind that the explosive growth and rapid expansion of Hispanics in this country necessitates that exponential methods of church planting be employed. Cell-based churches and house churches have the greatest potential for reaching the largest number of Hispanics possible.

In our discussion of Church Growth among Hispanics we outlined the principles that most significantly contribute to the health and growth of Hispanic congregations. A discussion of evangelism, church planting, and church growth would not be complete with focusing on marvelous new vision that Hispanics are catching to move from being a mission field to becoming a missionary force. While the dedicated commitment of Evangelical Christians of all of the cultural groups in America is needed to respond to the unprecedented growth and expansion of the Hispanic population, it is indeed vital for Hispanics to respond to the calling of God not only to reach Hispanics in this country, but to be willing to go to the ends of the earth with the message of salvation.

At the turn of the previous century, thousands of Latin Americans fled revolutions and persecutions in their lands to come to North America. Upon their arrival, they were as shepherds without sheep. Spanish-speaking priests and ministers were in very short supply, and the new comers were receptive to the Evangelical message. While heroic measures were taken by a limited number of Baptists, Methodists, and Presbyterian missionaries, the fact remains that many fields were not harvested because the laborers were few, the vision was limited, and the resources were scarce. What a difference it would have made if Evangelicals had had the vision, the resources, and the personnel to respond to this challenge.

Today, at the dawn of the 21st Century we face a similar challenge. The Hispanic population has exploded. Their receptivity to the Gospel is unprecedented. They are now found in every region of the country. What will future generations say of us? "If they had only..." or "Thank God that they had the vision, the passion, and the willingness to make what ever changes were necessary to lead untold numbers of Hispanics to a personal faith in Christ for the glory of God!"

As we look at the astounding task of reaching unprecedented numbers of Hispanics for Christ, we must challenge and encourage one another to work together more closely, to try new approaches, to make the necessary structural changes, to call on mission agencies to assist, and to do whatever it takes to get the job done. And we must do all of this strictly in the power of God and for His glory.

---

**Endnotes**

[407] Pew Hispanic Center/Kaiser Family Foundation, 2002 National Survey of Latinos, 6.

[408] Pew Hispanic Center/Kaiser Family Foundation, 2002 National Survey of Latinos, 6.

[409] Pew Hispanic Center/Kaiser Family Foundation, 2002 National Survey of Latinos, 7.

[410] *"Latino Growth in Metropolitan America,"* The Brookings Institution Center on Urban & Metropolitan Policy and the Pew Hispanic Center, 10.

[411] *"Latino Growth in Metropolitan America,"* The Brookings Institution Center on Urban & Metropolitan Policy and the Pew Hispanic Center, 11.

[412] *"Latino Growth in Metropolitan America,"* The Brookings Institution Center on Urban & Metropolitan Policy and the Pew Hispanic Center, 10.

[413] *"Latino Growth in Metropolitan America,"* The Brookings Institution Center on Urban & Metropolitan Policy and the Pew Hispanic Center, 11.

[414] This observation is made by the members of the Hispanic Task Force

Made in the USA
Lexington, KY
02 July 2019